# BYRON AND GOETHE
## Analysis of a Passion

1. *Frontispiece.* Model of the statue of Byron at the Grammar School, Aberdeen, by Pittendrigh Macgillivray.

# Byron and Goethe

## ANALYSIS OF A PASSION

E. M. Butler

PROFESSOR EMERITUS OF GERMAN IN
THE UNIVERSITY OF CAMBRIDGE

BOWES & BOWES
LONDON

*First published in 1956 by*
*Bowes & Bowes Publishers Limited,*
*42 Great Russell Street, London, W.C.1*

*Made and printed in England by*
STAPLES PRINTERS LIMITED
*at their Rochester, Kent, establishment*

To

H. D.

# Author's Note

In the year 1924, the centenary of Byron's death, the English Goethe Society brought out a monograph of Goethe and Byron by Professor J. G. Robertson of the University of London. This superseded A. Brandl's pioneering sketch in the twentieth volume of the *Goethe-Jahrbuch* in 1899 which had been used by Protheroe in the fifth volume of Byron's *Letters and Journals*. Brandl had printed some interesting new material; but Robertson broke fresh ground. His learned, scholarly and profusely documented study gave all the data then available about the connection between the two poets. In some 130 pages everything relevant was mentioned with references to the sources in footnotes crammed with extra information. This admirable piece of research is the corner-stone of the present study; and it is all the more necessary to signalize the debt here, since it will rarely be evident in the text or the notes. Like the author, and guided by him, I have consulted the original documents, and therefore I cannot quote him as my authority; but he is the authority behind it all and supplied the initial impetus.

The second impetus came from Sir John Murray, who drew my attention to some unpublished material connected with Goethe among his Byron papers; and it was here that I first made the acquaintance of Professor Benecke who played such an important and hitherto unrecognized part in the drama of Byron's dedications to Goethe. In placing this material at my disposal with permission to publish it, in allowing me access as well to Kinnaird's and Murray's letters to Byron, and in permitting me to quote extensively from the complete edition of Byron's works and letters, Sir John Murray has shown that generosity of mind and liberality of spirit which characterized his great forbear and has incurred my lasting gratitude.

Besides the unpublished material I have mentioned, this study is based on the works, letters, diaries and reported conversations of the two protagonists and their satellites. An impressive bibliography could be compiled from the abundant literature about Goethe who has been an object of study during the greater part of my life; and from the many admirable books about Byron which I have read with pleasure and (I trust) with profit during the course of this investigation. But it has seemed best to indicate by foot-notes only those works whose direct bearing on this particular subject has been shown by quotations or references in the text.

In conclusion I should like to express my gratitude to Professor Kayser of the University of Göttingen for consulting the authori-ties at Weimar on my behalf and for his lively interest; and to Mr. George Rylands for encouragement and sympathy when they were most needed and for his invaluable assistance in reading the proofs.

# ABBREVIATIONS

J. W. von Goethe, *Werke*, Weimar,  = *Werke* (55 vols.)
1888-1919, 133 vols.

= *Tagebücher* (15 vols.)
= *Briefe* (50 vols.)

J. P. Eckermann, *Gespräche mit Goethe*,  = Eckermann
ed. Beutler, Zürich, 1948.

*Gespräche mit Goethe*, ed. Beutler,  = *Gespräche*
Zürich, 1948, 2 vols.

*The Works of Lord Byron*, London,
1903–1922, 13 vols.
*Poetry*, ed. Coleridge, 7 vols.  = *Poetry*
*Letters and Journals*, ed. Protheroe,  = *Letters and Journals*
6 vols.

T. Medwin, *Conversations of Lord*  = Medwin
*Byron* . . .
A new edition, London, 1824.

T. Moore, *Life of Lord Byron*, London,  = Moore
1854.

---

I have italicized all titles in quotations where the writers have either omitted them or used quotation marks. Single quotation marks have been used throughout for the sake of consistency; they have also been supplied when necessary. Omission marks, unless otherwise stated, are mine. I have put "Orginal in German" in the foot-notes when Goethe and Benecke are addressing English correspondents.

ix

# Contents

# Illustrations

# Illustrations

PROLOGUE

# Prologue

## a. THE ARCHES OF THE YEARS

Two utterly dissimilar voices will be heard in this book: Byron's (incisive, vivacious, challenging) rings out clearly and carries far. Goethe's (mellow and sonorous) sends out prolonged and reverberating echoes. They are talking about each other and also hailing each other from afar across the gulf of forty years between them: intermittently but urgently; hopefully but bootlessly. When Byron fell silent, Goethe spoke on, uttering words in poetry and prose which were to ring down the generations and affect the course of history. They never met; they hardly wrote; they spoke a different language and belonged to a different race; yet their conjunction was to influence European literature and the future of mankind.

In an age in which impersonal forces are held accountable for more and more and single individuals however outstanding for less and less, this must seem very strange; and the strangeness is undeniable. The seeming incongruity between cause and effect becomes glaring in the third part of this study, but it is inherent in the whole situation; and the strangest feature of all is Goethe's passionate obsession with Byron, a man young enough to be his grandson, and surely altogether outclassed by the colossal figure of the German?

For Goethe ranks with the immortals: with Homer, Dante and Shakespeare in a fellowship of four. Yet his position, however well established by common consent, rests on narrower foundations. There is a monumental stability, an organic unity in the life-work of the other three which is not to be found in his. Mastering all literary forms, he is supreme in none. Homer, Vergil, Dante, Milton and Mickiewicz surpass him immeasurably in the epic, for heroism was not his theme. Aeschylus, Sophocles and Shakespeare tower above him in the drama, for he held aloof from tragedy. He has no standing as a satirist; and he cannot compete as a novelist with Dickens or Balzac, with Flaubert or Stendhal, with Tolstoy, Turgenev, Dostoyevski or Proust. His essentially lyrical genius, if unsurpassed in Germany, has peers and rivals elsewhere. But he stands shoulder to shoulder with the greatest because of his masterpiece *Faust*.

Homer immortalized and made radiant the world of pagan

antiquity. Dante transfigured the vision which medieval Christianity projected on to the screen of eternity. Shakespeare captured the spirit of life surging in the men and women of the Renaissance, its indestructible validity, its infinite significance and power. Goethe made incarnate in one symbolical figure the spiritual desolation of modern man. He experienced life quite as intensely as Homer, Dante or Shakespeare, the whole of life, but not life as a whole. The dualism at the core of his inmost being prevented that; but in his lyrical outpourings, and above all in the tragic questionings of *Faust* he achieved supremacy. The hero uplifts his voice at the beginning of that ever-changing dramatic rhapsody, defiantly registering despair. He dies at the end, a blind old man, defeated by life but under the cruel delusion that he has triumphed. This manifestation of the Faustian spirit, striving, questioning, doubting and despairing; ruthless, reckless and distraught; impatient of limitations and piteously limited, swept through Europe like a forest-fire with romanticism in its wake.

This may seem oddly at variance with the other side of Goethe: the great classical poet, the humane and conciliatory thinker, the serene Olympian sage; but both spirits cohabited in the same breast; and, until the end of his life, now the one and now the other was in command. *Faust* was conceived in early manhood when despair and defiance were uppermost, and relinquished when calm and serenity were revealed to him in the art and poetry of Greece. But he himself had not come to rest. *Faust* was taken up again, and again allowed to lapse; then resumed and brought up to a point where it could be abandoned temporarily; left at that point for nearly twenty-five years and finally completed just before Goethe died. In the ever increasing intervals he sought to recapture for himself and the modern world something of the beauty, harmony and wholeness which he venerated in Greek life. In fact he was attempting by natural means what Faust was endeavouring to perform by magic. His hero conjured up the Earth Spirit to learn the secrets of nature; Goethe undertook extensive scientific studies in search of an organic unity underlying all the manifestations of life. Faust evoked the spirit of Helen with the aid of necromancy to appease the longing of his spirit for Homer's glorious spring-time world which Goethe had tried for half a century to bring back into modern life. Helen vanished away and her world dislimned when reality intruded; and the final answer to Faust's restless striving was given by medieval Christianity, invoked in all its Catholic splendour to save the hero's soul and give meaning and coherence to his disrupted and sterile existence. This was accomplished by Goethe in 1825. When he died in 1832 he left behind him a strange document and some oral records offering a different interpretation of the problem of man in this mysterious universe. It was neither pagan nor Christian; it provided no sublimation of life on earth and no real hope of life beyond. It was a mythological rationalization of the fearful dualism he had experienced in himself and apprehended elsewhere; and this interpretation he owed very largely to Byron.

To Byron? We are back where we started from, except that the anomaly has increased; for, granted that both were animated by the same restlessly questioning spirit, it would be more reasonable to suppose that any spiritual or intellectual debt must be owing from Byron to Goethe and not vice versa; moreover have we not always been told that *Manfred* was a barefaced plagiarism from *Faust?* Something of *Faust* in *Manfred* there certainly was; but this shrinks almost to nothingness when compared with all that there was of Byron in Goethe's latter-day vision of life; for a power for which there is no rational accounting went out from the younger man; nor is it quite so certain as has been generally assumed that Byron's was the lesser spirit. Before approaching that question, Goethe's longevity and the brevity of Byron's life must be taken into account. For, if the German poet had also died when he was in his thirty-seventh year on the eve of his departure for Italy in 1786, there would have been considerably less to his credit than the English poet has to show, and he would have made no comparable mark on men's minds. The obituary notices would have stressed the fact that the author of *Götz* and *Werther* had risen to be a minister of state in the small duchy of Weimar; but there would have been no troubling of international waters; and the literary critics would have been much hampered by lack of material. The wonderful early poetry was there; but *Faust*, *Wilhelm Meister* and *Tasso* were only unpublished fragments; even *Egmont* was not yet finished, and *Iphigenie* was still in prose. These would doubtless have all been published posthumously with other schemes and sketches; and the letters too would have been collected and recognized for what they were: the torrential outpourings of a young man of genius, sobering down noticeably after the removal to Weimar. There would further have been a considerable number of heartfelt and resounding tributes from friends and admirers, among them Wieland's poem *An Psyche*, entranced and entrancing verses, but slight and light indeed when compared with Lamartine's address to Byron as *chantre d'enfer* in the *Méditations poétiques*.

This would be all the material which the literary critic of a later age, supposing him to be comparing the two poets, would have at his disposal to put beside the whole body of Byron's works, including his fascinating autobiographical fragments and his incomparable letters, all bearing witness to an intensely powerful and baffling personality who gave up the poetical ghost in a brilliant display of breath-taking fireworks, and died in harrowing circumstances with unpretentious heroism. And, as if all this were not enough, a spate of contemporary descriptions and conversations go to swell his legend, which, like a river in full flood, swirls through wrathful deeps and sparkling shallows, hurtling onwards to re-enact the awe-inspiring fall, when the world reverberated with the shock, and Europe mourned the un-crowned king of Greece. But it also passed through noisome swamps of controversy, stirring up malodorous mud on its way, everything about the legend looming larger than life-size, and yet not as great as the real events which it inspired. Faced with so much evidence of creative and posthumous vitality, and looking back at Goethe's truncated existence, such a critic could hardly fail to conclude that Byron was by many cubits the greater.

But if he were worth his salt he would remember that *Werther* had scattered broadcast over Europe the seeds of romanticism on to the soil prepared by Rousseau; he would reflect that René, Atala, Adolphe, Olympio and Rollo in France, perhaps Jacopo Ortis in Italy and certainly Childe Harold in England all derived ultimately from Goethe's hero, and he would ponder the matter more closely. *Werther*, he would then admit, mirrors more than the sorrows of an unrequited passion in an individual human soul; it also reflects the questing, dissatisfied, potentially revolutionary spirit of the age, uttering a deep note of protest against the sins of society, the divorce from nature and a natural life. Dealing apparently with a mere piece of private history, it seems to have absorbed into itself and reflected back the mystery of nature, life and the universe itself. It is as if the marvels and menaces of the sky above are mirrored in a dew-drop. No wonder that the self-consciousness of human suffering incarnate in the hero produced such a numerous progeny. Werther at one end of the scale and Childe Harold at the other are both children of Rousseau, both in part projections of their creators' personalities, each of them drawing sustenance from private experience and conditioned by personal grief. But (might not the critic now have told himself?) *Childe Harold* has much greater proportions than *Werther*; it un-rolls the panorama of history and brings far-distant countries into view; whereas *Werther* is located in a sleepy little provincial town in eighteenth-century Germany, and the hero hardly looks be-yond it. Even allowing for the signal effect produced by this tragic confession of a young man of genius, can it be compared with the power sweeping through the third and fourth cantos of *Childe Harold* and giving it those almost mythological proportions which Goethe's novel lacks? 'No', the hypothetical critic would reassert at this stage; 'there is no comparison; Byron is by far the greater'.

For how could such a critic know that Goethe, on the completion of his thirty-sixth year, was barely at the beginning of his creative life; that volume after volume of poetry, dramas, epics, novels and reminiscences were to come from his pen, and that the strange and lovely embryo which posterity has called the *Urfaust* was to develop into one of the great masterpieces of world-literature? Ignorant of all this, he would perhaps have assumed that Goethe had given in *Werther* the best that was in him to give, a possibility which should make one very chary of supposing that Byron at the age of thirty-seven had reached the end of his powers with *Don Juan*. Yet it remains true that Byron, living at a much greater speed than Goethe, came to maturity much earlier, and might have burnt himself out much sooner; although even a cursory survey of the years of their youth and early manhood discovers such striking coincidences in their life-lines that it is impossible to dogmatize even about that.

Goethe's childhood, it is true, was normal and happy enough. Adored by his gay young mother, and kept within due bounds by his staider and severer father, he was the king of his company abroad, and his upbringing had all those valuable qualities of middle-class decency, security and stability which Byron's distressing childhood so notoriously lacked. On the other hand Goethe's schooling, though thorough and sound enough, was not fundamentally formative. An outstandingly brilliant day-boy, he profited by his lessons, amused himself with his schoolmates, and that was all. Byron went to Harrow, where he was 'never seen reading, but always idle, and in mischief, or at play'; but where he somehow acquired the inspiring elements of a liberal education, not to mention life-long memories of friendships and adolescent intimations which enriched his later years. If in this respect he already seemed to be overhauling Goethe, they were equally precocious in other ways, entering as schoolboys on that never-ending series of love-affairs which chequered both their lives. Before they went to the university, at the early age of fifteen, both had been violently in love with a girl slightly older than themselves and had suffered similarly in consequence. Goethe fell dangerously ill from the shock of his rejection by the Frankfort 'Gretchen', a shock rendered all the greater because it was bound up with his first realization of the seamy side of life. But when the fever left him, the wound was healed, and no scar remained; whereas Byron's hopeless passion for Mary Chaworth, and the shock of her words: 'Do you think I could care anything for that lame boy?'

marked him for life. But both, however their fancies might stray, felt themselves bound to their sisters by no common tie. Goethe's feeling for Cornelia had elements of passion in it, which Byron's love for his half-sister Augusta was later to display.

On proceeding to the university both Goethe and Byron ran off the rails. In endeavouring to shed his provincialisms, Goethe acted the coxcomb and played the fool. His sarcasms and his sentimentalities, his languishing airs during the pursuit of his landlady's daughter; his paroxysms of jealousy, his floods of tears, his declamatory letters to Behrisch (a man eleven years his senior), all make the impression of very bad theatre, and his pre-Leipzig friends were disgusted with his affectations. Byron must have been quite as intolerable, with his 'tumultuous passions' and the bear he brought with him 'to sit for his fellowship'; whilst, scorning his pastors and masters, the wayward young scholar took his 'gradations in the vices with great promptitude'. Both he and Goethe were running true to type as young men of genius who had not yet found their feet. The ground became solid under Goethe's when he removed to Strasbourg and fell in with Herder who opened his eyes to the real nature of poetry and helped him to discover himself; stimulating him and transporting him, but also baiting and mocking him at times almost past endurance. It was painful but salutary. Goethe now began to write in earnest and to crave for the necessary freedom from ties. Disentangling himself from Friederike Brion, he made off, ostensibly to practise the law he had arduously acquired, in reality to let his genius have its way. At exactly the same age Byron broke away from his home immediately after attaining his majority and set off on the Grand Tour. He had also by now discovered his genius which had lashed out in fury against *The Edinburgh Review*; and he instinctively chose as its hunting-ground those travels in the near-East which represented then and ever afterwards the golden age of his life. They were in the strongest possible contrast to Goethe's provincial and outwardly humdrum existence in Wetzlar; but both periods have become equally famous in the eyes of posterity; for *Werther* is penetrated with emotions quite as intense and had an effect almost as electrifying as the first two cantos of *Childe Harold*. Goethe's remarkable resilience sent him back to Frankfort at the age of twenty-two in a state of creative and poetic fervour, at which age Byron was back in London making speeches in the House of Lords and taking society by storm with his 'stanzas in the Spenserian manner'.

It was at this point in their lives, in their early twenties, that the men and women around them became vividly aware of genius in their midst. In provincial Germany of the seventeen-seventies, quiet as a mill-pond and as dull as ditch-water, the sudden appearance of a glorious young Titan struck rapture but terror too into the minds of onlookers:

Goethe is a genius from the crown of his head to the soles of his feet, what is more, he is like one possessed. . . . You would worship him, he is the most terrible and the most lovable of men. . . . He should be a king. . . . A heart full of feeling, a mind all aflame, a spirit with eagle's wings . . . a great genius, a most formidable man. . . . The most beautiful, vital, original, ardent, impetuous, the tenderest and most seductive of human beings, and the most dangerous to a woman's heart that has ever existed. . . . One of the most extraordinary and mighty men of genius who have ever visited the world. . . . My soul is as full of Goethe as a dew-drop of the morning sun.

These paeans were raised by Jacobi, Heinse, Lavater, Zimmermann and Wieland in 1774 (the year in which *Werther* was published) ushered in, accompanied and ushered out by similar acclamations, but also by dissentient voices raised between 1771 and 1776:

. . . said to be man of genius, but intolerably conceited . . . crows very loudly on the slightest provocation . . . success has turned his head . . . even luke-warm praise of an adversary infuriates him. Genius makes a bad bed-fellow. . . . Unyielding arrogance. . . . Goethe is both loved and hated here. . . . This monster cannot go through the world behaving like this . . . eternal lampooning . . . indecent conduct, cursing and swearing . . . low and vulgar expressions . . . a male coquette. . . . 'That is either the devil or Goethe', I exclaimed. . . . 'Both', he replied, 'the devil's in him again today . . . better keep your distance'.

Thus spake a forgotten Pfeiffel, Herder, Merck, Count Stolberg, Charlotte von Stein (before she had tamed him) and that most Prussian of poets, old Father Gleim. Charlotte, dazzled by Goethe's intellect, also likened him to a fallen angel, which inevitably recalls Caroline Lamb's description of Glenarvon, her transparent pseudonym for Byron:

Calantha felt the power, not then alone, but evermore. She felt the empire, the charm, the peculiar charm, those features – that being must have for her. She could have knelt and prayed to heaven to realize the dreams, to bless the fallen angel in whose presence she at that moment stood, to give peace to that soul, upon which was plainly stamped the heavenly image of sensibility and genius.[1]

But even outside the pages of this sensational novel, the same kind of excitement prevailed among the observers of Byron:

. . . a mystery in a winding-sheet, crowned with a halo . . . his dwelling-

[1] [C. Lamb], *Glenarvon*, 3 vols., London, 1816; II, p. 32.

place was amidst the murk and the mist, and the home of his spirit in
the abysm of the storm, and the hiding-places of guilt. . . . So beautiful
a countenance I scarcely ever saw . . . his eyes the open portals of the
sun – things of light and for light. . . . Don't look at him, he is dangerous to look at. . . . The beauty of Byron makes me dream. . . . Mad,
bad, and dangerous to know. . . . When I think of the expression a
great painter should give to genius, I always have before me that
magnificent head. . . . He is a demon.

Galt, Coleridge, Lady Liddell, Walter Scott, Caroline Lamb,
Stendhal and Madame de Staël swelled this murmurous tumult,
in which the sinister note is more often heard than in the descriptions of Goethe, who made a 'terrible' or 'formidable' or 'mon-
strous' or even 'indecent' impression on some observers, but was
evidently innocent of that '*under* look' of Byron's which caused
sensitive ladies to swoon. Both young men were endowed with
personal beauty in a high degree, but there was evidently more of
magic in Byron's and his impact on society was even more strongly
felt:

He was now the universal talk of the town: his speech and his Poem
had not only raised his fame to an extraordinary height, but had disposed all minds to bestow upon him the most favourable reception. . . .
Crowds of eminent persons courted an introduction, and some volun-
teered their cards . . . never was there such a sudden transition from
neglect to courtship. Glory darted thick upon him from all sides. . . .
He was the wonder of greybeards, and the show of fashionable parties.[1]

From morning till night, the most flattering testimonies of his success
crowded his table . . . he now not only saw the whole splendid interior
of High Life thrown open to receive him, but found himself, among its
illustrious crowds, the most distinguished object.[2]

Most telling of all perhaps was the spellbound murmur *Byr'n-
Byr'n-Byr'n* travelling round and round the London dinner-
tables during the season of 1812 when he was unable to grace
such gatherings with his presence. Even Wieland's description of
Goethe at the Court of Weimar in the early days cannot compete
with that:

Goethe lives and reigns and rages, and brings rain and sunshine turn
by turn as you know, and he makes us happy, do what he will.[3]

But then to leave Weimar in 1775 for London in 1812 is not
unlike exchanging a beer-garden for a gala night at Covent
Garden. The Age of Elegance, as it has well been called, was
then in full swing. Dominated by the Whig aristocracy, powerful,
scintillating and sophisticated, it represents a peculiarly brilliant

[1] R. C. Dallas, *Recollections of the Life of Lord Byron*, London, 1824, pp. 232 f.
[2] Moore, p. 159.
[3] *Gespräche*, i, p. 104. May 1776

period in our social and political history, when British prestige
stood dizzily, if dangerously, high. Whereas the petty German
states, ground between the upper and nether millstones of Austria
and Prussia, had much ado to exist at all, let alone graciously.
Under the combined influence of Wieland, Goethe, Herder and
Schiller Weimar was to achieve great renown; but that was still
in the future; and meanwhile Goethe himself was far enough in
1775 from being polished or urbane. One need only compare the
letters he wrote to the Countess Stolberg in the throes of his
passion for Lili Schönemann with Byron's epistles to Lady
Melbourne about *his* affairs of the heart, to realize the different
levels of civilization from which these two poets sprang. Goethe
poured out his soul to his unknown correspondent in lava-like
eruptions of disordered, frenzied, exclamatory prose. Byron
wrote to Lady Melbourne no less naturally and quite as openly;
but he appears mature and sophisticated beyond belief when his
informal conversational style is contrasted with the *furor Teutonicus*
of Goethe's explosive utterances. Both were then twenty-four, and
both were half-flirting, half-struggling with love; but neither at
this stage would have tolerated the other. Goethe (who likened
himself to an unlicked bear in Lili's menagerie of lovers) would
have been outraged by Byron's cynical airs; and Byron would
have been supercilious in the extreme about Goethe's unbridled
deportment. Yet the essential similarity between them, allowing
for the difference in social climate, is apparent in the descriptions
of the bystanders; and they also reacted in a very similar way to
the sensation they were causing. Both played up to it and showed
off shamelessly by giving their temperaments the rein; and if
Goethe was noisier and more uncouth, Byron was more histrionic;
but much was forgiven to both because their genius was recognized. Women worshipped them both; but men raved more
violently about Goethe, although the cult of exalted friendships
between men, prevalent in his youth, partly accounts for that.
The Jacobis, the Stolbergs and Lavater could indulge in paroxysms
of ecstasy which a Hobhouse, a Lord Holland or a Thomas Moore
would have considered the acme of bad taste.

Whilst all this excitement was seething round them, the young
poets themselves occupied the intervals between their public lives
and their love-making in writing reams of poetry and cultivating
the acquaintances their fame had made: Goethe by a romantic
and rollicking journey down the Rhine and into Switzerland with
hero-worshipping, sky-larking and dithyrambic friends; Byron by
successive visits to country houses where dalliance was the order
of the day. Then, at the age of twenty-six, they both took a
fateful, even ominous, step which completely altered the course of

their lives. In both cases the reason was basically the same: they wished to put an end to their aimless drifting and anchor themselves in life, Goethe by accepting harbourage and responsibility at the court of Weimar; Byron by the marriage-tie. It would have needed no prophet to foretell disaster as the certain result of any matrimonial venture of Byron's then, although it would have demanded the utmost in second sight to foresee the particular form the catastrophe was to take. But hostile and friendly critics alike are unanimous in labelling the marriage with Anna Isabella Milbanke as the supreme error of Byron's life. The resulting separation-scandal which was the prime determining factor in his subsequent existence was the ruin of his personal happiness, but it proved the salvation of the poet and, ultimately, of the man. In Goethe's case the situation is more doubtful. Weimar was certainly a fateful choice, as he (and others) felt at the time, and very vividly in retrospect. It was also fully as potent in conditioning the rest of his life as Byron's star-crossed marriage. But was it equally disastrous? Few of his biographers and critics allow and most of them dislike the suggestion that the flight to Weimar imperilled his poetical gifts and was the undoing of the natural man. Be that as it may, Weimar can no more be thought out of Goethe's life than 'Annabella' can be wished away from Byron's. At the still youthful age of twenty-six both poets met their fate.

During the eight years which remained to him after he left England, Byron's life was even more rudderless than it had been before, until just before the end. Or so at least it seemed. But quite apart from his active efforts to support the Carbonari in Italy, he was in the grips of a furious creative energy which was sending masterpieces of 'imperishable excellence of sincerity and strength' hurtling across the Channel to Albemarle Street. And whatever may be thought of his dramas, the sustained intellectual effort that went to their composition counteracts the superficial impression of restless, indecorous, aimless and languid drifting. He was in poetical harness. The reverse is true of Goethe's life between the ages of twenty-six and thirty-six. *He* was harnessed to the service of the state, and seemed (as his mother wrote at the time) to be on bad terms with the Muses. But in one important respect their fates ran strictly parallel. *L'Anglico Mylord*, that unrepentant sinner, was being domesticated by the Countess Guiccioli; and 'the monster' whose indecent conduct had so much scandalized Charlotte von Stein was being chastened into polite behaviour by that well-bred Egeria. Meanwhile the poet in Goethe fell silent and the ebullient young man was eclipsed by the minister of state, who disconcerted and sometimes alienated the friends of his youth. Yet beneath the surface his genius was bent on survival and determined to escape, even if only for a time, from an atmosphere so inimical to poetic creation. Regeneration was Goethe's watchword as he stole away from Weimar on his way to Italy, where no one was to accompany him, least of all Charlotte von Stein. The Duke of Weimar knew that he was going; but only his secretary knew where he had gone. Had death stricken him down on the completion of his thirty-sixth year as he made his last furtive arrangements in Karlsbad for travelling under an assumed name, posterity would certainly have judged that Weimar had written *finis* to his poetical career.

Regeneration was also Byron's watchword as he set out for Greece: the regeneration of that tormented country, but his own regeneration too, and his own rehabilitation in the eyes of the world; and, like Goethe, he experienced a sense of release in leaving behind him a woman too well known and too well loved in the past. Similar also in this, both men (it is no exaggeration to say) were driven by despair; and it is equally certain that both attained their hearts' desire. No one who reads the accounts of Byron in Greece and his own letters will deny that he redeemed himself; and no one who reads Goethe's works subsequent to the sojourn in Italy will deny that he rescued the poet.

*      *      *

Goethe unlike Byron survived his desperate remedy; and many other things were to happen to him before his life-line began to cross Byron's in the year 1816, which saw the latter's disaster and exile. The German poet returned to the Cimmerian North as he called it in 1788, the year of Byron's birth, and eased his heart-ache for the halcyon days in Rome by his *liaison* with Christiane Vulpius. She bore him a son on Christmas Day 1789, whilst the French Revolution, thundering unnoticed over Byron's head, was profoundly disturbing and antagonizing Goethe. The source of his poetry, liberated in Italy, was choked up again, troubled and muddied, and finally reduced to the merest trickle. But the friend-ship with Schiller (1794–1805) retrieved him from isolation and sterility, revived and restored him to literature and life. Then Schiller died; and Goethe, his mind laid waste, looked vainly for comfort and stability in a desolate and menacing world. Finally he decided to legalize his relationship with Christiane which time had sanctioned whilst depriving it of glamour; but hardly had he accomplished this chivalrous if belated act, before his passion for Minna Herzlieb caused him to regret it. His anguish can be witnessed in the lyrics in *Pandora* and in the sufferings of Edward and Ottilie in *Die Wahlverwandtschaften*; but the flesh-and-blood heroine knew nothing about it; for Goethe was now entering on a period of relinquishments, renunciations and losses. Yet his fame and his glory outpaced his sorrows; and the death of his mother in September 1808, whatever it may have meant to him, was probably not vividly present in his mind during the historic interview with Napoleon which took place on October the second of that year.

A few months later Byron came of age; and the towering figure of Napoleon was an invisible link between the two poets, since both of them recognized in their great contemporary the true portent of the age. To both he was an object of hero-worship; and both, strangely enough, experienced the same violent revulsion in 1814, expressed by Goethe with uncharacteristic ferocity in *Timur* and by Byron in the headlong vituperation of the *Ode to Napoleon Buonaparte*; both were won back by the escape from Elba and the Hundred Days; and both of them procured and devoured the Memoirs of Las Casas. This might seem to bridge the gulf of forty years between them; but the love-affairs in which they were both engaged in 1814 show how deep it was. Byron, distraught by the sensational antics of Caroline Lamb was in a state of youthful frenzy; Goethe was basking in the spring sunshine of Marianne von Willemer's love and the autumnal splendour of his own. Yet, in the teeth of the years that separated them, time was bringing them together at a psychological moment. Byron left England in April 1816, and on May 8 Knebel brought his name to Goethe's notice, with the result that Goethe procured *The Corsair* and *Lara* and read them on May 22, 23 and 24. He was in the right frame of mind to listen to the tones of passion and grief ringing through both poems, being still shaken by the agony of his final farewell to Marianne on September 25, 1815. Byron certainly struck a related chord, which may even have seemed prophetic. For towards the end of May Christiane fell dangerously ill, and by the second of June her condition was critical. Yet on June the fourth Goethe found time in the middle of harrowing scenes to write with curious urgency:

I have taken cognisance of the English poet Lord Byron, who deserves to interest us. His strange nature shines out in his poems, which find much favour because of his wild and yet controlled talent. If you could tell me where I might find more detailed information about the life, character, etc. of this amazing man, you would be doing me a particular kindness.[1]

Poets pass our comprehension; the words 'particular kindness' sound like a cry for help; and how could Byron help Goethe?

My wife is in the utmost danger. . . . My son is the helper, counsellor

[1] *Briefe*, xxvii, pp. 47 f. To Professor Eichstädt in Jena.

and only rock to cling to in this turmoil. . . . Death of my wife. Last
terrible struggle of her whole being. She died at midday. Emptiness
and deathly stillness in and around me.[1]

> Du versuchst, O Sonne, vergebens
> Durch die düsteren Wolken zu scheinen!
> Der ganze Gewinn meines Lebens
> Ist ihren Verlust zu beweinen.
>
> .        .        .        .
>
> Vainly, oh sun, you are trying
> To break through the clouds' dark veil;
> For the rest of my life is but sighing,
> And my gain is her loss to bewail.

Goethe's sense of desolation and loss may have been increased
by remorse; for, if Christiane had many faults, he himself was no
saint; nor (and in this he also resembled Byron) was he of the
stuff of which husbands are made. Both poets were now suffering
a common sorrow: the loss of a wife and the resultant devastation
of their private lives. Goethe grieved and Byron raged (*his* wife
was still alive); yet the German was only saying in other words
what Byron frantically proclaimed:

> Seared in heart – and lone – and blighted –
> More than this I scarce can die.

The basic similarity between the situation of the two poets in
1816 was the decisive factor in Goethe's spontaneous sympathy
with Byron. Mere literary criticism was swamped by emotion;
mind and heart were stirred. Aged sixty-seven, the famous author
of *Götz, Werther, Iphigenie, Egmont, Tasso, Römische Elegien, Wilhelm
Meister, Hermann und Dorothea, Die Natürliche Tochter, Faust I,
Pandora, Die Wahlverwandtschaften* and *Dichtung und Wahrheit I–III*
(not to mention many lesser and some decidedly minor works)
began in his own phraseology to take cognizance of Byron.

## b. SOUND-BARRIER

He came up against the sound-barrier at once, although he was not
aware of it; for he was by no means at home with Byron's language. A fair reading knowledge of English was the utmost he
could claim; but he had no real feeling for it, and no facility in
speaking or writing it. He never attempted the latter feat after his
youth, when as a high-spirited young genius of seventeen he made
delightful hay of it both in prose and verse:

The father as he wrote in an appendix to Luptons letter, would see if
I write as good english as Lupton german. . . . Let us speak a little

[1] *Tagebücher*, v, p. 239. June 5 and 6, 1816.

sister, the fathe may judge. Lupton is a good fellow, a marry, invetious fellow as I see it in his letter, which is wroten with a spirit of jest, much laudably moderated by the respect, he owes to his master. . . . Any worlds of my self. Sister I am a foolish boy. . . . Many time I become a melancholical one. I know not whence it comes. Then I look on every man with a starring owl like countenance. . . . In like a situation of my soul, I make english verses, /: a science more than Lupton:/ english verses, that a stone would weep. In that moment thou shallt have of them. Think on it sister thou art a happy maiden, to have a brother who makes english veses. I pray thee be not haugty thereof.

### A SONG OVER THE UNCONFIDENCE TOWARDS MY SELF

An other tought is misfortune
   Is death and night to me:
I hum no supportable tune,
   I can no poet be.

When to the Altar of the Nine
   A triste incense I bring;
I beg let Poetry be mine
   O Sistres let me sing.

But when they then my prayer not hear,
   I break my whisp'ring lire;
Then from my eyes runns down a tear,
   Extinguish th'incensed fire.

Then curse I, Freind, the fated sky,
   And from th'altar I fly;
And to my Freinds aloud I cry,
   Be happier then I.

Are they not beautifull sister? Ho yes! Senza Dubbio. . . . Often Sister I am in good humor. In a very good humor! Then I go to visit pretty wifes and pretty maiden. St! say nothing of it to the father. . . . I seek further to please to the uttermost part of men, wise and fools, great and littles, I am diligent, I am mirthy, and I am luky. Adieu.[1]

Teutonic to the backbone, even the rhythmic verve; and this was as far as Goethe ever got (with an English tutor and an English friend at his elbow) in mastering the written language. He was alien to its idiom; and although he declared in 1825 that he knew the literature, life and institutions of England so well that he would be no stranger if he ever visited our shores, one cannot but feel that he would have appeared conspicuously a stranger to us, a distinguished foreigner, very much on everyone's mind. But

[1] *Der junge Goethe*, ed. Max Morris, 6 vols., Leipzig, 1901–12. Cf. i, pp. 129 ff. for the complete text. To Cornelia Goethe from Leipzig, May 11–14, 1766.

he never came to this country, and his knowledge of English life was gained at second-hand. As for speaking the language, that he resolutely avoided, forcing his English and American visitors to talk German if they were capable of doing so, and conducting the conversation in French if they were not. This he spoke with 'not a good accent' as young Thackeray noted; and was 'not quite easy' in it according to an American observer. But he kept on relapsing into French when attempting to express in English his opinion of a translation of *Faust* by Leveson-Gower and of *Tasso* by Charles Desvoeux. 'I understand English à ma manière', he assured his visitor, speaking perhaps more truly than he knew.

On another occasion he remained obstinately mute rather than converse with an Englishman in the latter's language; and his engaging young daughter-in-law Ottilie (*née* von Pogwisch) was responsible for the straits into which he was put. As she is closely connected with the story of Byron and Goethe, she cannot be allowed to slip into this book without a word of introduction. Married to August von Goethe in 1817 at the age of twenty-one, she became the life and soul of Goethe's household where the young married couple occupied rooms of their own, and where she dealt as best she could with poor unhappy August. Loutish and badly brought up (for Goethe like Byron was unequal to parental responsibilities), intemperate, unstable, and in fact a pathological case, this love-child and child of genius was like a standing reproach to his father and the bane of Ottilie's life. Yet she somehow managed to continue to be naturally happy and gay. Extravagantly pretty, with a delicate figure and great dark-blue eyes, cordial, charming and a winning hostess, she was the Queen of Hearts in Weimar and the apple of Goethe's eye. He called her a 'crazy angel', for he delighted in her spirited nonsense, teased her, made much of her and came to depend on her more and more. In her own rather *gamine* way, she was also devoted to him, profuse in marks of affection, interested in all his doings and nursing him when he was ill. But she had all the defects that go with such qualities. Wilful, flirtatious, giddy and capricious, she was also wantonly extravagant; and such a shocking housekeeper that, two years before his death, Goethe, like Byron,

> Dreading the climax of all earthly ills,
> The inflammation of his weekly bills,

deprived her of the office, slept with the keys under his pillow and saw to it that every ounce of bread was weighed out. Her flirtations also often overstepped the bounds of decorum; and during an affair with a certain Mr Wemyss Goethe stigmatized her conduct as empty-headed and hollow hearted, inspired, not by passion, but by her rage for excitement and general sensationalism. Perhaps he felt some unconscious jealousy; for he told Chancellor Müller after August's death in 1830 that a second marriage on her part would be a portcullis cutting her off from his love (and out of his will). Considering what life with August had been like, this sounds very harsh; but it never came to that. The old poet and the 'crazy angel' remained together till the end.

It was possibly not pure 'sensationalism' that threw Ottilie into the arms of Wemyss. He was an Englishman, and she was Anglophil to a degree that amounted to Anglomania; she would do anything for the English; and so it came about that on one occasion she succeeded in inducing her father-in-law to receive (evidently in her own absence) one of her cherished English *protégés*, an intelligent, amiable and highly entertaining young man, she assured him; Goethe gave in, reluctantly we may be sure, since this paragon spoke no German:

The young man was announced [Goethe told a hilarious dinner-party next day]; I went down to receive him, and bowed him into a chair, politely but in pantomime. He sat down and I sat down opposite to him. He was silent, I was silent, we were both silent together. After a good quarter of an hour, or perhaps not quite so long, I got up and he got up. I took leave, again in pantomime, he did the same, and I accompanied him to the door. Then my conscience began to prick me because of Ottilie, and I felt that I could not let him go without a word. So I pointed to Byron's bust and said: 'That is the bust of Lord Byron'. 'Yes', said he, 'he is dead'. And that is all I got out of this intelligent, amiable, lively and loquacious Englishman.[1]

One likes to think of the bust of Byron presiding over this encounter. It was very far from a masterpiece, being the work of one Jean Jacques Flatters, a Franco-German sculptor who had never seen Byron. But Goethe prized it greatly, and told the artist that 'a highly esteemed traveller who saw Lord Byron in Corfu' vouched for its perfect resemblance to the original. It had arrived towards the end of 1824; and now, placed in a conspicuous position, witnessed the discomfiture of a fellow-countryman and Goethe's lack of spoken English.

His reading knowledge was in better case, but even that was shaky, as his various efforts to translate Byron reveal. There are several mistakes in sense in the passages he rendered from *Manfred*, amongst which the reading of 'joke' for 'yoke' deserves to rank with the howlers. He failed entirely to reproduce the hypnotic

*Gespräche*, ii, pp. 766f. August 25, 1831. F. Förster.

effect of the *Incantation*, and may even have been unaware of its
nature, since he translated it into penny-plain rhymeless verse;
and he never communicated the inspiring energy which is the
soul of Byron's poetry, as can be seen, or rather felt, in his version
of the opening stanzas of *Don Juan*. He was defeated at the outset
by *English Bards and Scotch Reviewers* and gave up the unequal
struggle; but *The Vision of Judgment* aroused his enthusiasm to
such a pitch, that he read and re-read it with the help of a dictionary and finally mastered it completely. Otherwise Byron's language was a dead language to Goethe. He could follow the
meaning and recognize the nature of the works, but the vital
spirit escaped him.

*         *         *

If Goethe was a *dilettante* in English, Byron was an ignoramus in
German and claimed to be a dunce:

When I was a boy I studied German, which I have now entirely
forgotten. It was very little I ever knew of it.[1]

Of the *real* language I know absolutely nothing,–except oaths learned
from postillions and officers in a squabble! I can *swear* in German
potently, when I like – 'Sacrament – *Verfluchter – Hunds-fott*' – and so
forth; but I have little else of their energetic conversation.[2]

This was undoubtedly a handicap in German-speaking countries:

Dined at Interlachen. Girl gave me some flowers, and made me a
speech in German, of which I know nothing: I do not know whether
the speech was pretty, but as the woman was, I hope so.[3]

This was far from being the only pretty speech made about him
in German of which he knew nothing; for his vogue in Germany
was probably greater than anywhere else on the Continent:

Um! [mused the young author of the piles of *Harolds* and *Giaours*
Lord Leveson-Gower was taking with him to Berlin in 1813] – have I
been *German* all this time, when I thought myself *Oriental*?[4]

This was by no means a welcome thought; for from a very
early age Byron's mischievous sense of humour was apt to be
aroused by Germans:

---

[1] Medwin, p. 150.

[2] *Letters and Journals*, v, p. 172. Diary for January 12, 1821. Protheroe reads 'little
less of their energetic conversation'. I adopt Quennell's reading in *Byron, A Self-Portrait*,
London, 1950, ii, p. 565; but I think it possible that Byron meant to write: 'little of
their less energetic conversation'.

[3] Ibid., iii, p. 362. Diary for September 25, 1816.

[4] Ibid., ii, p. 372. Journal for December 10, 1813.

C

*Abel* was one of the first books my German master read to me; and whilst he was crying his eyes out over its pages, I thought that any other than Cain had hardly committed a crime in ridding the world of so dull a fellow as Gessner made brother Abel.[1]

German sentimentality did not go down well with Byron; and neither did German pedantry and pretentiousness, of which a remarkable specimen came under his notice in the person of August Wilhelm Schlegel. The latter was living with Madame de Staël at Coppet in 1816, where Byron and Hobhouse saw him frequently in company with the Abbé de Brême, who took a fiendish delight in poking fun at the German and showing him up. From the stories retailed by Hobhouse in his diary it would seem that Schlegel (whom Heine also ridiculed for his vanity) was very easy game:

Madame de Staël was one day saying that she was glad she published her *Allemagne* some time ago; if she had done so now it would have been too late. Nobody cares about Germany – literature was on the decline. 'Quoi, Madame; vous osez dire ça du pays de Frederick Schlegel devant William Schlegel!' 'Ah', said Madame de Staël, throwing herself back in her chair, 'comme la vanité est bête!'

Schlegel was one day talking English to Miss Randall. Brême said, 'It seems to me that the English, for a man that does not understand it, is rather a hard language'. Schlegel went up to Madame de Staël, and said, 'I see, Madame, that there is a conspiracy in your house against me; everybody is resolved to offend me'. Madame de Staël was writing; she threw down her pen: 'Dites-moi donc, M. de Brême, qu' avez-vous fait pour offenser M. Schlegel?' Brême explained, but in vain. He said that he did not know that Schlegel was hired defender of all nations. 'Sir', said Schlegel, 'any one could see you meant to laugh at my way of pronouncing English. . . .'

Schlegel has a habit of walking in with some great book, and throwing it down with a great noise; also of leaving Oriental books, and when he saw anybody turning over the pages, to go up to him and say, 'What, sir, don't you know that Oriental books always begin by the end?' Brême got an Armenian book and took him in. Schlegel made the same remark, only saying, 'It is odd that this work begins with "finis" '. Brême exposed him![2]

This 'dreadfully national behaviour', as Hobhouse called it, recurred vividly to Byron's mind several years later when reading a translation of Friedrich Schlegel's *History of Literature* and finding the author high-flown and unintelligible:

I dislike him the worse . . . because he always seems upon the verge of meaning; and, lo, he goes down like sunset, or melts like a rainbow,

---

[1] Medwin, p. 150. This was Gessner's epic *Der Tod Abels* (1758).
[2] Lord Broughton (John Cam Hobhouse), *Recollections of a Long Life*, 6 vols., London, 1909–11; II, pp. 42 ff. Diary for October 14, 1816.

leaving a rather rich confusion – to which, however, the above comparisons do too much honour.

Continuing to read Mr Frederick Schlegel. He is not such a fool as I took him for, that is to say, when he speaks of the North. But still he speaks of things *all over the world* with a kind of authority that a philosopher would disdain, and a man of common sense, feeling and knowledge of his own ignorance, would be ashamed of. The man is evidently wanting to make an impression, like his brother. . . .

Of Dante he says 'that at no time has the greatest and most national of all Italian poets ever been much the favourite of his countrymen'. 'Tis false! There have been more editors and commentators (and imitators, ultimately) of Dante than of all their poets put together. *Not* a favourite! Why, they talk Dante – write Dante – and think and dream Dante at this moment (1821) to an excess, which would be ridiculous, but that he deserves it.

In the same style this German talks of gondolas on the Arno – a precious fellow to dare to speak of Italy! . . .

I have found out, however, where the German is right – it is about the *Vicar of Wakefield*. 'Of all romances in miniature . . . the *Vicar of Wakefield* is, I think, the most exquisite'. He *thinks*! – he might be sure. But it is very well for a Schlegel.[1]

It was not 'very well for a Schlegel' however, when Byron heard a few months later that August Wilhelm was proposing to launch an attack against him; then his innate dislike of the country, its inhabitants and above all its language merged with his memories of Schlegel at Coppet to produce a furious reaction:

They write from Paris that Schlegel is making a fierce book against ME: what can I have done to the literary Col-captain of late Madame? *I*, who am neither of his country nor of his horde? Does this Hundsfott's intention appal *you*? if it does, say so. It don't *me*; for, if he is insolent, I will go to Paris and thank him. There is a distinction between *native* Criticism, because it belongs to the Nation to judge and pronounce on natives; but what have *I* to do with Germany or Germans, neither my subjects nor my language having anything in common with that Country? . . .

The disloyalty of such a proceeding towards a foreigner, who has uniformly spoken so well of Me. de Stael in his writings, and who, moreover, has nothing to do with continental literature or Schlegel's country and countrymen, is such, that I feel a strong inclination to bring the matter to a *personal* arbitrament, provided it can be done without being ridiculous or unfair. . . . The Man was also my personal acquaintance; and though I refused to flatter him grossly . . . yet I uniformly treated him with respect – with much more, indeed, than any one else: for his peculiarities are such, that they, one and all, laughed at him; and especially the Abbe Chevalier di Breme, who did nothing but make me laugh at him so much behind his back, that

---

[1] *Letters and Journals*, v, pp. 191 ff. Diary for January 28 and 29, 1821.

nothing but the politeness, on which I pique myself in society, could
have prevented me from doing so to his face. . . .

It appears to me that there is a distinction between *native* and *foreign*
criticism in the case of living authors, or at least should be; I don't
speak of *Journalists* (who are the same all over the world), but where a
man, with his name at length, sits down to an elaborate attempt to
defame a foreigner of his acquaintance, without provocation and
without legitimate object: for what can I import to the Germans? What
effect can I have upon their literature?[1]

Posterity was to answer those questions in no uncertain tones:
in the second part of Goethe's *Faust*, in the works of Heine and
Lenau, in the Young German movement, and in the person of
history itself. Yet Byron felt himself utterly alien from the country
which housed his most fervent admirers, and amongst them (most
fervent of all and most eminent) Wolfgang von Goethe. Flaring
up at the very notion that a *German* should venture to attack him,
he was never unduly elated by the plentiful evidence of his
popularity in Germany, although he owned that it was some
compensation for the 'brutality' of the English. Goethe's praise
was a different matter; but otherwise the feeling that he could have
little or nothing in common with a country whose language he
did not know was his overriding and understandable sensation:

I like, however, their women (I was once *so desperately* in love with a
German woman, Constance), and all I have read, translated, of their
writings, and all I have seen on the Rhine of their country and people –
all, except the Austrians, whom I abhor, loathe, and – I cannot find
words for my hate of them, and should be sorry to find deeds correspondent to my hate; for I abhor cruelty more than I abhor the
Austrians. . . .[2]

It was the political oppression of Italy by Austria which made
Byron 'hate and utterly despise and detest those *Hun brutes*, and
all they can do in their temporary wickedness', words he would
certainly have applied to the Germans in our day; but having
himself no experience of German savagery (though he abominated
that 'drunken corporal, old Blücher'), he had no quarrel with the
nation as such, but not much enthusiasm for it either:

> From Poland they came on through Prussia Proper,
>     And Königsberg, the capital, whose vaunt,
> Besides some veins of iron, lead, or copper,
>     Has lately been the great Professor Kant.
> Juan, who cared not a tobacco-stopper
>     About philosophy, pursued his jaunt

---

[1] *Letters and Journals*, v, pp. 337 and 340 f. To Murray from Ravenna, August 4
and 7, 1821. Goethe sometimes applied the epithet *Hundsfott* to persons he disliked.
[2] Ibid., p. 172. Journal for January 12, 1821.

To Germany, whose somewhat tardy millions
Have princes who spur more than their postillions.
. . . . . . . . . . . . . . . . . .
On with the horses! Off to Canterbury!
    Tramp, tramp o'er pebble, and splash, splash through puddle;
Hurrah! how swiftly speeds the post so merry!
    Not like slow Germany, wherein they muddle
Along the road, as if they went to bury
    Their fare; and also pause besides, to fuddle
With 'schnapps' – sad dogs! whom 'Hundsfot', or 'Verflucter',
Affect no more than lightning a conductor.[1]

A backward country, tyrannical rulers, drunken postillions and
a barbarous language; iron, lead and copper and the late Professor Kant – this is not the voice of a Germanophil, but the tones
of insularity itself. Yet how little could Byron have imagined the
grisly part two of the racial characteristics so gaily noticed here
were to play in Missolonghi a few weeks before he died. He was
just recovering from a fearful attack of epilepsy and was lying
exhausted and barely conscious on his bed, when two drunken
Germans raised an unfounded alarm that the Souliots had risen
and were marching on the Seraglio. Panic-stricken, Gamba,
Parry and Stanhope rushed out to deal with the situation. In
burst the two drunken Germans, wildly waving their arms and
shouting in German that the arsenal had been stormed by the
Souliots, but that they would protect Lord Byron. In his damp
and dimly lighted room, bewildered, helpless and alone, unable to
make any sense of what the men were saying, conscious only of
noise, confusion and horror, hideously contorted faces and uncouth and brutish sounds, Byron may well have felt that he was in
one of the circles of Dante's *Hell*, expiating those lines in *Don
Juan*.[2]

\* \* \*

Though Byron was no Germanophil, he fell many degrees short
of Goethe's Anglophobia:

All Englishmen as such are without the power to reflect. . . . In no
country does egoism predominate more than in England, and no nation
perhaps is so fundamentally inhumane in politics and private affairs. . . .
Nowhere are there so many hypocrites and so much sanctimoniousness
as in England. . . . Whilst the Germans work like galley-slaves to solve
philosophical problems, the English, strong in their great practical
common sense, laugh us to scorn and conquer the world. Everyone
remembers their fulminations against the slave-trade; and whilst they

---

[1] *Poetry*, vi, pp. 418 and 421.
[2] Cf. the striking account given of this incident by Sir Harold Nicolson in *Byron.
The Last Journey*, London, 1948, pp. 223 f.

tried to make us believe in the incredible humanity of their motives, it
now turns out that they were in fact actuated purely by motives of
material gain, without which, as is well known, the English never do
anything.[1]

This sounds uncompromising enough; but Anglophobia is often
an ambivalent emotion. Goethe, like many another, half admired
what he wholly condemned; and he evidently could not help
liking the mettlesome young Englishmen who kept on dribbling
into Weimar to be taught German by Eckermann and to flirt with
Ottilie. He admired their self-confidence and considered them
greatly superior in every way to their German contemporaries. He
particularly liked their easy and assured manners, he told Eckermann; and added that the very fact of being English, and of
enjoying the blessing of personal freedom as members of a race so
highly esteemed by other nations gave them the courage to be as
nature made them, complete human beings, even when they were
complete fools. They never betrayed awkwardness at being in a
foreign country. On the contrary, they behaved as naturally as if
they were the lords of creation and as if the whole world belonged
to them. And how attractive they were to women! Goethe's heart
always sank when Ottilie announced to him the imminent arrival
of yet another young Englishman, for he saw in advance the floods
of tears that would be shed when he left. Yes, they were dangerous
young men; it was part of their charm.[2] Poor Eckermann, not
altogether relishing this panegyric, tried to put in a good word
for German youth, but Goethe swept this aside. Had Ottilie been
present, she would have been delighted to find her father-in-law
so amiably disposed to the representatives of a race not otherwise
much liked; for he often complained that the English bothered
him with their visits more than the natives of any other country
and bored him with their idle curiosity. He was not proof however
against their individual acts of courtesy; as for instance when
Charles Desvoeux had a copy of his manuscript translation of
*Tasso* printed expressly for Goethe and when Lord Leveson-Gower
presented him with a magnificent copy of his translation of *Faust*,
printed in large letters on vellum. These attentions caused him
to declare that in matters of high courtesy and good breeding
Englishmen had not their equal in the world.

Goethe's championship of Eckermann's pupils is all the more
striking, because these young men whom the ladies of Weimar

---

[1] Cf. Eckermann, pp. 148 and 371; and *Gespräche*, ii, pp. 451 and 590.
[2] Cf. Eckermann, pp. 687 f. for this conversation, which is given under the date
March 12, 1828.
[3] Cf. *Gespräche*, ii, p. 502. August 31, 1827, E. Gans; and ii, pp. 588 f., May 1829,
F. Förster.

adored were often markedly deficient in the high courtesy and good breeding of a Leveson-Gower or a Charles Desvoeux. Ottilie (self-styled British Consul at Weimar) and her almost equally Anglomaniacal women friends would not hear a word against them; but the men were less indulgent and seem to have had serious grounds for complaint:

Her Excellency Countess Henckel had given a ball at which Young-Old-England was as usual very much to the fore and at which some of the specimens had made themselves highly objectionable. All the gentlemen were outraged; all the ladies made placatory excuses; and as usual Goethe's daughter-in-law had been conspicuous by her wit and her obvious party spirit. . . . The anti-Anglomaniacs liked to send me ahead as a skirmisher when a luncheon-party or a tea-fight was contemplated against the English colony; and at dinner after that ball I accordingly opened proceedings with a will and, by this bold example, encouraged others to follow suit. Doctor Vogel, physician to the Grand Duke and Goethe's family doctor . . . rushed into the fray after me, and gave as a particular instance of my general criticisms the extraordinary behaviour of the sons of Albion who, in the intervals between dances, had stretched themselves out full length on the sofas, whilst their partners stood by them. This certainly seemed very striking, but Madame Ottilie was not in the least at a loss. 'I told grandmama ages ago', she replied, 'that the sofas in the corners of the big ball-room are absolutely useless. They are set so deeply into the wall and are so wide, that in order to sit in any kind of comfort one finds oneself involuntarily adopting a recumbent attitude'. 'I can't quite agree with you there', answered Vogel very diffidently; 'I sat on one of them with Madame X' (incidentally a very ugly lady), 'and —'. 'And yet', Goethe interrupted him, 'neither of you felt any desire to lie down? Oh, what models of virtue!'[1]

The joke was almost on a par with the conduct of the sons of Albion, which Goethe would certainly not have approved in the ordinary way, but he was breaking a lance for Ottilie. Also, though his Anglophobia was deep-seated, it was intermittent and intimately associated with his admiration for Byron. Both began to appear sporadically at the same time. For it was the attitude of the English towards Byron which led Goethe to dislike and even to despise the whole nation; he could not take their censoriousness calmly; nearly all the passages quoted above and others still to come occur in that connection. Not only that, but Goethe's frequent hymns of hate against the English were often in the nature of apologias for Byron's shortcomings; whereas Byron's attitude to Germany, Germans and the German language conditioned his response to Goethe by acting as a brake.

[1] *Gespräche*, ii, p. 799. Not earlier than 1828. Karl von Holtei.

Partly because of the sound-barrier between them, their relationship got off to a very slow start, being bogged down at the beginning by a series of blunders of Goethe's making. This set the tone of Byron's responses; and his intermittent overtures were sadly hampered by the intermediaries he was forced to use. With so much against it, the course of Goethe's love for Byron was not destined to run smooth; and the precarious relationship which eventually came into being would probably have borne no fruit had it not been for the overriding passion which the younger poet (unaware of it throughout) inspired in the mind of his great contemporary.

# PART I

# SYMPATHIES AND DISPATHIES (1816–1824)

# CHAPTER I

# Cross-Purposes (1816-1819)

## a. MISCONCEPTIONS

BYRON impinged on Goethe's consciousness in May 1816, on a suffering, melancholy and remorseful consciousness which made him peculiarly susceptible to the accents of despair in *The Corsair* and the mysterious mourning in *Lara*. Almost simultaneously Byron became vividly aware of Goethe during the most tragic months of his life, in the early period of exile projected against a spectacular background of ruin and disgrace. He already knew something of the German poet through Madame de Staël's *De l'Allemagne* which he read enthusiastically in 1813; he had also perused *Die Wahlverwandtschaften* in French and, like everyone else at the time, he was familiar with *Werther* to which he referred light-heartedly in *The Waltz* (1813):

> Seductive Waltz! – though on thy native shore
> Even Werter's self proclaimed thee half a whore;
> Werter – to decent vice though much inclined,
> Yet warm, not wanton; dazzled but not blind –[1]

And now he was to become acquainted with Goethe's master-piece, if acquainted is the right word for what can at most have been a series of vivid impressions gathered from an oral rendering into English of parts of *Faust I*. The translator was Monk Lewis, who repaid Byron's hospitality at the Villa Diodati in Coligny in August 1816 by this poetical service; and one would give a good deal to know how well or how ill he acquitted himself of the task. But sensitive and suggestible poets such as Byron find food for their imaginations in the slightest of hints; and he saw in a flash how well the magic framework accorded with the tormenting and conflicting emotions which were seeking for utterance:

But in all this – the recollections of bitterness, and more especially of recent and more home desolation, which must accompany me through life, have preyed upon me here; and neither the music of the Shepherd, the crashing of the Avalanche, nor the torrent, the mountain, the Glacier, the Forest, nor the Cloud, have for one moment lightened the weight upon my heart, nor enabled me to lose my own wretched

---

[1] *Poetry*, i, p. 494.

identity in the majesty, and the power, and the Glory, around, above,
and beneath me.[1]

His 'own wretched identity' perhaps seemed easier to lose when
objectified dramatically and projected into the person of a titanic
human being seeking certainty in the unhallowed practice of
magical evocations; for Byron had not been able to lose himself
in the hero of the almost contemporaneous third canto of *Childe
Harold*, explicitly undertaken:

> So that it wean me from the weary dream
> Of selfish grief or gladness – so it fling
> Forgetfulness around me –[2]

In the turmoil of his mind ('half mad . . . between meta-
physics, mountains, lakes, love unextinguishable, thoughts un-
utterable, and the nightmare of my own delinquencies'),[3] what
more fitting symbol could be found than the figure of the tragic
magician, whom he had glimpsed in Goethe's *Faust*? This basic
debt Byron certainly owed to Goethe; and he probably also
recognized the affinity between them which Goethe had felt when
reading *The Corsair* and *Lara*. The Faustian spirit in both drew
them together; but that was as far as Goethe's influence went and
Byron completed *Manfred* which was published on June 16, 1817,
entirely unconscious of breakers ahead; nor, unlike Goethe, does
he seem to have felt any curiosity about the personality, the
character or the private life of his German predecessor in the
field.

Had he done so, he would have had an excellent opportunity
for satisfying it at Coppet in the autumn of 1816, since both
Madame de Staël and August Wilhelm Schlegel knew Goethe
personally and had very definite opinions about him. But Hobhouse and Byron seem to have been too much occupied watching
de Brême make a fool of Schlegel, to spend any time gossiping
about the Sage of Weimar, although his name did occur once in
connection with a very unfavourable critique of *Dichtung und
Wahrheit I–III* in *The Edinburgh Review* for June 1816. This naturally
interested Byron as a fellow-victim, and he mentioned it to
Murray:

I have been twice to Copet [*sic*] this week. Madame is very well and
particularly agreeable; her daughter (the Duchess) is with child. There
were the Duchess of Ragusa and a Prince of –, I forget the name, – but
it was of fifty consonants, – German of course, – there; both very

---

[1] *Letters and Journals*, iii, p. 364. Journal for September 29, 1816; sent to Augusta.
[2] *Poetry*, ii, p. 218.
[3] *Letters and Journals*, iv, p. 49. To Moore from Venice, January 28, 1817.

worthy and pleasing personages. I have read the last *E.R.* They are very severe on the Germans – and their Idol Goethe.[1]

This review certainly formed one of the topics of conversation at Coppet then; for Byron remembered later that Schlegel had been 'wroth about *The Edinburgh Review* of Goethe, which was sharp enough, to be sure'.[2] But otherwise no comments are recorded, and no eagerness or interest was shown.

The reverse was true in Weimar where Goethe was reading the separation-poems, *Fare Thee Well* and *The Sketch* and evidently gossip-columns too. So much at least can be deduced from a conversation reported by George Ticknor, one of a little group of brilliant young Harvard men, all destined to play a distinguished and sometimes a conspicuous part in the history of their own country, who came over to the Old World in the first decades of the nineteenth century to sit at the feet of the learned in Göttingen and to pay their respects to Goethe and Byron as they wended their way through Europe. This almost forgotten episode in the literary relations between the two hemispheres played no negligible part in increasing the mutual awareness between the two poets; and indeed the intervention of one of the young Americans marked a turning-point later in their joint history. Ticknor for his part, on the face of it an ideal go-between, developed into a mischief-maker and made trouble between them. This young man (1791–1871), the future professor of French and Spanish in Harvard University, had been in London in 1815 and, launched into society by Murray, had been kindly received by everyone and in particular by Byron of whom at that time he spoke with the utmost warmth:

... his manners are so gentle, and his whole character so natural and unaffected, that I have come from him with nothing but an indistinct, though lively impression of the goodness and vivacity of his disposition. ... I think I have received more kindness from Lord Byron than from any person in England on whom I had not the regular claim of a letter of introduction.[3]

This was a description which would have fanned Goethe's enthusiasm; but when Ticknor in company with his friend Edward Everett visited the German poet in Weimar, the young American was obviously too much overawed to hazard any opinions of his own; and he was all the more reticent probably because, the separation-scandal having now broken out, his views

---

[1] *Letters and Journals*, iii, pp. 370 f. To Murray from Diodati, October 5, 1816.

[2] Ibid., v, p. 334. To Moore from Ravenna, August 2, 1821.

[3] G. Ticknor, *Life, Letters and Journals*, 2 vols., Boston, 1876; i, pp. 67 and 68; Journal for June 25 and 27, 1815.

of Byron had changed; whereas Goethe was completely unmoved by the commotion it had occasioned in England:

> Of Lord Byron, he spoke with interest and discrimination, – said that his poetry shewed great knowledge of human nature and great talent in description; *Lara*, he thought, bordered on the kingdom of spectres; and of his late separation from his wife, that, in its circumstances and the mystery in which it is involved, it is so poetical, that, if Lord Byron had invented it he could hardly have found a more fortunate subject for his genius.[1]

Though undeterred by the slander surrounding Byron's name, Goethe was nevertheless a prey to conflicting emotions on the subject of his personality and his writings; for, from the beginning almost to the end, he felt fascinated and repelled by them in varying degrees of intensity. Intimately attracted by Byron's poetry, he recoiled from his hypochondria as he termed it; for he knew that insidious emotion far too well himself; and the sinister spirit of despair counselling self-destruction was also no stranger to him; but, after his early manhood, he refused to entertain it; and his attitude towards Byron was compounded in almost equal parts of resistance to his pessimism and subjection to his genius:

> My interest in foreign literature [so he summed up in retrospect the year 1816] was chiefly directed to *Byron's* poems; for he appeared increasingly significant and gradually attracted me more, as he had earlier repelled me by hypochondriacal passion and violent self-hatred, which threatened to estrange me completely from his Muse when I sought to approach his great personality.[2]

The attempt to approach that great personality in 1817 through the third canto of *Childe Harold* and *Chillon and Other Poems* which Goethe ordered after reading Sir Walter Scott's review in the *Quarterly* seems to have misfired; and the next step was disastrous. He began to read *Glenarvon* on October 7, 1817, in order to obtain some information about Byron's life and loves; and at this unpropitious moment Young America intervened with a presentation-copy of *The Lament of Tasso* from Edward Everett and a similar gift of *Manfred* from Theodore Lyman, another Harvard man. The books arrived on October 11; and curiously enough Goethe ignored *Tasso*, obviously chosen because of his own famous drama on the same theme, and addressed himself to *Manfred* instead. He finished it in three sittings (October 11, 12 and 16); but before he had completed it he had jumped to two false conclusions, writing exultantly to Knebel:

---

[1] Ibid., i, p. 114. Journal for October 28, 1816. Also in *Gespräche*, i, p. 866.
[2] *Werke*, xxxvi, pp. 107 f. *Tag-und Jahreshefte* for 1816.

The most amazing event for me was the appearance a day or two ago of Byron's *Manfred*, presented to me by a young American. This strange and gifted poet has completely assimilated my *Faust* and derived the strangest nourishment from it for his hypochondria. He has used all the *motifs* in his own way, so that none remains quite the same, and for that reason alone I cannot sufficiently admire his mind. The remodelling is so complete that very interesting lectures could be given about it, as well as about the similarity with the original and the dissimilarity from it; although I certainly do not deny that the sombre glow of an unlimited, abounding despair becomes tedious in the end. Yet the displeasure felt on this account is always mixed with admiration and respect. As soon as our ladies, who are passionate votaries of Byron, have devoured the work, you shall have your share in it.[1]

There are two deeply dyed errors here, clearly due in the first place to hasty and feverish reading; but both of them so plausible, and one of them so flattering to Goethe's feelings, that he adhered to them rigidly for many a long year. In the first place he postulated a far deeper knowledge of *Faust* than Byron in fact possessed and drew the erroneous conclusion that the divergences were one and all attributable to skilful and deliberate remodelling. This was a serious misconception, arguing a dependence upon himself which went far beyond the choice of a similar theme, a family likeness in the opening monologue and some half-conscious reminiscences to be found in Byron's poem. But the whole is so totally different in effect as to underline Byron's originality. Different especially (and here the second error comes into the picture) in its much stronger affirmation of man's mastery over his own fate. The ethical content is the triumph of the unconquerable spirit of man, symbolized in the figure of a direct descendant of the mighty magicians of old who had power over the spirits and were in no way subject to them. The great central necromantic scene, the calling up of Astarte, follows the precedents of antiquity; there was nothing similar in the first part of Goethe's *Faust*, for the two heroes belong to different schools of magic:

> my past power
> Was purchased by no compact with thy crew,
> But by superior science – penance, daring,
> And length of watching, strength of mind, and skill
> In knowledge of our Fathers – when the earth
> Saw men and spirits walking side by side,
> And gave ye no supremacy: I stand
> Upon my strength – I do defy – deny –
> Spurn back, and scorn ye! –
>
> . . . . . . . . . . . . . . . . . . . . . . . .
> *Thou* didst not tempt me, and thou couldst not tempt me;

---

[1] *Briefe*, xxviii, pp. 277 f. October 13, 1817.

I have not been thy dupe, nor am thy prey –
But was my own destroyer, and will be
My own hereafter. – Back, ye baffled fiends!
The hand of Death is on me – but not yours![1]

This speech, and in particular the denial of a pact, shows that Byron was adhering to a much older tradition than the one which inspired Goethe's *Faust*, whose hero descended from the black magician of medieval times, selling his soul for knowledge, riches and power, and doomed to expiate this crime by an eternity in hell. Goethe it is true was to bring about his salvation in *Faust II* and had already promised to do so in the Prologue to *Faust I*; but this did not alter the status of his hero, who signed the pact and thereafter in a state of rebellious subjection to the evil spirit began slipping and sliding down the road to perdition. Despair and passion, guilt and remorse assail both Faust and Manfred; they are more clamorous in Byron's poem, but there is a certain exhilaration in the spectacle of a hero who remains undefeated against all odds. Moreover the extraordinary energy of the language, the vivid beauty and power of the natural descriptions, the grandeur of the spirit-world and the course of the action lift the poem far above the dismal level of hypochondria. In its essence it is a drama of purification, and as such should be compared with the final act of *Faust II* rather than with *Faust I*. But in so far as similar *motifs* come into play, Byron's divergences are all in the direction of a nobler estimate of man and a more grandiose conception of the powers of evil. This ethical superiority over Goethe (which by no means involves aesthetic superiority) has been noted by Samuel Chew, who stresses the message of encouragement and hope in *Manfred*, since it represents the triumph of the mind and soul of man and therefore ultimately of the forces of good.[2] Where he saw greatness vindicated, Goethe saw unrelieved gloom; and yet he was penetrated with admiration for the mind which had drawn such strange nourishment (as he believed) from his *Faust*. The conviction that Manfred was none other than Faust in a hypochondriacal disguise was and remained very dear to him. It not only witnessed to the strange spiritual kinship he had felt from the first, it also convinced him that Byron had felt it too and was now confessing it publicly. In a word he took it as a tribute of the highest order, and determined to acknowledge it openly as such.

How such an acknowledgement might affect Byron can easily be seen by the distress he felt on hearing that the critics in England were fathering *Manfred* on Marlowe's *Faustus*; and, curiously

---

[1] *Poetry*, iv, p. 135.
[2] S. Chew, *The Dramas of Lord Byron*, Göttingen, 1915, pp. 83–84.

enough, the letter he wrote to Murray on this subject was dashed
off the day before Goethe's epistle to Knebel:

Many thanks for the *Edinburgh Review* which is very kind about
*Manfred*, and defends its originality, which I did not know that any
body had attacked. I *never read*, and do not know that I ever saw, the
*Faustus* of Marlowe . . . but I heard Mr Lewis translate verbally some
scenes of *Goethe's Faust* (which were some good, and some bad) last
summer; – which is all I know of the history of that magical personage;
and as to the germs of *Manfred*, they may be found in the Journal which
I sent to Mrs Leigh. . . . I have the whole scene of *Manfred* before me,
as if it was but yesterday, and could point it out, spot by spot, torrent
and all.[1]

This strikes at the root of Goethe's misconception; the germs of
*Manfred* were embedded in the tragic triangular catastrophe which
had laid Byron's life waste; the inspiration came from 'the
majesty, the power, and the Glory' of the Alpine scenery; the
form was suggested by *Faust*; and Byron, ever quick to acknowledge debts of which he was conscious, was the first to inform
Murray on that score. But unluckily for him, critics both in
England and in Germany were far more conversant with Goethe's
*Faust* than he was; and the hunt was up. A writer in the *Critical
Review* was already speaking of 'gross plagiary';[2] and only a week
after Goethe had made his exciting 'discovery' and communicated
it to Knebel, Byron heard repercussions of it in Venice:

The Review of *Manfred* came very safely, and I am much pleased
with it. It is odd that they should say (that is, somebody in a magazine
whom the *Edinburgh* controverts) that it has been taken from Marlowe's
*Faustus*, which I never read nor saw. An American who came the other
day from Germany, told Mr Hobhouse that *Manfred* was taken from
Goethe's *Faust*. The devil may take both Faustuses, German and
English, – I have taken neither.[3]

It was the truth; but with Goethe proclaiming the contrary,
who was going to believe it? And why should Ticknor (for the
malicious American was George Ticknor) have been so ready to
make bad blood between the two poets? He had been impressed,
but not greatly attracted by Goethe, and was now highly critical
of Byron because of the separation-scandal; so that he was in no
mood to do either of them a good turn in their relation to each
other when, 'still feeling curious to see him', he called on Byron at
La Mira on October 20, 1817. The poet was not yet up (at eleven
in the morning!). However, Hobhouse, who 'after a youth of

---

[1] *Letters and Journals*, iv, pp. 173 f. October 12, 1817.
[2] Cf. *Poetry*, iv, p. 81.
[3] *Letters and Journals*, iv, p. 177. To Murray from Venice, October 23, 1817.

D

dissipation has now become a severe student', did the honours and the censorious young American took the opportunity to drop his poison into the ears of Byron's friend whilst the poet was dressing:

In a short time Lord Byron came in, looking exactly as he did in London two years and a half ago. In conversation he was more lively and various, and came nearer to what a stranger might expect from him, but still he did not attain it; for I have never heard him make one extraordinary or original observation, though I have heard him make many that were singular and extravagant.[1]

In 1815 Ticknor had found Byron's conversation 'gay, pleasant and interesting in an uncommon degree . . . simple and unaffected . . . he speaks . . . with sincerity . . . without ostentation . . . with modesty . . . with justice, generosity, and discriminating praise'.[2] But times had changed; Byron might look exactly the same; Ticknor felt very differently about him, and, determined to make the charge of plagiarism stick, he brought the conversation round to *Faust*:

He [Byron] told me incidentally that M. G. Lewis once translated Goethe's *Faust* to him extemporaneously, and this accounts for the resemblance between that poem and *Manfred*, which I could not before account for, as I was aware that he did not know German.

'Incidentally' is disingenuous; Ticknor had evidently angled for that piece of information, and one can imagine the meaning look he directed towards Hobhouse when he got it. Now would have been the moment, since Goethe's name had been introduced, to pass on some of the praise which the latter had bestowed on Byron in Ticknor's hearing; but instead of doing that, Ticknor, obliquely hinting at his interlocutor's ostracism, tried to get a rise out of him by bringing forward Goethe's unpopularity:

When I happened [!] to tell Lord Byron that Goethe had many personal enemies in Germany, he expressed a kind of interest to know more about it that looked extremely like Shylock's satisfaction that 'other men have ill luck too'; and when I added the story of the translation of the whole of a very unfair *Edinburgh* review into German, directly under Goethe's nose at Jena, Byron discovered at first a singular eagerness to hear it, and then, suddenly checking himself, said, as if half in earnest, though still laughing, 'And yet I don't know what sympathy I can have with Goethe, unless it be that of an injured author'. This was the truth, but it was evidently a little more than sympathy that he felt.

[1] Cf. G. Ticknor, op. cit., i, pp. 165 f., for the complete account of the visit. Journal for October 20, 1817.

[2] Ibid., op. cit., i, pp. 59 and 64. Journal for June 20 and 23, 1815.

The half-malicious amusement Ticknor provoked in Byron on the subject of Goethe was replaced by exasperation when Hobhouse told him of the charge made by the departed guest, who also revived in a very tenacious memory the damaging language used by *The Edinburgh Review* about Goethe. Yet the statement that there was no real bond between himself and the German poet (made before he knew of his alleged indebtedness) gives the truth of the situation as he saw it at the time, and this must have added to his annoyance at the glib accusation of plagiarism brought against his most passionately personal poem.

## b. SHADES OF GLENARVON

As soon as Goethe had finished *Manfred*, he turned back to *Glenarvon*, thus sandwiching Byron's witch-drama between Lady Caroline's blood-and-Gothic. It was an unholy combination; for, though the novel bored him dreadfully, he read it from cover to cover under the impression that he was gleaning reliable information about Byron's private life:

> The novel *Glenarvon* was said to give information about many love-affairs of Byron's; but the interest of this voluminous work is not equal to its size; situations are repeated, especially intolerable ones. It must be admitted that it has a certain value; but one would be more ready to admit this, had it been in two modestly sized volumes.[1]

He waded through it conscientiously, however, finishing it on October 30, 1817, before embarking on his review of *Manfred* on November the second. This, together with the translation of several passages from the drama, was finished by the end of the year; and whilst Goethe was staying with Knebel during the first fortnight in November, he was completely absorbed in this task and could talk of nothing else. But he delayed publication until 1820, and it remained in cold storage for more than two years, thus very much retarding the action engaged between him and Byron. In view of its nature, Goethe may possibly have hesitated to print it at the time; for, when he finally released it, he was in no mood to be scrupulous about the story it contained. The opening paragraph was almost word for word a repetition of what he had written to Knebel in the first flush of paternal pride; but the review as a whole was written under the shadow of *Glenarvon*, and in the misguided belief that one of the sensational tales it contained was literally true. This story had been adapted by Lady Caroline from *The Giaour*, of which Byron said in the Advertisement:

---

[1] *Werke*, xxxvi, p. 128. *Tag-und Jahreshefte* for 1817.

The story, when entire, contained the adventures of a female slave, who was thrown, in the Mussulman manner, into the sea for infidelity, and avenged by a young Venetian, her lover.[1]

It was the tale of a double murder, a tale of love and revenge; and it was founded on fact – an eleventh-hour rescue by Byron of a girl in Athens about to suffer the same fate as the heroine in *The Giaour*:

The new governor [thus Lord Sligo summed up at Byron's request the rumours he had heard about the affair in Athens] . . . had, of course, the barbarous Turkish ideas with regard to women. In consequence, and in compliance with the strict letter of the Mohammedan law, he ordered this girl to be sewed up in a sack, and thrown into the sea – as is, indeed, quite customary at Constantinople. As you were returning from bathing in the Piraeus, you met the procession going down to execute the sentence of the Waywode on this unhappy girl. Report continues to say, that on finding out what the object of their journey was, and who was the miserable sufferer, you immediately interfered; and on some delay in obeying your orders, you were obliged to inform the leader of the escort that force should make him comply; that, on further hesitation, you drew a pistol, and told him, that if he did not immediately obey your orders, and come back with you to the Aga's house, you would shoot him dead. On this the man turned about and went with you to the governor's house; here you succeeded, partly by personal threats, and partly by bribery and entreaty, in procuring her pardon, on condition of her leaving Athens. I was told that you then conveyed her in safety to the convent, and despatched her off at night to Thebes, where she found a safe asylum.[2]

It would be hard to imagine a more exciting story or one more greatly to the credit of the hero; but Byron was never quite satisfied with it, hinting darkly both in letters and his Journal that there was considerably more behind it:

It was a strange and not a very long story, and his report of the reports . . . is not very far from the truth. Don't be alarmed. There was nothing that led further than to the water's edge; but one part (as is often the case in life) was more singular than any of the *Giaour's* adventures.[3]

I showed him [Galt] Sligo's letter on the reports of the Turkish girl's *aventure* at Athens soon after it happened. He and Lord Holland, Lewis, and Moore, and Rogers, and Lady Melbourne have seen it. Murray has a copy. I thought it had been *unknown*, and wish it were; but Sligo arrived only some days after, and the *rumours* are the subject of his letter. That I shall preserve, *it is as well*. Lewis and Galt were both *horrified*; and L. wondered I did not introduce the situation into *The*

[1] *Poetry*, iii, p. 83.
[2] *Letters and Journals*, ii, p. 258, footnote. August 31, 1813.
[3] Ibid., 11, p. 311. To Professor Clarke, December 15, 1813.

*Giaour*. He *may* wonder; – he might wonder at that production's being written at all. But to describe the *feelings* of *that situation* were impossible – it is *icy* even to recollect them.[1]

This tallies more or less with Byron's later statement (or alleged statement) to Medwin, that he was the lover of the Turkish girl, and only discovered her identity after the rescue. That certainly would have been an *icy* situation. But even this account stops short of the double murder which is the theme of *The Giaour* and which was evidently circulating as a true story in London in 1813. Byron hoped to kill it by means of Sligo's version as he explained to Thomas Moore:

This letter was written to me on account of a *different story* circulated by some gentlewomen of our acquaintance, a little too close to the text [of *The Giaour*].[2]

Lady Caroline Lamb was obviously one of the gentlewomen in question; and one cannot help suspecting that Byron (like Goethe, much given to mystifications) had been dropping dark hints of guilt and bloodshed in her ear, and was now sorry for it. But if so, repentance came too late; although it is also perfectly possible that 'little *Mania*', as Byron called her, had indentified Byron with the hero of *The Giaour* entirely on her own account. He had played up altogether too successfully to the lurid reputation *Childe Harold* had procured him to escape from the consequences of his imaginary crimes. They came home to roost in *Glenarvon*, and amongst them the double murder committed in *The Giaour*, now figuring as a *crime passionnel* in Florence involving the super-Byronic hero:

The victim of his unfortunate attachment had fallen a prey to the revengeful jealousy of an incensed husband; but her death was not more sudden, more secret, than that of the tyrant who destroyed her. Every one knew by whose hand the fair and lovely Fiorabella had perished; but no eye bore witness against the assassin, who, in the depths of night had immediately revenged her loss. The murderer and the murdered were both alike involved in the impenetrable veil of mystery. . . . Lord Glenarvon was seen no more at Florence: he had been the cause of this tragic scene.[3]

Glenarvon had said, there was a horrid secret, which weighed upon his mind. He would start at times, and gaze on vacancy; then turn to Calantha, and ask her what she had heard and seen. His gestures, his menaces were terrific. He would talk to the air; then laugh with convulsive horror; and gazing wildly around, enquire of her, if there were

---

[1] *Letters and Journals*, ii, p. 361. Journal for December 5, 1813.
[2] Ibid., ii, p. 258. September 1, 1813.
[3] *Glenarvon*, ii, pp. 83–85. Cf. also i, pp. 28 f., for a shorter version. This is one of those 'intolerable situations' of whose repetition Goethe complained.

not blood upon the earth, and if the ghosts of departed men had not been seen by some.[1]

Unnerved by such behaviour, Calantha was still further terrified by the well-meant warnings of one Gondimar:

'Lost woman', he cried, fiercely seizing her, 'you know not what you love; – look to his hand, there is blood on it!'[2]

It hardly needed the sinister apparition of a black monk haunting her feverish dreams next night and embroidering the same dark theme to convince the unfortunate Calantha that her lover had committed murder. But should it have been sufficient to satisfy Goethe that Byron was in sober fact the guilty and conscience-stricken hero of this turgid tale? Like Catherine Morland in *Northanger Abbey* he applied to persons and situations in real life the lore imbibed from a tale of horror; but, unlike Catherine, he had no Henry Tilney at his elbow to put him straight. On the contrary, the story was widely accepted as true on the Continent, and pursued Byron all the more unflaggingly for the rest of his life because the weight of Goethe's authority was behind it. For Goethe, reading *Glenarvon* simultaneously with *Manfred*, had come across what he probably believed to be arresting internal evidence. 'Look to his hand, there is blood on it!' exclaimed Gondimar:

MANFRED: Her faults were mine – her virtues were her own –
              I loved her, and destroyed her!
WITCH:                       With thy hand?
MANFRED: Not with my hand, but heart, which broke her heart;
              It gazed on mine, and withered. I have shed
              Blood, but not hers – and yet her blood was shed;
              I saw – and could not stanch it.

        . . . . . . . . . . . .

              If I had never lived, that which I love
              Had still been living; had I never loved
              That which I love would still be beautiful,
              Happy and giving happiness.[3]

Take *Glenarvon* as gospel truth and *Manfred* as straight autobiography, and there is no escaping the conclusion reached by Goethe. Granted the premises, his logic was sound. But the author of *Werther*, who had lived emotionally through the suicide of his double, should have known better than to foist Manfred's murder on Byron. It was *Glenarvon* that misled him and 'little *Mania*' who befooled him; so that when Manfred, considering the precedents for calling up the dead, mentioned Pausanias, who

---

[1] *Glenarvon*, ii, p. 183.
[2] Ibid., ii, p. 257.
[3] *Poetry*, iv, pp. 106 and 109.

slew
That which he loved, unknowing what he slew,
And died unpardoned –,[1]

Goethe took this as yet another proof of the tragic blood-guilt of the author. It would be idle to deny that he misinterpreted *Manfred* grossly, gravely over-estimating his own part in the poem, entirely misunderstanding its purport and showing extreme gullibility on the subject of the 'crime'. But in this connection it should be re-emphasized that some crucial passages in *Manfred* fitted the Florentine episode in *Glenarvon* like a glove; just as other passages can be used (and have been used) to substantiate the charge of incest. If a dramatic poem is to be given the weight of a deposition, then both crimes are proved to the hilt in *Manfred*, and should stand or fall together. In this respect Goethe, Harriet Beecher-Stowe and Lord Lovelace belong to the same school of thought.

The mention of those last two names throws a lurid light on the position Goethe had taken up in his review; but (unlike either of them), it was with no moral questionings. He deprecated Byron's hypochondria, and explained it by murder; but he betrayed no symptoms of shock, uttered no condemnation, and took it so calmly that his biographers and critics have taken his accusation with a like unruffled calm, as if the mistake were the most natural thing in the world, and certainly nothing to merit the word libellous. But truth to tell, the tie-up with *Glenarvon* is so fantastic that it is difficult to be serious about it; it underlines the unreality based on ignorance of Goethe's whole approach to the subject of Byron then; and his notions of the younger poet were not likely to be rectified when Karl August, Duke of Weimar, sent him the April number of *The New Monthly Magazine* for 1819 with the comment: 'My wife tells me that there is a marvellous piece of invention by L. Bayron in this number'. When he had read it, Goethe solemnly replied: 'The story your Royal Highness has sent me may well be the strangest production of this strange man'.[2] Strange indeed; for Byron, though he had initiated the idea, was not the author of *The Vampyre: a Tale by the Right Hon. Lord Byron*, preceded by *A Letter from Geneva*, both of them the work of his temperamental young physician, Polidori. It all went back to a rainy week in June 1816 when the circle gathered round Byron and Shelley at Geneva decided to while away the time by writing ghost-stories. The stimulus came from a French translation of a German volume of uncanny tales which had come their way; and Shelley and Mary, Monk Lewis, Polidori and Byron himself all

---

[1] *Poetry*, iv, p. 108.
[2] *Briefe*, xxxi, pp. 350 and 143. Weimar, May 6, 1819.

tried their hands at it. Mary produced *Frankenstein*; and according to Byron:

Lewis told a story something like *Alonzo and Imogene*; and Shelley himself . . . conjured up some frightful woman of an acquaintance of his at home, a kind of Medusa, who was suspected of having eyes in her breasts.[1]

According to Mary:

The noble author began a tale, a fragment of which he printed at the end of his poem of *Mazeppa*. Shelley . . . commenced one founded on the experience of his early life. Poor Polidori had some terrible idea about a skull-headed lady . . . but . . . he did not know what to do with her, and was obliged to dispatch her to the tomb of the Capulets, the only place for which she was fitted.[2]

Byron's tale, as can be deduced from the printed fragment as well as from his statement to Medwin,[3] was in fact a vampyre-story; and Polidori used the idea for the version he published in *The New Monthly Magazine*, in which form it is all 'Pollydolly's' and sad enough stuff. The introductory letter contained, beside some vampyre-lore, a certain amount of irresponsible gossip about Byron and Shelley, Polidori being decidedly hostile to the latter; and it was he who attributed Shelley's vision of the woman with eyes in her breasts to Byron's rendering of Coleridge's *Christabel*, at that time still unpublished:

. . . the whole took so strong a hold of Mr Shelly's [*sic*] mind, that he suddenly started up and ran out of the room. The physician and Lord Byron followed, and discovered him leaning against a mantlepiece, with cold drops of perspiration trickling down his face . . . they found that his wild imagination having pictured to him the bosom of one of the ladies with eyes (which was reported of a lady in the neighbourhood where he lived) he was obliged to leave the room in order to destroy the impression.[4]

What with this and other titbits and Byron's reputed authorship of *The Vampyre* (which continued to be published as his in spite of his authoritative denial), Polidori's contribution to the April number of *The New Monthly Magazine* made good reading for sensation-mongers, and evoked an impression of the goings-on at Geneva which produced the following horrified comment:

In rival conclave there and deep divan
He met and mingled with the Vampyre crew

[1] Medwin, pp. 120 f.
[2] *Letters and Journals*, iii, p. 447.
[3] Medwin, p. 120. For Byron's Vampyre-fragment, see *Letters and Journals*, iii, pp. 449–453.
[4] *New Monthly Magazine*, London, vol. xi, p. 195.

Who hate the virtues and the form of man,
And strive to bring fresh monsters into view;
Who mock the inscrutable Almighty's plan
By seeking truth and order to subdue –
Scribblers, who fright the novel-reading train
With mad creations of th' unsettled brain.

There Frankenstein was hatched – the wretch abhorred,
Whom shuddering Sh—y saw in horrid dream
Plying his task where human bones are stored,
And there the Vampyre quaffed the living stream
From beauty's veins – such sights could joy afford
To this strange coterie, glorying in each theme,
That wakes disgust in other minds – Lord Harold
Sung wildly too, but none knew what he carolled.[1]

Luckily this poem, containing many more distorted facts and
hostile fictions about Byron, was unknown to Goethe. The tales
would probably not have estranged him from the author of *Manfred*,
but he might have believed them; and his belief that Byron had
written Polidori's *Vampyre* was shortly to precipitate him into a
critical error even more glaring than his misinterpretation of
*Manfred*. At the moment it did nothing worse than sustain (and
indeed increase) his admiration for the poet. This had reached a
high pitch of enthusiasm when Joseph Cogswell (yet another
gifted young American) paid his second visit to Goethe in May
1819. He had gone to him in a state of violent prejudice two years
earlier, but had been won over during the interview, and they
were now on the most friendly terms:

Goethe . . . was not merely gracious, but affectionate and playful
even, – but he is breaking and will never do much more to increase his
fame. I spent all my time in Weimar with him, which was one evening
only: at supper he was unusually gay. His only remaining friend Meyer
[the painter], was present, a Baron chose [Chancellor von Müller],
whom [I] did not know, and a pretty little lively girl [Ottilie's sister
Ulrike]. We sat till midnight, and of course you will conclude we must
have been in glee, as such things are not often done in Germany. I
made him talk of the literature of the day, and he confirmed all I wrote
from Hamburg about the low state in which it is. He was enthusiastic
in his praises of Byron, pronounced him the greatest and only living
poet, which was no small gratification to me from its coincidence with
my own opinion.[2]

'Baron chose' also left an account of this meeting, remarking

---

[1] S. Chew, *Byron in England*, London, 1924; p. 31. Taken from *Don Juan: with a
Biographical Account of Lord Byron. . . . Canto III* (1819).
[2] A. E. Ticknor, *Life of Joseph Green Cogswell as sketched in his Letters*, Cambridge,
Mass., 1874; p. 98. To G. Ticknor from Dresden, May 18, 1819. Also in *Gespräche*,
ii, p. 54.

on Goethe's unusual animation and gaiety, owing to the presence of the 'interesting young American from Boston', also mentioning Cogswell's enthusiasm for Byron, and adding that Goethe had declared him to be the only great poet of the present age.[1]

This inspiring evening had as its sequel the presentation of Goethe's works in bulk to the Harvard University Library, a munificent gift already promised after the first meeting; for Goethe had taken a great liking to Cogswell, his 'dearest friend', as he addressed him in a German letter, which was answered in English, because 'it is the language of my heart and in writing to you my heart must speak'. Speaking the language of his heart to Goethe, it was inevitable that this ardent admirer of both poets should also speak of Byron, whom, like Goethe, he never met:

A friend of mine [Ticknor?] writes me that Byron's new poem of *Don Juan* is far inferior to all his former productions, but I am too great an admirer of Byron to think he can ever take a retrograde step.[2]

Theodore Lyman had ushered in the period of cross-purposes with his gift of *Manfred*, setting a whole train of events in motion which only ended with Goethe's death. Joseph Cogswell all unwittingly heralded the approach of an ice-age by his mention of *Don Juan*.

[1] *Gespräche*, ii, pp. 53 f. May 10, 1819.
[2] L. L. Mackall, *Briefwechsel zwischen Goethe und Amerikanern*, Goethe Jahrbuch, Frankfort am Main, 1904; vol. xxv, pp. 14 f. From Dresden, August 8, 1819.

# CHAPTER II

# The Ice-Age and After (1819-1823)

## a. SHOCK

COGSWELL followed up his letter by a final visit to Goethe towards the end of August 1819, during which highly emotional parting Byron's name was not mentioned. But Goethe was soon to hear it again in connection with the first two cantos of *Don Juan* in a report from London by Johann Christoph Hüttner, official interpreter to the Foreign Office and literary agent to the Duke of Weimar, who wrote in scandalized tones:

This poem has made an amazing sensation here because it was known . . . it was by Lord Byron, and because religion, morality, propriety and everything that is dear to us is here trampled underfoot in the most shameless manner. . . . For all that, it cannot be denied that he proves himself a genius in this work, a bold thinker and a fiery poet, from whom as such it is impossible to withhold one's admiration. Indeed many regard this rhapsody as his most successful work. But, as far as the subject-matter is concerned, the profligate Lord treats all opinions with contempt.[1]

We are now embarking on the treacherous ground of moral values, and it is amusing to find that a certain young American called George Bancroft (1800–91) who had been studying German literature at Göttingen University, had come to much the same conclusion about Goethe's writings as Hüttner had about *Don Juan*:

I am only more and more astonished at [Goethe's] indecency and immorality. . . . He appears to prefer to represent vice as lovely and exciting sympathy, than virtue, and would rather take for his heroine a prostitute or a profligate, than give birth to that purity of thought and loftiness of soul, which it is the peculiar duty of the poet to raise, by connecting his inventions with the actions of heroes, and embodying in verse the merits of the benefactors of mankind.[2]

Bancroft was to become a famous historian and statesman, ambassador to London in the wake of Edward Everett, later representing his country with dignity and distinction in Berlin;

[1] Mackall, op. cit., pp. 32 f. London, September 10, 1813.
[2] M. A. DeWolfe Howe, *Life and Letters of George Bancroft*, 2 vols., New York, 1908; i, p. 38. Diary for August 1818.

but, though he lived to attain the age of ninety, he never outgrew his early dislike of Goethe's morals as reflected in his writings, a dislike which he shared with the majority of cultivated Americans and Englishmen of that period. Recoiling from Goethe's 'prostitutes and profligates', Bancroft was still less disposed to think well of their creator when he learnt from his friends the Blumenbachs (who were also friends of Goethe), that the poet was a large, stout man of about seventy, fond of eating, drinking, mirth and good company. This picture of a robust philistine, even though said to be ennobled by 'majesty of form', did nothing to reconcile Bancroft to the indecency and immorality he had discovered in his writings. Happily the original proved to be less gross and less distressingly jovial than the Blumenbachs' portrait:

As for his person, Goethe is somewhat large, tho' not very, with a marked countenance, a fine clear eye, large and very expressive features, well built, and giving at once a favourable impression. In his manners he is very dignified, or rather he has a sort of dignified stiffness, which he means should pass for genuine dignity. He walks amazingly upright. I found him quite in dishabille. He had on an Oberrock – *i.e.* a surtout, but no waistcoat, a ruffled shirt, not altogether clean, a cravat like the shirt, fast inclining to dark complexion. His boots were of quite an ordinary cut. No Dandi would have worn them. He received me in the garden.[1]

This was at Jena, where Goethe was wont to retire to escape from public life at Weimar, which accounts for his undress. To a correct young man of nineteen, such slovenliness was not commendable and did not go well with the dignified stiffness. However, Goethe was talkative and affable, full of the pleasure the visits of Cogswell (that 'dear fellow') had given him, and Bancroft began to sound him:

At length I, gathering courage from talking with him, took occasion to bring him upon the British poets. Byron he praised in the highest terms, declared himself one of a large party in Germany who admired him unboundedly and seized on and swallowed everything that came from him. Of Scott we had time to talk; of Wordsworth, Southey he knew nothing; of Coleridge, the name – had forgotten however his works. The author of *Bertram* [C. R. Maturin] was praised. 'The tragedy', said Goethe, 'has many beautiful passages.' Byron, however, seemed to remain the most admired of all.

In connection with this and other matters Bancroft's tongue ran away with him, and he kept on 'coming into a strait', as he put it; or, as Byron would have said, 'getting into a scrape':

[1] Cf. Howe, op. cit., i, p. 68, for the complete account. Diary for October 12, 1819. Also in *Gespräche*, ii, pp. 65 f.

Of Byron I said his last poem [*Don Juan*] was reported to contain the most splendid exertions of poetical power, mixed with the lowest and most disgraceful indecencies. I did not think at the moment of Goethe's *Faust*. I mentioned, too, Byron's wife, forgetting that Goethe had not been happy in the married state. . . . I spoke a word, too, of Eichhorn's writing so many books, forgetting that Goethe had found no end with writing many.[1]

Goethe, serenely unaware of his visitor's unintentional *double entendre*, thought well enough of Bancroft to have him presented to his son and daughter-in-law in Weimar, where Bancroft arrived next day, and was charmed with Ottilie:

. . . a very pretty little woman, of lively sprightly manners, witty and agreeable and spirituelle, saying all things, even common ones, very prettily, never coming into embarrassment, knowing always what to say. The son seem'd rather a stupid and ignorant fellow.[2]

Ottilie, sister under her skin to Philine in *Wilhelm Meister*, the most reprehensible of those captivating 'profligates' who roused Bancroft's ire in Goethe's works, made a conquest of the susceptible young American, whereas Goethe never did. As late as 1855 in his *Studies in German Literature*, Bancroft, whilst admitting his genius, assigned to him the lowest place among all contemporary writers, as far as firm principles, love of truth, humanity and love of freedom were concerned. Byron, Voltaire and Shelley were far superior to him in magnanimous feelings, he declared; nor were Goethe's industry and genius, let alone his morality, equal to Voltaire's. This severe judgment, made in Bancroft's maturity, forms an entertaining commentary to Goethe's strictures on *Don Juan*.

He came to it entirely unmoved by the deleterious reports of Cogswell, Hüttner and Bancroft. What the English thought about Byron was never a safe guide; here they were as usual, extolling him to the skies one moment and carping at him the next.[3] In this at least Goethe strongly resembled the perfidious sons of Albion, although up till now it had been Byron's hypochondria rather than his immorality which had distressed him; but the first two cantos of *Don Juan* altered his perspective. They were presented to him on December 6, 1819, by the Duke of Weimar, who was decidedly unlucky in his gifts of Byroniana to Goethe, but who would have enjoyed *Don Juan* himself, had he been able to read it, with the exuberant gusto he brought to life and sport and women and war. In the early Weimar days Goethe and the

---

[1] The omission marks are not mine.
[2] Howe, op. cit., i, p. 69. Diary for October 13, 1819.
[3] *Briefe*, xxxii, p. 73. To Frau von Pogwisch (Ottilie's mother). October 13, 1819. Obviously inspired by Bancroft's report the day before.

rumbustious princeling unofficially in his charge had been hand in glove; but other times, and other customs. The minister had eliminated Prince Hal in himself and rejected Falstaff in the duke. Yet in spite of recurrent strained relations, appearances were always kept up by Goethe and cordiality kept on breaking in on the part of Karl August. It was therefore entirely in keeping with his genial and open-handed ways that he should have sent Goethe the first instalment of *Don Juan* the moment he procured it from London. The poet was delighted to receive it, read the two cantos at once, and wrote gratefully to his Highness when he had finished them, thanking him warmly for 'this remarkable and witty work which is shortening the long winter evenings'.[1] So far so good; and history even seemed to be repeating itself when he began to translate the opening stanzas of the poem, following this up with a commentary, completed by December 18, 1819, although not published until 1821. It looks like the story of *Manfred* all over again; and though one could not and perhaps one should not hope for another biographical tale of horror, still a review on somewhat similar lines to the previous one would appear to be pending.

Similarity there certainly was, for the feelings expressed were at least as mixed as before. The translation was naturally a good deal worse, it being beyond Goethe's powers, as he acknowledged himself, to give a German version of the 'untranslatable *Don Juan*'. Yet he printed his five lifeless and spiritless stanzas at the head of his review with a very awkward preamble:

If we had earlier scruples about inserting a passage from the perhaps translatable *Conte di Carmagnola*, and now make a bold attempt to grapple with the untranslatable *Don Juan*, it will probably be regarded as an inconsistency; we must therefore not fail to draw attention to the difference. Signor Manzoni is still little known among us; consequently we ought to get to know his merits in their entirety, and this is only possible from the original; when that is done, a translation by one of our younger friends will certainly be in order. But concerning Lord Byron's talent we are sufficiently initiated and cannot either help or harm him by translation; the originals are in the hands of all educated people. Such an attempt, even if it is undertaking the impossible, will always bring us some advantage; for even if a false reflection does not reproduce the image correctly, it at least draws our attention to the surface of the mirror itself and its more or less noticeable defects.[2]

This strained and stilted opening gambit, reflecting the confusion in Goethe's mind, shows that *Don Juan* had been too much for him and had disturbed his equilibrium:

[1] *Briefe*, xxxii, p. 117. December 14, 1819.
[2] Cf. *Werke*, xli, i, pp. 245 ff. for the complete text of this review and the translation of Canto I, stanzas 1–5.

*Don Juan* is a work of boundless genius, manifesting the bitterest and most savage hatred of humanity, and then again penetrated with the deepest and tenderest love for mankind. And as we already know and esteem the author and would not have him other than he is, we gratefully enjoy what with excessive licence, nay with audacity, he dares to set before us. The technical handling of the verse is quite in harmony with the strange, wild, ruthless content; the poet spares his language as little as he spares humanity; and as we approach closer we become aware that English poetry is already in possession of something we Germans totally lack: a cultured comic language.

With an almost audible sigh of relief, Goethe then clambered on to the safer ground of German comic writers, who attained their effects, he said by content rather than by form. Much might be learnt from *Don Juan* here:

. . . only in one form of wit we cannot imitate him, namely, that which frequently arises from the peculiar and questionable pronunciation of many words which on paper are quite differently written.

This sentence alone shows that Goethe was labouring under the severest of all handicaps in grappling (as he put it) with *Don Juan*; he realized that humour and wit abounded, and could appreciate the 'cultured comic language' academically, but without spontaneous enjoyment. Fundamentally it remained for him a poem in which the deepest and tenderest affection was swamped by savagery, ruthlessness, wildness, audacity and licence; whereas Canto I has been described by Chew as 'witty, sprightly, entertaining, vulgar'.[1] Dazzled by *Don Juan* Goethe certainly was, but also profoundly discomposed by it. Circling back warily to his attempt at a translation, he asserted that he was not printing it as a model to be imitated, but as an encouragement to others to undertake a difficult but linguistically rewarding task; then, still very much the cautious pedagogue, he added:

Should we be reproached for acting irresponsibly in endeavouring, by translation, to circulate such a work among the Germans, and thus to make an honest, sober and solid nation acquainted with the most immoral work poetic art has ever produced, we would reply that such an attempt need not, in our opinion, be destined for publication, but may well serve as an exercise for intelligent and talented minds. Closely considered, however, no particular harm to morality is to be feared today by printing such poems. Poets and authors would have to cut strange antics indeed to be more subversive of morals than the daily newspapers.

Yet, in his heart of hearts Goethe did consider *Don Juan* dangerous to morality; for, when presenting his copy of Cantos

[1] Chew, *Byron in England*, p. 28.

I and II to the Weimar library, he suggested that they might be lent out to intimate acquaintances and friends,[1] which was tantamount to saying that they should not circulate freely.

Goethe's review is moderation itself when compared with the torrents of abuse *Don Juan* called forth in England. Entirely free from any personal animus, it is also generous in its praise; but that one sentence 'the most immoral work poetic art has ever produced' is completely in accord with what Byron's best friends, and worst enemies were saying at home. One would be willing to concede that even a genius like Goethe cannot rise entirely superior to his times where notions of public morality are involved, were it not for Shelley's verdict 'I think that every word is pregnant with immortality'; and if Shelley is thought to be the kind of exception that disproves every rule; then let us listen to the voice of calm contemporary common sense raised among the nation of hypocritical shopkeepers:

As to PRINCIPLES, all the world, and you, Mr Murray, *first of all*, have done this poem great injustice. There are levities here and there, more than good taste approves, but nothing to make such a terrible rout about – nothing as bad as *Tom Jones*, nor within a hundred degrees of *Count Fathom*.[2]

Goethe may be exonerated from any knowledge of those two novels; but, as Robertson unanswerably said:

The mind reverts to a considerable library of French and German books, widely read in Goethe's age, which might have raised a blush even on *Don Juan's* cheeks.[3]

The mind reverts, even more perplexedly, to some of Goethe's own works: to the eroticism of *Römische Elegien*, for instance, with their pagan amoralism and deliberate voluptuousness. But Goethe has an answer to that:

There is a mysteriously great effect inherent in the various poetical forms. Should one attempt to transpose the content of my *Römische Elegien* into the tone and metre of *Don Juan*, the impression created would be one of depravity.[4]

> Oftmals hab' ich auch in ihren Armen gedichtet,
>     Und des Hexameters Mass leise mit fingernder Hand
> Ihr auf den Rücken gezählt. . . .

[1] Cf. *Briefe*, xxxii, p. 252. To F. T. Kräuter from Jena, April 21, 1820.

[2] S. Smiles, *A Publisher and his Friends*, 2 vols., London, 1891; i, p. 414. To Murray from J. W. Croker, March 26, 1820.

[3] J. G. Robertson, *Goethe and Byron*, Publications of the English Goethe Society, London, 1925, p. 64.

[4] Eckermann, p. 90. February 25, 1824.

Often too have I written verses, lying wrapped in her arms,
    And the hexameter's beat, softly, with fingering hand
Counted out on her back. . . .

And thus they form a group that's quite antique,
Half naked, loving, natural and Greek.[1]

It would occur to no one today to call either of these descriptions depraved. But Goethe's is much the more sophisticated, and by so much the nearer to what he condemned in *Don Juan*. There are also certain scenes in *Wilhelm Meister* which go quite as far in depicting sexual irregularity as anything in the Julia episode in *Don Juan*. Moreover when Goethe and Byron are ironical on this subject, there is a striking similarity between them. Julia's husband Alfonso, it may be remembered, having ransacked his wife's bedroom in vain to find the lover whose presence he suspects but cannot prove, listens dumbly and finally humbly to Julia's torrential self-defence, implores her pardon, and is in the process of being half-forgiven,

When, lo! he stumbled o'er a pair of shoes.

Wilhelm Meister went through much the same kind of experience in reverse, finding Philine's slippers in front of his bed one night on retiring, and jumping angrily to the obvious conclusion. In vain did he apostrophize the rogue secreted behind the bed-curtains to get up and come out and leave the room immediately, not a sound was to be heard; not a movement to be seen; then, tearing back the curtains:

To his great susprise he found that his bed was empty, the pillows and blankets quite undisturbed. He stared round the room, hunted round the room, ransacked everything and found never a trace of the rogue. Behind the bed, behind the stove, behind the wardrobe; – there was nothing to be seen. More and more diligently he hunted high and low; and indeed a malicious observer would have thought that he was seeking in order to find.[2]

The mind which conceived that scene was the last mind in the world to be shocked by the adventure of Juan and Julia; and the creator of Gretchen was of all men least likely to condemn the idyll between Juan and Haidée ('so loving and so lovely'). The sombre realism of the shipwreck on the other hand, with its blood-chilling alternation between the sublime and the grotesque, tragic grief submerged ever and again by a wave of strident laughter, would not be at all to Goethe's taste; and indeed the apparent heartlessness of those scenes caused great offence to all Byron's

[1] *Poetry*, vi, p. 136.
[2] *Wilhelm Meisters Lehrjahre*, Book V, end of Chapter 10.

E

critics, as did also his parody of the ten commandments ('Thou shalt believe in Milton, Dryden, Pope'), one of the audacities which Goethe for his part probably enjoyed. The shock he sustained on reading these first two cantos of Byron's masterpiece was partly no doubt attributable to the shipwreck, but mainly I think to receiving without prior warning the total impact of Byron's personality, and the total revelation of his mind. He had until now been thinking of him as a poet of soaring genius, crippled by misanthropy, self-hatred and hypochondria and bearing the intolerable weight of a fearful crime on his conscience. He now met the full blast of his humour and wit allied with tragic pessimism; love, sympathy and scorn for humanity, savagery and tenderness, interpenetrating each other in the most bewildering fashion, and in a tone and metre which gave to the whole an aspect of 'depravity'. More than anything else, Goethe now became aware of something in Byron which he felt to be dangerous; if not to himself, then to the world at large; so that his voice swelled the warning chorus uplifted against *Don Juan* as a corrupting influence on life, whereas he had taken mere murder in his stride.

George Bancroft would have been well worth hearing on the subject of Goethe's right to call *Don Juan* the most immoral work ever produced by poetic art, but Byron himself would have been still more rewarding, although probably in lighter vein:

> If any person should presume to assert
>   That this story is not moral, first, I pray,
> That they will not cry out before they're hurt,
>   Then that they'll read it o'er again, and say
> (But, doubtless, nobody will be so pert)
>   That this is not a moral tale, though gay. . . .[1]

Exasperated by the timorousness of his publisher and his friends ('there is *no indelicacy*'), brought to bay but undefeated by the fury of his foes, Byron would in all probability have greeted Goethe's disapproval with gales of delighted laughter; for, during the period of 'promiscuous debauchery' in Venice (1819–20) whilst he was composing the first four cantos of *Don Juan*, he was apt to speak of Goethe with marked hilarity, a fact duly recorded by a companion in revelry. This was a certain Count Stroganov, at that time a wild young man and several years Byron's junior, who had overcome the poet's prejudice against all Russians by his overflowing high spirits and *joie de vivre*:

It is true that Byron generally treated me like a naughty child and in his difficult moods often roughly; but at the same time he confided

[1] *Poetry*, vi, p. 75.

more in me (treachery from whom he had no cause to fear) than in any of his other acquaintances of that period, who often enough surrounded him for selfish reasons. Our intercourse was not that of like-minded venerators of art, but of two insatiable lovers of life.[1]

Although this gay young spark is by no means easy to identify, he certainly existed; and Byron smuggled him into one of the stanzas in *Don Juan* in which Julia protests her unassailable virtue to her husband:

> 'Did not the Italian *Musico* Cazzani
>     Sing at my heart six months at least in vain?
> Did not his countryman, Count Corniani,
>     Call me the only virtuous wife in Spain?
> Were there not also Russians, English, many?
>     The Count Strongstroganoff I put in pain,
> And Lord Mount Coffeehouse, the Irish peer,
> Who killed himself for love (with wine) last year.'[2]

According to his own account 'Strongstroganoff' was often privileged to hear interesting disquisitions about poetry inter-woven in the perpetual discussions about beautiful women 'whom we both ardently pursued'. In this connection Goethe's name kept on cropping up, pronounced with great benevolence and goodwill by Byron, but always accompanied by laughter:

For instance he would often speak of Goethe's hypocrisy with much humour but little reverence, and said on one occasion: 'He's an old fox who won't come out of his lair and preaches moral sermons from it.' He called his *Werther* and his *Wahlverwandtschaften* a persiflage of marriage which his familiar spirit Mephistopheles could hardly have bettered; the conclusion of both works was the summit of irony.[3]

Goethe's feelings for Byron were torn between helpless admira-tion for his genius and dismay at its direction; Byron's for Goethe swayed this way and that between genuine esteem for his powers and a mischievous delight in something ridiculous which seemed to surround him. This found expression not only to Stroganov at the time, but in one of the stanzas in the third canto of *Don Juan* which there is every reason to hope and believe that Goethe never saw.[4] Leading up to his wonderful hymn to the isles of Greece, Byron began blithely by enumerating the models of the 'trimmer' poet who

---

[1] *Gespräche*, ii, p. 789. Date uncertain.
[2] *Poetry*, vi, p. 56. Cf. also ibid., vi, p. 306; Strongenoff.
[3] *Gespräche*, ii, p. 790.
[4] Goethe seems to have abandoned *Don Juan* after reading Cantos I and II. He told Eckermann in 1827 that he knew very little of the poem. In 1829 he read Cantos XIII and XIV.

> when *he* was asked to sing,
> He gave the different nations something national;

and then continued, very much in vein:

> In France, for instance, he would write a chanson;
>     In England a six canto quarto tale;
> In Spain he'd make a ballad or romance on
>     The last war – much the same in Portugal;
> In Germany the Pegasus he'd prance on
>     Would be old Goethe's – (see what says De Staël);
> In Italy he'd ape the 'Trecentisti';
> In Greece he'd sing some sort of hymn like this t'ye.[1]

'Much humour but little reverence' here too; an iridiscent jet of gaiety playing round the only contemporary poet found worthy of being named: 'old Goethe' prancing past on Pegasus. If Byron had seen what Goethe was writing about *Don Juan* whilst he was composing that passage, he would surely have expanded it to include a picture of the 'old fox' sermonizing him from his lair; and it is certainly a beguiling coincidence that just at the period when Byron was laughing about this tendency of Goethe's to Stroganov, the German poet should have been preparing such a signal example of it for posterity in his review of *Don Juan*.

Having written it, he probably felt bound to withhold it from publication until after the appearance of his review on *Manfred*, which came out early in 1820, the protest against immorality following in 1821. Meanwhile far greater symptoms of estrangement than are manifest in what is on the whole a kindly review are to be found in Chancellor Müller's diary, a reliable, factual, unpretentious and singularly revealing source. Tantalizingly brief in reporting conversations, Müller gives the impression of complete trustworthiness in his day by day record of events, which unfolds a dismal story of disillusionment on Goethe's part as far as Byron was concerned in the early months of 1820. On January 18, about four weeks after the completion of the review, Müller noted laconically that the talk had been about Byron and the translation of *Don Juan* and had then turned to Ottilie's love for the poet. She was, need it be said? a perfervid admirer; and 'jests about Ottilie's affection for Lord Byron' were the chief topic of conversation a week later.[2] It would seem from that as if Goethe's love were in abeyance; and although on February 18 Müller told him the story of *Mazeppa*, this evidently produced no reaction in favour of the author; for a few days afterwards, in the presence of a company of friends including Ottilie's mother but fortunately not Ottilie herself, Goethe announced that he would probably

---

[1] *Poetry*, vi, p. 168.
[2] *Gespräche*, ii, p. 69. January 29, 1820.

declare himself against Byron in six months' time; and before the reader has assimilated that startling piece of news, he is faced with the categorical statement that the best thing Byron had written was *The Vampyre*.[1] Goethe, who was totally unacquainted with Byron's prose style, cannot be blamed overmuch for accepting the advertised authorship; but to call *The Vampyre* Byron's best work immediately after reading *Don Juan* was a tribute to the genius of poor 'Pollydolly' which could well be spared. It seems to suggest that Goethe had recoiled in greater distaste from *Don Juan* than he had permitted to appear in his guarded and embarrassed review; and that the leaven of what he took to be its baneful brilliance was working violently in his mind; so violently that he was now meditating an open declaration of war. Whether, had this ever taken concrete shape or form, he would have completely freed himself from the spell Byron's personality had cast over him must remain a moot point. But this was emphatically the moment to attempt it. Now or never was the chance to escape. Goethe allowed that moment to pass, although his disaffection continued.

This was manifest in a letter written about a month after the outburst recorded by Müller to Johann Sulpiz Boisserée (1785–1854) whose work on Cologne Cathedral (1822–31), produced in collaboration with his brother Melchior, became a classic. His second claim to fame rests on his friendship with Goethe, who honoured him at one time with confidences and intimations reserved for his ears alone:

> In Heidelberg Goethe made a habit of watching the sunsets from a summit in the district; and on such occasions he would express his feelings at the spectacle of the sublime natural drama to his friend Sulpiz Boisserée in the most affecting manner. This was known in the town. One evening, when Goethe was ascending the height with his friend to watch the sunset, two ladies, who wished to overhear what he said, had hidden themselves behind some bushes. Goethe noticed this, but pretended not to see them; and when he reached the top, he began to preach such an intimidating sermon on the ageing of the sun and the wanness and pallor already stealing over it, that the figures behind the bushes vanished forthwith. Never, Sulpiz later told his friends, had Goethe's reflections been greater and more soulful than on that glorious evening after the two unbidden eavesdroppers had disappeared.[2]

Boisserée had been one of the first to hear the exciting news that *Manfred* had been taken from *Faust* and the young artist had naturally made all haste to read Byron's poem, and also Goethe's review as soon as it appeared, taking it in all good faith as the *ne plus ultra* in criticism:

---

[1] *Gespräche*, ii, p. 70. February 25, 1820.
[2] Ibid., i, p. 769. September 25–October 9, 1814; J. B. Bertram

I agree heart and soul with what you say about Byron. The story of the horrible event in Florence has shed new light on many relationships which until now I could only ascribe to the gloomy nature of the poet in general. Could he but free himself from his ludicrous arrogance and his self-complacency in despair, and cast himself with his whole heart down into the dust before God! He would then soon arise and be able to view the world, if not perhaps in the freshness of dawn, then at least in a mild and peaceful evening twilight. As it is, he has nothing but storms and thunder; and, when these have raged themselves out, the most repulsive grey fog.[1]

Poor Byron! He had hardly deserved that; but new lights are not always true lights; and, though the picture of the poet as a gloomy and ridiculously arrogant and self-complacent murderer is a good deal blacker than Goethe had painted it, nevertheless the latter was responsible for this caricature. The vision of Byron prone in the dust before God was not one that would ordinarily have appealed to Goethe; for such pious *clichés* were foreign to his nature and not at all to his taste; and the fantastic suggestion that Byron (of all people) might thereafter view the world perpetually bathed in a peaceful evening twilight remains preposterous even when it is remembered that Boisserée believed himself to be speaking about a murderer desperately in need of divine pardon. Yet, far from protesting against the exaggerated conclusions drawn from his review (as he surely would have done in the pre-*Don Juan* days), Goethe actually acclaimed them:

Have you met with *Don Juan* by Byron? [he replied]. This poem is crazier and more grandiose than his others. Always the same themes, but handled with the highest talent and mastery. Were he a painter, his pictures would be worth their weight in gold. But as it is, his volumes belong to everybody, and what you so aptly express begins to appear all too plainly. And as by external repetitions he wears out our sympathy, so in the end he will wear out our patience.[2]

That last sentence has an ominous ring; and Goethe's confession that his sympathy for Byron was a thing of the past has also a direful sound. Moreover what had Boisserée so aptly expressed? 'Ludicrous arrogance . . . self-complacency in despair . . . nothing but storms and thunder and . . . the most repulsive grey fog'. Did any of this in truth apply to *Don Juan*? Yet Goethe took it as particularly applicable to that poem; not one word to Boisserée about the riotous humour informing it, unless 'crazier' be taken as his epithet for that. 'Always the same themes . . . eternal repetitions'. No one could guess from this that *Don Juan* was, as

[1] *Sulpiz Boisserée*, ed. M. Boisserée, 2 vols., Stuttgart, 1862; ii, p. 275. March 13, 1820.
[2] *Briefe*, xxxii, p. 205. Weimar, March 23, 1820.

Shelley realized 'something wholly new and relative to the age, and yet surpassingly beautiful'. Whether it were in fact all due to the horror induced by the shipwreck scenes (for Goethe always recoiled from scenes of this nature), or whether something more elemental entered in, Goethe was experiencing a revulsion from Byron, comparable to the aversion Kleist's *Penthesilea* inspired in him, which caused him to repudiate and crush the author, as he alone knew how:

He could kill . . . with one glance, with one breath from his mouth, with one lift of his Olympian shoulders: he could turn a human heart to stone; he could kill a soul and then turn his back on it as if nothing had happened, and then walk off to his plants, to his stones, to his colours. . . . Yes, who killed the soul of Heinrich von Kleist, who was it? . . . The Wizard of Weimar. . . .[1]

## b. DEDICATIONS AND DEADLOCKS

Byron's soul was in no danger from the Wizard of Weimar; but the two years' time-lag between the writing and printing of the review of *Manfred* created a situation which might well have ended in open hostility between the two poets. Almost two months to the day after Goethe had told Boisserée that his sympathy for Byron was at an end and that his patience was wearing thin, Byron was thrown into a state of great suspense by receiving a copy of Goethe's review of *Manfred*:

A German named Ruppsecht [Rupprecht] has sent me, heaven knows why, several Deutsche Gazettes, of all of which I understand neither word nor letter. I have sent you the enclosed to beg you to translate to me some remarks, which appear to be *Goethe's upon Manfred*, – and if I may judge by *two* notes of *admiration* (generally put after something ridiculous by us) and the word *hypochondrisch*, are anything but favourable. I shall regret this, for I should have been proud of Goethe's good word; but I shan't alter my opinion of him, even though he should be savage.

Will you excuse this trouble, and do me this favour? – Never mind – soften nothing – I am literary proof – having had good and evil said in most modern languages.[2]

Hoppner flung himself with such a will into the linguistic breach, that Byron had the translation in his hands a few days later, and Hoppner's sufficiently faithful if not very elegant rendering is reproduced here just as Byron read it more than a hundred years ago:

[1] H. v. Hofmannsthal, *Selected Prose*, tr. Hottinger and Stern, London, 1952; pp. 298 f.

[2] *Letters and Journals*, v, pp. 33 f. To Richard Belgrave Hoppner, Ravenna, May 25, 1820.

Byron's tragedy, *Manfred* [Goethe began almost exactly as he had written to Knebel], was to me a wonderful phenomenon, and one that closely touched me. This singular intellectual poet has taken my *Faustus* to himself, and extracted from it the strangest nourishment for his hypochondriac humour. He has made use of the impelling principles in his own way, for his own purposes, so that not one of them remains the same; and it is particularly on this account that I cannot enough admire his genius. The whole is in this way so completely formed anew that it would be an interesting task for the critic to point out, not only the alterations he has made, but their degree of resemblance with, or dissimilarity to, the original; in the course of which I cannot deny that the gloomy heat of an unbounded and exuberant despair becomes at last oppressive to us. Yet is the dissatisfaction we feel always connected with esteem and admiration.[1]

Byron, who had shied at the word *hypochondrisch* as almost certainly derogatory, now found it rubbing shoulders with the more damning charge of plagiarism; for although the pill was liberally coated with the best sugar, still it was there: ('He has taken my *Faustus* to himself'), and he was expected to swallow it. Moreover after labouring that point, though without a single example to prove it, Goethe harked back in far from flattering terms to the subject of hypochondria:

We find thus in this tragedy the quintessence of the most astonishing talent born to be its own tormentor. The character of Lord Byron's life and poetry hardly permits a just and equitable appreciation. He has often enough confessed what it is that torments him. He has repeatedly pourtrayed it; and scarcely any one feels compassion for this intolerable suffering, over which he is ever laboriously ruminating.

Anything less likely to lighten the gloom of the author of *Manfred* it would be hard to imagine; but Byron's sense of humour probably came to the rescue as he read on:

There are, properly speaking, two females whose phantoms for ever haunt him, and which, in this piece also, perform principal parts – one under the name of Astarte; the other without form or actual presence, and merely a voice. Of the horrid occurrence which took place with the former the following is related: When a bold and enterprising young man, he won the affections of a Florentine lady. Her husband discovered the amour, and murdered his wife; but the murderer was the same night found dead in the street, and there was no one on whom any suspicion could be attached. Lord Byron removed from Florence, and these spirits haunted him all his life after. This romantic incident is rendered highly probable by innumerable allusions to it in his poems.

---

[1] Cf. *Letters and Journals*, v, pp. 506 f. for the complete text of Hoppner's translation; and pp. 503 ff. for the original German and the passages from *Manfred* which Goethe translated.

The 'horrid occurrence' or 'romantic incident' (whichever is preferred), leading back through *Glenarvon* to *The Giaour* and now reappearing in a most unexpected quarter must have taken Byron aback. For it was one thing to bruit abroad the factual basis behind *The Giaour* as far as the rescue and even the love-interest were concerned, and quite another to find himself calmly (even benevolently) labelled a murderer by Goethe. It all came from pandering in the past to the wild imaginings of 'little *Mania*', the

... one human being whom I do utterly *detest* and *abhor*.... She has been an adder in my path ... she has often belied and sometimes betrayed me; she has crossed me everywhere, she has watched and worried and grieved and been a curse to me and mine.[1]

The spectacle of the adder crossing his path again in Goethe's review might have infuriated Byron had it not been so outrageously comic; as it was it ministered to that sense of the ridiculous which 'old Goethe' seemed doomed to inspire. He gaily christened the libel 'Goethe's Florentine husband-killing story', and it became a standing joke between himself and Thomas Moore, causing the Irishman to suggest half in earnest:

... that it would be but a fair satire on the disposition of the world to 'bemonster his features', if he would write for the public ... a sort of mock-heroic account of himself, outdoing, in horrors and wonders, all that had yet been revealed or believed of him, and leaving even Goethe's story of the double murder in Florence far behind.[2]

It is particularly amusing to find that Goethe believed the 'double murder' to be practically proved because of the 'innumerable allusions' to it to be found in his poetry, which was certainly putting the cart before the horse as far as *Glenarvon* was concerned; and when the German poet elaborated at length Byron's passing allusion to Pausanias, recreating in detail the tragic occurence of the accidental murder of Cleonice, Byron must have chuckled at the biographical conclusion drawn:

That poet must have a lacerated heart who selects such a scene from antiquity, *appropriates it to himself*, and burdens his tragic image with it. The following soliloquy, which is overladen with gloom and a weariness of life, is, by this remark, rendered intelligible. We recommend it as an exercise to all friends of declamation. Hamlet's soliloquy seems improved upon here.[3]

In spite of this *bonne bouche* at the end, Goethe's review of *Manfred* ('a strangely futile production', as Robertson called it)

---

[1] *Correspondence*, i, pp. 261 f. To Lady Melbourne, June 26, 1814.
[2] Cf. *Letters and Journals*, v, p. 113, with Moore, p. 545, footnote.
[3] The italics are mine.

was of a nature more apt to irritate than to please. The gratifying
'quotabilia' it contained: 'genius . . . admiration . . . astonishing
talent' occurred in a context which gravely diminished their
value; for a review which reproached the poet with wearisome
hypochondria and taxed him with plagiarism and murder, even
though congratulating him on the one score and withholding
blame on the other, contained much matter to take amiss, however 'literary proof' the author. But the tone of the whole, impregnated with admiration and interest, and entirely free from
hostility must have come like water in the wilderness to a poet
who was at that time facing the utmost in vilification and vituperation from critics at home in connection with *Don Juan*. Goethe's
fame also shed its own lustre and gave the whole a consequence it
would otherwise have lacked; and Byron, fully aware that he had
made an important conquest, announced this to Murray and
thereby also to the comminatory Synod in Albemarle St, with a
resounding flourish of trumpets:

Enclosed is something which will interest you, (to wit), the opinion
of *the* Greatest man of Germany – perhaps of Europe – upon one of the
great men of your advertisements (all 'famous hands', as Jacob Tonson
used to say of his ragamuffins,) – in short, a critique of *Goethe's* upon
*Manfred*. There is the original, Mr Hoppner's translation, and an
Italian one; keep them all in your archives, – for the opinions of such
a man as Goethe, whether favourable or not, are always interesting,
and this is moreover favourable.

Then, touching on the vexed question of plagiarism, he repeated
what he had already told Murray twice before and was to re-assert
to others again and again:

His *Faust* I never read, for I don't know German; but Matthew
Monk Lewis, in 1816, at Coligny, translated most of it to me *vivâ voce*,
and I was naturally much struck with it; but it was the *Staubach* [*sic*]
and the *Jungfrau*, and something else, much more than *Faustus*, that
made me write *Manfred*. The first Scene, however, and that of *Faustus*
are very similar.[1]

Well might those two opening scenes be very similar, since
they both represent the hero resorting to magic in the extremity
of despair, a situation Goethe had found in the puppet-plays
which opened with a mangled Marlovian monologue, and which
(as Marlowe had done before him) he irradiated with his genius.
'Something else' in Byron responded to this; and, just as Goethe
had thereafter gone his own way which was not the way of the
puppet-plays, so also Byron went his way, which was not the way
of Goethe. Yet the German, steeped as he was in Faustian folk-

---

[1] *Letters and Journals*, v, pp. 36 f. To Murray from Ravenna, June 7, 1820.

lore and tradition, owed considerably more to his humble predecessors in the field than Byron owed to his bowing-acquaintance with Goethe's masterpiece. This had served him as a diving-board; but the sublimity of the Swiss scenery was a more vital factor than *Faust*; and the real origin of *Manfred* lay far deeper: in the whirlpool of dark emotions at the centre of his being. Knowing all this, Byron would not have been human if Goethe's assumption of paternity had not rankled, and he would not have been Byron if he had ever been able to forget it; but he made no public protest either then or later; and he might have refrained altogether from answering the review as a whole, had he not received from Murray four months later

. . . a *German* translation of *Manfred*, with a plaguy long dissertation at the end of it; it would be out of all measure and conscience to ask you to translate the whole; but, if you could give me a short sketch of it, I should thank you, or if you would make somebody do the whole into *Italian*, it would do as well; and I would willingly pay some poor Italian German Scholar for his trouble.[1]

The translation of *Manfred* was by A. Wagner, uncle to the composer; and the dissertation was 'about the *Fausts*', as Byron told Murray when acknowledging its receipt. Hoppner once more obliged with the utmost speed; and Byron discovered a quotation from Goethe in the appendix to the effect that 'the predominant character of the whole body of the present English poetry is a disgust and contempt for life'. This challenging statement was just what he needed for a veiled reply to the review of *Manfred*, and his pen began racing over the page with such verve and gusto and so fast, that he was able to write to Murray a bare week after his appeal to Hoppner:

Enclosed is the dedication of *Marino Faliero* to *Goethe*. Query? is his title *Baron* or not? I think yes. Let me know your opinion, and so forth. . . . I enclose you an Italian abstract of the German translator of *Manfred's* appendix, in which you will perceive quoted what Goethe says of the *whole body* of English poetry (and *not* of one in particular). On this the dedication is founded, as you will perceive, though I had thought of it before, for I look upon him as a Great Man.[2]

Delighted to point out to Murray that Goethe's strictures on 'hypochondria' were not confined to *Manfred*, Byron also leapt at the heaven-sent opportunity to answer the personal charge impersonally; and, by dedicating *Marino Faliero* to Goethe, to repay his interest and express his own gratitude without mentioning

---

[1] *Letters and Journals*, v, p. 98. To Hoppner from Ravenna, October 13, 1820.
[2] Ibid., v, p. 100. To Murray from Ravenna, October 17, 1820. The quotation is from *Dichtung und Wahrheit*, Part III, Book 13.

the review. For it would have been downright impossible to acknowledge that document and yet leave the accusations of plagiarism and murder unanswered; and it was equally unthinkable to notice them. But here was a pretext for responding in kind with a bitter-sweet cordial mixed by a master-hand. Goethe had uttered *ex cathedra* weighty and solemn periods in which the highest praise and admiration were shot through with daunting censure while grave sympathy ushered in a nonsensical and libellous story. Byron chose a direct personal approach, informal and topical, in which due reverence alternated with mock reverence, homage with teasing, and inopportune jests with genuine esteem. Full of a high-spirited determination to prove that the writer was anything but hypochondriacal, the dedicatory letter was also a vigorous attempt to establish personal contact with Goethe: to woo and win him with *Marino Faliero*; to predispose him against the 'Lakers'; to pay signal tributes to the *doyen* of German letters and yet to put him in his place; and throughout is heard that undercurrent of laughter which 'Goethe's Florentine husband-killing story' had made it almost impossible to suppress. All these mixed and mutually incompatible elements made of Byron's first effort to approach Goethe personally something unique in the annals of dedications: nonchalant, flippant, impertinent, and then again belauding in the grand manner the Great Man.

Tackling the question of hypochondria firmly, Byron quoted Goethe's statement about English literature in general, and then gaily instanced *Werther* as outdoing in this respect the whole body of contemporary English poets, referring in particular to the spate of suicides it had occasioned. As a Rowland for an Oliver, *Werther* for *Manfred* could hardly have been bettered; but the sly hint that Goethe's prejudice against English literature might be due to the 'acrimonious judgment' passed on him by the redoubtable *Edinburgh Review* involved an anachronism; for the remarks in question had been made in the third book of *Dichtung und Wahrheit*, in the very work in fact which had been so adversely noticed by the 'celebrated Northern journal'. Erring (and rather grossly too) through ignorance, Byron was nevertheless teasing better than he knew. For Goethe's criticisms of the suicidal gloom of contemporary English poetry had been made in connection with *Werther*; and its influence on that novel had been played up in order to play down the passion for Lotte which had come so near to destroying him forty years earlier. Unwilling or unable in 1814 to acknowledge its devastating effect, Goethe blamed on English literature what Byron was now blaming on *Werther*, a situation full of ironical charm for the historian of literature. Whether philologists will be equally charmed by Byron's gibe at the

grotesque names of most German poets (completely unpronounce-
able and therefore doomed to be forgotten by posterity, with the
happy exception of Goethe's) is a different matter. It disfigures a
dignified and sincere tribute in a highly flippant manner; and the
most that can be said for it is that it reads like the first draft of
certain stanzas in *Don Juan* poking fun at Russian.[1]

Twice and twice only in this extraordinary epistle did Byron
achieve those ceremonious heights which dedications as from one
poetical potentate to another demand; and on each occasion he
came slithering down into banter and persiflage. It was a daring
essay in shock-tactics, an attempt to batter his way through to his
eminent admirer and force him to reconsider his strictures on
English (and Byronic) temperamental gloom. Considering the
nature of the provocation Goethe had given him and the wit of
the writer, the retort courteous was mercifully mild; nor was it
undeserved. By animadverting so strongly against the 'hypochondria' of *Manfred*, Goethe had certainly laid himself open to a
reminder of the suicidal effect of *Werther*; and to be teased about
*The Edinburgh Review* was at least no worse than to be publicly
patted on the back for appropriating Goethe's *Faust*. As for the
fling at the German language, that was harmlessness itself when
compared with the tale of the double murder in Florence. But
over and above all this, just as the total impression of Goethe's
review is that of a tribute to Byron, so too Byron's answer leaves
the reader in no doubt that he was paying sincere (if mischievous)
homage to the literary giant of the age.

But how would Goethe have taken it, if it had reached him at
the time? He was still meditating a public declaration against
Byron when the latter was composing his challenging and provo-
cative dedication; and one hardly knows whether to rejoice or
regret that Murray advised against publication. Not, I fear, to
spare Goethe's feelings; but almost certainly because of the fero-
cious ridicule poured over Wordsworth and Southey in the
opening passage which took up a large part of the letter. It was
totally out of place in that context, and its presence can only be
accounted for by Byron's regretful withdrawal of the savage
dedication to Southey at the beginning of *Don Juan*, which he
could no longer allow to stand once he had decided that the poem
should be published anonymously. And so it came about that in
his cathartic reckoning with the GREAT GOETHE (as he
ceremoniously entitled him) he included a still more cathartic
exposure of the pretentiousness (as he deemed it) of his two
favourite butts. To hold them up publicly to Goethe's scorn was
to insult them twice over; Murray evidently protested, and Byron

---

[1] *Poetry*, vi, pp. 306 f.

gave in without a murmur. '*Omit* the dedication to Goethe',[1] he said laconically at the fag-end of a very long letter chiefly devoted to frantic suggestions as to how the appearance of *Marino Faliero* on the London stage might be averted. That was the crying need of the moment. Dedications, to whomsoever and howsoever addressed, were of very minor importance compared with that; and the one written to be prefixed to *Marino Faliero* remained a dead letter for many years. The first attempt to open a channel of communication between himself and Goethe had failed.

Simultaneously with Byron's withdrawal of his dedicatory epistle in January 1821, the intended recipient was immersed in the study of a book which brought Byron vividly to the forefront of his mind. This was an account by a German lawyer called Jacobsen of contemporary English literature given in a series of letters to Elise von Hohenhausen, one of Byron's admirers and translators. His portrait adorned the frontispiece, and much space was devoted both to him and to Thomas Moore. Wordsworth, Southey, Coleridge, Crabbe, Scott, Rogers and Campbell were also represented; but of Keats and Shelley there was no word. The author extolled Byron as 'one of the greatest poets, and in spirit the first among all his contemporaries in the whole world'.[2] Goethe had used almost identical expressions to Cogswell in the summer of 1819; but that was before the ice-age had set in with *Don Juan*; and one could hardly expect the ice to melt when he read: 'You will not misunderstand me, if I call Byron the greatest of now living poets. I do not place him above Goethe in his manhood, but above Goethe in his old age'.[3] What must (or should) have been even more disconcerting was to find the following reference to his review of *Manfred*:

I have heard and read a great deal to Lord Byron's detriment; but never even the slightest hint of what Goethe erroneously reports in his Journal, to the effect that the poet had fallen in love in Florence and that a catastrophe had transformed his love into sorrow and grief. Actually he was not in Florence until much later, long after deep melancholy had seized upon his heart; and his evil star seems to have presided over his fate from very early days.[4]

Predisposed against Byron as Goethe was just then, this outright denial of the episode which had formed the basis of his critique of *Manfred* must have been peculiarly aggravating, since it put him

---

[1] *Letters and Journals*, v, p. 226. To Murray from Ravenna, January 19, 1821.
[2] F. J. Jacobsen, *Briefe an eine deutsche Edelfrau über die neuesten englischen Dichter*, Altona, 1820; p. 4.
[3] Ibid., p. 635.
[4] Ibid., p. 608. The Journal was *Über Kunst und Altertum*, published by Goethe.

in the wrong about the poet whose own wrongheadedness had disturbed him so much. Yet even so, it would have shown better in Goethe if he had now or even later acknowledged the error of which he stood convicted; but he let it stand; and the only positive result of reading Jacobsen's study was that it drew his attention to *English Bards and Scotch Reviewers*. He occupied himself with this satire during the greater part of the month, and even began to translate it; evidently (as a fellow-victim) interested and gratified by the Nemesis which had overtaken Byron's 'feeble and unworthy critics',[1] and always ready to incline a willing ear to censure of the English. *English Bards and Scotch Reviewers* did Byron no disservice with Goethe who later frequently referred to it with high praise; and it may well have determined him to withhold public condemnation from a poet who had won his spurs in his first encounter with his contemptible countrymen. Certainly when young Bancroft paid him a second visit in March 1821, Goethe said nothing to lead his visitor to suppose that his earlier enthusiasm for Byron was dimmed, although he was altogether unenthusiastic in his manner, showing no very lively interest in the subjects discussed. Bancroft vainly tried to make him talk about German literature, but drew a blank. Goethe greeted Tieck's name with silence and damned the Schlegels with faint praise. He was not much more forthcoming about Byron:

Byron's *Don Juan* Goethe has read and admired its humour. 'The humour of the rimes', said he, 'is capable only in your language where words differently written are often pronounced alike. This peculiarity of your language has been cultivated and exercised by a series of comic writers, Swift, etc., etc.'[2]

That was all and it was tepid enough, dealing chiefly with the question of those punning rhymes which figured so ponderously in Goethe's review. But Bancroft saw nothing amiss. He had already heard from others that Goethe now lived a very secluded life, associating with none of the inhabitants of Weimar and appearing neither at the Court nor at any of the parties, so that his comparative unresponsiveness about Byron passed unnoticed, and Bancroft was far from suspecting that in mentioning *Don Juan* he had once more been 'coming into a strait'. Active hostility now seemed to be on the wane; but the blight on Goethe's former feelings was still there when R. P. Gillies, then 'a humble student of Edinburgh', visited Goethe in June 1821 in company with his brother-in-law Captain James Macdonnell. They were given to understand that Goethe was slowly recovering from a long illness,

---

[1] *Werke*, xxxvi, p. 192. This is a retrospective notice in *Tag-und Jahreshefte*.
[2] Howe, op. cit., i, p. 98. Diary for March 7, 1821. Also in *Gespräche*, ii, pp. 122 f.

which his appearance certainly confirmed. Unfavourably impressed by the gloom, bareness and chill (even on a summer's day) of the reception-room, they were eyeing its discomforts critically, when:

. . . as the door opened from the farther end . . . and His Excellency's tall, gaunt form, wrapped in a long, blue surtout which hung loosely on him, slowly advanced, he had veritably the air and aspect of a revenant. His was not an appearance, but an apparition. Evidently and unmistakeably he had belonged to another world which had long since passed away. . . . Goethe advanced in profound silence, in a mood, seemingly, of utter abstraction, and after the manner of ghosts in general, he waited to be spoken to! The spirit had been evoked from his other world, had condescended to appear, and now the question was what sort of conversation ought to be, or might be, without impropriety addressed to him?[1]

Half paralysed with fright, Gillies 'in sheer desperation' hit upon a topic of practical interest to Goethe: the desire of the two young Scotchmen to settle for a time in Weimar. This led by easy stages to memories of other Britishers who had taken up their residence in Weimar in times gone by, some of whom Goethe had much esteemed. Luckily for his visitors Gillies happened to be an intimate friend of the most highly valued of all, the diplomat Sir Brooke Boothby (1743–1824). Goethe became quite animated about this mutual acquaintance whose only failing had been that he would not take the trouble to learn German thoroughly. A countryman of his, a certain Mr Mellish, had been much more praiseworthy in that respect; and not only in that respect. Joseph Charles Mellish (1769–1823), a writer as well as a diplomat, translated several of the works of Goethe and Schiller; but he was first and foremost a convivial soul, a man after Goethe's own heart. During the years 1792–1802 when Mellish was in Weimar, he and Goethe had punished many a bottle of wine together; so many indeed that when Mellish revisited Goethe many years later, he was greeted ecstatically with the one word: 'Champagne!' Yes, and Goethe had been very near indeed to falling in love with his charming daughter. The 'revenant' did not touch on those jovial days to his visitors; but he became a different person, cordial and expansive, thus greatly delighting the two young men who had been given to understand (like many another) that the lion they had come to beard was generally very reserved, nonchalant and taciturn with strangers. On one subject however Goethe resolutely refused to be drawn. Having finished with Boothby and Mellish, Gillies tried, as he put it, to introduce other literary characters, but in vain:

[1] Cf. *Gespräche*, ii, pp. 129 ff. for this interview which took place on June 22, 1821.

I . . . could only bring him thus far, that he desired to be particularly informed whether Sir Walter Scott had quite recovered his health, to which I replied that, not only had he recovered, but seemed stouter than before; and that his industry was unequalled and indomitable. I then endeavoured to speak of the singular influence that *Faust* and *Wilhelm Meister* had exercised on English authors; of Lord Byron's debt to the former in *Manfred,* and so forth; but to this his answers were in a tone of perfect indifference. He cared not a straw about praise and was inaccessible to flattery.

It is certainly significant that Goethe did not even rise to the bait of that 'debt' which he had been the first to proclaim in tones of unconcealed triumph; and it strengthens the impression that he had come to a pass when 'he cared not a straw' about Byron. Gillies, it is true, told a slightly different tale in another account of his visit; but it comes to much the same thing:

Like Tieck, and our other friends at Dresden, he was . . . extremely desirous to hear all that we could tell him respecting leading characters among the English *literati* – of whom, it is superfluous to say, that Scott and Byron interested him the most. But whilst speaking of both, with ample deference as distinguished men, he could by no means be led into hearty praise of either one or the other on account of their works.[1]

All things considered, it was fortunate indeed that *Marino Faliero,* a copy of which Knebel presented to Goethe on July 18, 1821, was innocent of the intended dedication. That drama and Heinrich Döring's translation of *Manfred,* which reached him in October, Goethe may or may not have glanced at; he referred to them retrospectively with non-committal benevolence as works which 'kept that extraordinary and estimable man ever before our eyes'.[2] Perhaps he was relenting; but during the whole of the rest of the year and far into 1822 Goethe seems to have experienced no difficulty in keeping his eyes averted from that extraordinary and estimable character. He certainly never referred to him: he had banished Cantos I and II of *Don Juan* from his shelves the year before, and he evidently refrained from reading the second instalment which came out on August 8, 1821. This comprised Cantos III, IV and V and as it included the 'Pegasus' stanza, Byron's cause certainly did not suffer from Goethe's neglect; but the same cannot be said of his omission to read the volume of tragedies containing *Sardanapalus, The Two Foscari* and *Cain,* published on December 21, 1821.

\*     \*     \*

His apathy in this respect is in striking contrast to the energy

[1] *Frazer's Magazine,* London, January 1840; xxi, p. 70.
[2] *Werke,* xxxvi, p. 192. *Tag-und Jahreshefte* for 1821.

F

Byron was again putting forth in order to establish a closer relationship with him. His sense of gratitude for Goethe's notice was as lively as ever; and having vented what it would be exaggerated to call his spleen in the suppressed dedication to *Marino Faliero*, he decided to honour him in a less equivocal way:

To

THE ILLUSTRIOUS GOËTHE

A Stranger presumes to offer the homage of a literary vassal to his liege lord, the first of existing writers – who has created the literature of his own country, and illustrated that of Europe. – The unworthy production which the author ventures to inscribe to him is entitled SARDANAPALUS.[1]

Nothing could have been more seemly and more honourable to both; and Byron was also anxious that everything right and proper should be done in this connection:

My dear Douglas, – I intend to dedicate the *two Foscari's* to Walter Scott, *Sardanapalus* to Goethe, and *Faliero* to you. The two first I have sent to Murray; your own I enclose to *you*, that you may see it first, and accept it or not. If content, send it to Murray.

You are a good German Scholar, I am not even a bad one, but would feel greatly obliged if you would write two lines to the 'Grosser Mann' at my request, to tell him my intent, and ask his leave. See the inscription at Murray's; it goes by this post.[2]

It was the second edition of *Marino Faliero* which was to be dedicated to Kinnaird, who was evidently 'content' (as well he might be) with the flattering inscription enclosed;[3] and Byron wrote to him somewhat later: 'I rejoice that you accept the dedication – especially as you liked the play'.[4] Nevertheless it was not prefixed to the second edition of *Marino Faliero* in 1821; but was found after Byron's death and printed before the 1832 edition. This curious fact, for which no explanation is discoverable, is balanced by the equally inexplicable one that, when *Sardanapalus* appeared on December 21, 1821, bound up with *The Two Foscari* and *Cain*, the dedication to Goethe was lacking. *The Two Foscari* was also without an inscription; but that was because Byron had changed his mind and had decided to dedicate *Cain* to Walter Scott instead. The permission of the latter had been duly asked, and an unpublished copy sent to him at the same time, for it was rightly felt that *Cain* was a delicate matter. But Scott

---

[1] *Sardanapalus*, London, 1823. Cf. also *Poetry*, v, p. 7.
[2] *Correspondence*, ii, p. 197. To Douglas Kinnaird from Ravenna, September 4, 1821.
[3] *Poetry*, iv, p. 343. Dated from Ravenna, September 1, 1821.
[4] C. L. Cline, *Byron, Shelley and the Pisan Circle*, London, 1952; p. 49. To Kinnaird from Pisa, November 4, 1821. Original in the Pierpoint Morgan Library.

2. Portrait of Douglas Kinnaird, by kind permission of Lord Kinnaird.

was stout-hearted, and accepted the honour in a handsome letter in which he declared that Byron had matched Milton on his own ground in this 'very grand and tremendous drama'. Everything the most scrupulous author could demand had therefore been done as far as Sir Walter was concerned. Nothing whatsoever had been done about Goethe; and who was to blame for that?

Neither Kinnaird nor Murray can be absolved, or even exonerated, in this matter; although in the course of events to come extenuating circumstances present themselves in the guise of the dual control exercised over Byron's affairs by Kinnaird and Murray which often led to confusion. Kinnaird, a partner in the bank of Ransome and Morland, and famous for his brandy-parties when Byron was the idol of London, had been chosen by the poet as his financial adviser and trustee. He was a loyal friend and acquitted himself nobly of a task bristling with difficulties, excessively complicated and often thankless. Not that Byron was deficient in gratitude; he realized how much he owed to 'my trusty and trust-worthy trustee and banker, and crown and sheet-anchor, Douglas Kinnaird the Honourable'.[1] But his money-matters were in a state of great confusion when he left England, painful and perplexing problems were always arising and there were snarls and tangles without end. Looking through Kinnaird's letters to Byron preserved in Albemarle St, one would need to be lynx-eyed indeed to detect any signs of negligence or disregard of Byron's interests except in the one matter of the dedication of *Sardanapalus* to Goethe; and, as there are gaps in the correspondence between them (though nothing like such tantalizing *lacunae* as face one in Murray's letters to Byron, also in Albemarle St) judgment can sometimes be held in suspense. Kinnaird's portrait reveals an alert cast of countenance, as he sits with Byron's picture on the wall beside him and Byron's *Parisina* open in his hands. Indeed he looks as if he were just about to spring up and write to the author. Medwin was therefore probably accurate (anyway for once) when he quoted Byron as saying:

I don't know what would become of me without Douglas Kinnaird, who has always been my best and kindest friend.[2]

And yet this devoted, active and dependable friend totally disregarded Byron's request to write to Goethe for permission to print the dedication. He later excused himself to a third person on the grounds that, having accidentally discovered that Goethe spoke English and having passed this information on to Byron,

---

[1] *Letters and Journals*, vi, p. 287. To John Bowring from Cephalonia, December 13, 1823.
[2] Medwin, p. 204.

he had presumed that the latter would write direct to the 'Grosser Mann' himself.[1] There is no confirmation of this excuse either in his letters or in Byron's; and indeed the latter was still in ignorance of Goethe's proficiency in English as late as May 1822.[2] Kinnaird was possibly telling a white lie to save his face; and he may have hesitated to write in the first instance because he was not quite the 'good German Scholar' Byron believed him to be, in spite of his studies at Göttingen University from 1805–06. It was a bothersome little commission and Kinnaird ignored it. Byron for his part believed that it had been executed;[2] no more was said about it, and there for the moment the matter rested.

Murray's failure to print the dedication is less perplexing, although his excuse that it came too late will not bear close investigation. It was sent to him on September 4, 1821, and the volume it was to appear in was published on December 21, 1821. Letters from Italy to England took between ten days and a fortnight; and there were three months and a half at his disposal: ample time for Byron to change his mind about the dedication of *The Two Foscari* (sent by the same post); more than time enough for Murray to receive and act on his revised instructions and to communicate with Sir Walter Scott; time and to spare for the latter to read *Cain* and accept the dedication. No; time was not the trouble; and if Murray had been waiting to hear from Kinnaird that Goethe's permission had been granted, he would certainly have said so to Byron; but actually (owing to the system of dual control) he seems to have known nothing about the step Kinnaird had been asked to take. The truth is – yet one's heart rebels at telling the truth about Murray. In so many ways, in fact in nearly every way but one, this Anak of publishers, as Byron called him, was the *beau idéal* of authors. Generous to a fault, delicate, tactful, high-minded; renowned for his fair dealing and kind-heartedness, he called forth paeans of praise from member after member of the *genus irritabile*, Byron amongst their number. Imagine what it meant to the poet in 1815 when, beset by turmoils and torments domestic and financial, he received a cheque of £1,500 from Murray, who had heard that he was being forced to sell his library and who offered a similar sum in a few weeks, coupled with the proposal to sell all the copyrights of Byron's poems for the benefit of the author. Touched to the core, he replied:

I return your bills not accepted, but certainly not *unhonoured*. Your present offer is a favour which I would accept from you, if I accepted

---

[1] Information in a letter from L. L. Mackall to John Murray IV. Murray Papers. The third person was Professor Benecke.
[2] See below, p. 75.

such from any man. Had such been my intention, I can assure you I would have asked you fairly, and as freely as you would give; and I cannot say more for my confidence or your conduct.[1]

This is not the only acknowledgement Byron made of Murray's extreme liberality; and his letters until the last few years of his life plainly show the liking, confidence and friendship he felt for him. The relationship was completely wrecked towards the end, partly owing to Murray's half-heartedness and faint-heartedness about *Don Juan*, partly because of Byron's disastrous connection with the Hunts; but mainly, I think, owing to the mounting exasperation which Murray's maddening habits of procrastination, allied with his forgetfulness and what Kinnaird called the 'slovenliness' of his business methods produced. This finally enraged Byron so much that a breach between author and publisher became inevitable; and the part played in this by the star-crossed dedication of *Sardanapalus* was far from negligible, although at first Murray's failure to print it was an almost venial omission compared with his other sins:

I write to you in considerable surprise, that, since the first days of November, I have never had a line from you. It is so incomprehensible, that I can only account for it by supposing some accident. I have written to you at least ten letters, to none of which I have had a word of answer.[2]

Why do you not write? You should at least send me a line of particulars [about the threatened performance of *Marino Faliero*]: I know nothing yet but by Galignani and the honourable Douglas . . . do pray write: when there is anything to interest, you are always silent.[3]

Now I should be glad to know upon what principle of common or *un*common feeling, you leave me without any information but what I derive from garbled gazettes in English, and abusive ones in Italian . . . while all this kick up has been going on about the play? You SHABBY fellow!!! Were it not for two letters from Douglas Kinnaird, I should be as ignorant as you are negligent. . . . Yours, in haste and hatred, you scrubby correspondent![4]

. . . The *Doge* is longer than I expected: pray, why did you print the face of M[argarita] C[ogni] by way of frontispiece? It has almost caused a row between the Countess G[uiccioli] and myself. And pray, why did you add the note about the Kelso woman's *Sketches*? Did I not request you to omit it, the instant I was aware that the *writer* was a *female*?[5]

SIR, – I have just received the parcel, all right, and well. But I am greatly surprized to see that you have omitted the dedication of

---

[1] *Letters and Journals*, iii, p. 249. November 14, 1815.
[2] Ibid., v, p. 216. Ravenna, January 4, 1821.
[3] Ibid., v, pp. 292 and 294. Ravenna, May 19, 1821.
[4] Ibid., v, pp. 297 ff. Ravenna, May 25, 1821.
[5] Ibid., v, p. 308. Ravenna, June 14, 1821.

*Sardanapalus* to Goethe, which, if any opportunity of replacing it occurs, I desire may be done, and a copy forwarded to Goethe from the author. . . .

I am, etc., your obedt.

B.[1]

As a remonstrance it is mildness itself; but the tone tells its own tale. The SHABBY fellow and scrubby correspondent of the preceding May and June was a mere SIR the following January; and 'Yours, in haste and hatred' was now 'your obedt. B'. Murray's sins of omission and commission had been accumulating to such an extent, that Byron was losing heart; and with so much else to complain of, he was not in the mood to make an issue of the dedication to Goethe. That subject was now dropped between Murray and himself. Byron's second communication to '*the* Greatest man of Germany' was allowed to lapse and became for the time being another dead letter. Byron said no more about it to Murray; and Goethe for his part was maintaining the attitude of lofty indifference about Byron he had displayed to Gillies. An absolute deadlock had been reached.

## c. CONTACT

Young America now came to the rescue in the person of George Bancroft with the aid of an American squadron. It was lying off Leghorn in the merry month of May 1822 when the horrified student of *Faust* met the author of the horrifying *Don Juan* on board the Commodore's ship:

I must begin a new period to tell you what else I've seen: what do you think now: I went on board the Commodore's ship, Sir! the *Constitution* or *Old Ironsides* as she hath been rightly termed: Well! Is that all? Not quite. A short time after I had been on board a man, who wore his hair very long, with full fat cheeks, a healthy lively pair of dark eyes, a cheerful forehead, a man of gentle manners though of a misshapen foot, a man of rank and some note in our small world, came on board. Whom do you guess it was? Prince Borghese? No, the fat old goat I do not mean. The Tuscan Duke? No, he is a good fellow to be sure, quite a radical, an honest man, who wears a blue coat and a white hat, and is drawn about by six horses. 'Tis not he I mean. Who was it then? Why nothing but a poet; yet it was a pleasure to have a poet on board an American Squadron, and to have been presented to Lord Byron anywhere else, would not have given me half so much pleasure as it did to meet him on American boards and beneath the American flag.[2]

[1] *Letters and Journals*, vi, p. 8. Pisa, January 23, 1822.
[2] Howe, op. cit., i, pp. 151 f. To S. A. Eliot, May 29, 1822.

It was not only Bancroft who derived intense pleasure from an occasion as brilliant and impressive as the American Navy was determined to make it. The guest of honour was delighted, and greatly exhilarated by it; and he sadly needed heartening just then, shaken as he was by the death of his little daughter Allegra. Her body had been embarked for England only a few days before; and he wrote to Murray on May 26, 1822, giving instructions for her burial which he wished to be at Harrow with Henry Drury officiating if possible. Then, turning to 'other subjects', he continued:

Since I came here, I have been invited by the Americans on board of their Squadron, where I was received with all the kindness I could wish, and with *more ceremony* than I am fond of. I found them finer ships than your own of the same class, well manned and officered. A number of American gentlemen also were on board at the time, and some ladies. As I was taking leave, an American lady asked me for a *rose* which I wore, for the purpose, she said, of sending to America something which I had about me, as a memorial. I need not add, that I felt the compliment properly. Captain Chauncey showed me an American and very pretty edition of my poems, and offered me a passage to the United States, if I would go there. Commodore Jones was also not less kind and attentive. I have since received the enclosed letter, desiring me to sit for my picture for some Americans.[1]

All this was highly flattering as was also the 'distinguished civility' as Bancroft called it ('*more ceremony* than I am fond of') with which Captain Chauncey received Byron on the *Ontario* 'a salute was fired, the yards were manned: and three cheers given in most glorious and clear unison', said the young American exultantly. For, among the many conquests Byron made that day, he was certainly not the least enthusiastic:

I was out to see him afterward, and was treated by him with more civility than I have ever been by any man in Europe. I hardly know if I ever talked with a man so frankly. He is very gay and fashionable in his way of talking, will converse of duels and horses, rows and swimming and good principles of Liberty, and in short is one of the pleasantest men in the world. Of himself he spoke with the utmost openness, of his success and his enemies. I was taken into a room in his villa: as I believed to enjoy the prospect toward the west: when my eyes were suddenly dazzled by beauty almost more than human and my ears soothed by the sweetest Italian accents from sweet Italian lips. Who was the lady? I do not know. It was a beautiful apparition, and why attach harsh ideas and harsher words to one who looked so innocent and conversed so purely?[2]

Bancroft could hardly have said more plainly that, if he did not

---

[1] *Letters and Journals*, vi, pp. 72 f. Montenero, near Leghorn, May 26, 1822.
[2] Howe, op. cit., i, p. 152. To Eliot, same date as above.

know *who* the lady was, he realized vividly *what* she was. He was now in the same boat as Goethe, representing 'vice as lovely and exciting sympathy'; and his refusal to apply to Teresa Guiccioli the same 'harsh' epithets he had used for Goethe's heroines shows the amiable inconsistency of a man highly susceptible to charm. Captivated by Byron, he listened like a partisan to the poet's energetic defence against the charge of immorality in his writings; and Bancroft prized to the end of his life the autographed copy of *Don Juan* which Byron gave him, indifferent now to 'the lowest and most disgraceful indecencies' ambushed between its covers. During the course of the conversation and before Bancroft was introduced to Teresa, Byron who had latterly been hearing a good deal about Goethe and in particular about *Faust* from Shelley at Pisa, introduced his name:

We spoke of Germany. He asked if I knew Goethe. I answered I did, and reported faithfully what I had heard Goethe say of him. I then told him of the translations which have so often been made of his works, and of the great admiration, which all Germans had for him. This B. said was new to him, and would serve as some solace for the abuse which he was constantly receiving from home. . . . I mentioned Goethe's comparison of *Faust* and *Manfred*: and Byron observed, evidently in earnest, that he deemed it honour enough to have his work mentioned with *Faust*. As to its origin, Lord B. said that some time before he had conceived the idea of his piece, Monk Lewis had translated to him some of the scenes and had given him an idea of the plan of the piece.

Speaking of the immorality of his works, he said: 'Why what are Fielding and Smollett and those authors?' He seemed to think there were worse things in Smollett than in anything he had ever written. 'What would they say, too, to the introduction to Goethe's *Faust*?' . . . He had dedicated one of his late works to Goethe; but for some reason or other his publisher had omitted to print it. . . . Lord Byron related to me the late scrape, into which he or his servant got at Pisa. He laughed at the story Goethe tells of his murdering a man at Florence – hopes Goethe may not hear of this affair at Pisa, lest he should make a famous story out of it.[1]

Bancroft's communications about Goethe and Germany were meat and drink to Byron, who immediately passed them on to Murray and Kinnaird:

I am also told of considerable literary honours in Germany. Goethe, I am told, is my professed patron and protector. At Leipsic, this year, the highest prize was proposed for a translation of two Cantos of *Childe Harold*. I am not sure that this was at *Leipsic*, but Mr Bancroft was my authority – a good German Scholar (a young American), and an acquaintance of Goethe's.

[1] Howe, op. cit., i, pp. 148 ff. Diary for May 22, 1822, Leghorn.

Goethe and the Germans are particularly fond of *Don Juan*, which they judge as a work of Art. I had heard something like this before through Baron Lutzerode. The translations have been very frequent of several of the works, and Goethe made a comparison between *Faust* and *Manfred*.

All this is some compensation for your English native brutality, so fully displayed this year (I mean *not your* individually) to its brightest extent.[1]

Bancroft's report of Goethe's professed protection and patronage of Byron no longer applied in 1822; and his belief that the praise of the 'humour of the rimes' signified particular enthusiasm for *Don Juan* was wide indeed of the mark; but these partial misstatements made in all good faith came at a very opportune moment. Byron's admiration for Goethe's *Faust* had been greatly increased by Shelley's translations and expositions; so that a 'comparison' between that dramatic poem and *Manfred* now appeared in the light of an honour. But more important still, the unbounded admiration felt for him by Goethe in 1819, and believed by Bancroft to be still active in 1822, demanded an acknowledgement; and, if Byron remembered the murder-story, he also recalled the outstanding dedication to *Sardanapalus*, writing urgently to Kinnaird:

Would you write a *German* line to Goethe for me, explaining the omission of the dedication to *Sardanapalus* by the fault of the publisher, and asking his permission to prefix it to the forthcoming volume of *Werner* and the Mystery.[2]

The Mystery was *Heaven and Earth* which did not finally appear with *Werner*, but separately in *The Liberal*, and was heard of no more in connection with the dedication to Goethe which (it is obvious from the above) Byron believed that the German poet had already accepted through the agency of Kinnaird. This was far from being the case; Goethe was in complete ignorance of it, and remained so whilst Byron, now thoroughly roused, kept on bombarding Murray:

Please to send me the dedication of *Sardanapalus* to Goethe, which you took upon you to omit – which omission, I assure you, I take very ill. I shall prefix it to *Werner*, unless you prefer my putting another, stating that the former had been omitted by the publisher.[3]

I sent you the revise of *Werner* last week. As you thought proper to omit the dedication of *Sardanapalus* to Goëthe, you will please to append it to *Werner*, making only the necessary alteration in the title of the work dedicated.[4]

[1] *Letters and Journals*, vi, pp. 73 f. To Murray, May 26, 1822.
[2] *Correspondence*, ii, p. 225. Leghorn, May 26, 1822.
[3] *Letters and Journals*, vi, pp. 75 f. Leghorn, May 29, 1822.
[4] Ibid., vi, pp. 92 f. Pisa, July 3, 1822.

With regard to what you say about your 'want of memory', I can only remark, that you inserted the note to *Marino Faliero* against my positive revocation, and that you omitted the dedication of *Sardanapalus* to Goethe (place it before the volume now in the press), both of which were things not very agreeable to me, and which I could wish to be avoided in future, as they might be with a very little care, or a simple Memorandum in your pocket book.[1]

If this inscription did not appear prefixed to *Werner* which was published on November 22, 1822, Kinnaird was at least partly to blame; since he did nothing about the commission entrusted to him at the end of May until the end of October, when at long last the 'good German Scholar' got under way. There was considerably more to explain now than there had been earlier, far more certainly than would go into one '*German* line to Goethe'; and Kinnaird chose the less arduous course of writing in English to his former tutor, C. F. Benecke (1762–1844), Professor of German and English and Librarian in the University of Göttingen. Benecke is still remembered in his own country as a collaborator in the great Lachmann dictionary; in England, if at all, as having taught Coleridge German; yet he played such a vital part as a go-between in the dedication-imbroglio, that he and his *alma mater* deserve a moment's scrutiny.

Göttingen University was then past its glory, but still at the height of its fame, attracting many foreign students, among them a whole bevy of Harvard men as has been seen, and a good many English ones too. Yet, in spite of its international reputation, young Heinrich Heine thought less than nothing of it, and the professors in particular struck him as past praying for. He compared them for age and immobility with the pyramids of Egypt, but pyramids devoid of any hidden wisdom; and, when considering the terrible Nemesis that had overtaken the enemies of Napoleon, he produced as a savage anti-climax Professor Saalfeld 'who is *still* a professor in Göttingen'. At least one of Saalfeld's colleagues would have agreed with Heine about the horror of such a fate, as George Bancroft happened to know; and the young American for his part shared Heine's harsh opinions of the Göttingen professoriat, a coincidence all the more telling, because they were there at the same time (1819–20), although unfortunately for both of them they never met. But Heine would certainly have subscribed to the following adverse criticisms:

I go from Göttingen without much regret. The people here are too cold and unsocial, too fond of writing books and too incapable of conversation, having more than enough of courtesy, and almost nothing

---

[1] *Letters and Journals*, vi, p. 95. Pisa, July 8, 1822. Cf. also Medwin, p. 329. For the note to *Marino Faliero*, see above, p. 71.

of actual hospitality. I admire their industry; but they do not love labour; I consider their vast erudition with astonishment; yet it lies as a dead weight on society. The men of letters are for the most part ill bred; many of them are altogether without manners. Here is Harding, whose name is widely spread as the discoverer of a planet and a capital observer of the stars; but he has not a notion of what a gentleman ought to do on earth; the renowned Stäudlin, the cleverest of all the Göttingen theologians, talks quite as vulgarly as a common man about the 'cursed affair of the queen', and the '*hellish* bad situation of the ministers'; and our excellent Heeren, who has written the most acute book that has ever been written on the commerce of the ancients, hardly knows how to hold commerce with men of his own time. One of the most copious of the professors longs to get some petty office as clerk at Hanover, and often exclaims, 'Could I once get out of this hell on earth, I would never write a book again.' As it is he writes two octavos a year. And Eichhorn, than whom I have never seen a more amiable or a kinder man, speaks often of his labours, in a manner, which does not increase one's respect for him. . . . All these things seem to justify the Germans of higher rank in the little respect, with which they treat the learned; but they correspond poorly with the childish ideas I had formed in America of the superior culture and venerable character of the wise in Europe.[1]

Benecke's name does not figure on this list of boorish and disgruntled pedants; for he was a cut above most of them socially, and genuinely kind. Ticknor found his German lessons pleasant and useful on the literary side, and remarked on his unfailing punctuality; Bancroft commented gratefully on his kindness, but felt that he overdid his exactitude with regard to time:

. . . it was at first quite amusing to me to see how careful he was in observing the second when the hour had elapsed, and how uneasy and even disturbed he is when I am rude enough to stay a moment beyond the time. I must rise and fly at the instant, when the hand of time is on the point of the hour, even if in the midst of a line, aye, or of a long word.[2]

Cogswell found him so hopeless as a teacher of German that, following Ticknor's advice, he used him in his capacity of qualified librarian instead:

I have made two experiments with Benecke in the library, and rejoice that I now get an hour of very valuable instruction, for one which was worth nothing at all. He takes the library first according to the arrangement on the shelves, and goes through the whole with me in that way, giving minute accounts of all the divisions and subdivisions, and of the practical application of the principles of classification and distribution. Afterwards he will do the same with the catalogues.[3]

[1] Howe, op. cit., i, pp. 85 f. To President Kirkland from Göttingen, September 17, 1820.     [2] Ibid., i, p. 37. Journal for August 1818.
[3] A. E. Ticknor, op. cit., p. 67. To George Ticknor from Göttingen, July 27, 1817.

It sounds the reverse of inspiring; but it bore fruit; for Cogswell became the chief librarian at Harvard, and later the administrator of the famous Astor Library which owed its inception to him. So that Benecke had at least one outstanding success to his credit as a tutor; and was now the recipient of a most important and valuable document: the dedication to *Sardanapalus* in Byron's own hand; with a request from his former pupil Douglas Kinnaird to send it to Goethe for his approval together with an explanation of the circumstances which had delayed its publication. This was a highly honourable but excessively delicate task. Benecke hardly knew Goethe and stood in great awe of him: unapproachable, formidable, almost rigid with dignity, this was the impression he created when among strangers; and Benecke had seen him in Göttingen several years ago. On the other hand, he was devoted to Kinnaird and serviceable by nature. He executed the commission without a moment's delay; and, after some days of anxious suspense, he was able to reply to the Englishman's letter:

I would seek in vain for words to tell you how happy I was to see again the handwriting of an old friend whom I shall never forget, and what is more to hear there is a hope that I may see him again soon. But don't forget that I am already too old to count on hopes whose fulfilment lies far in the future.[1]

Benecke was only fifty-five at the time of writing, and another twenty-two years of existence still stretched before him; but, worn and harassed by life in 'this hell on earth', he felt that he had one foot in the grave. However, at the moment he was uplifted by the success of his diplomatic mission:

Your commission, my dearest friend, was a rather delicate one to execute. 'Why', Goethe might well ask, 'did Mr Kinnaird not write *immediately* on receiving Lord Byron's commission to his friend Benecke, if he did not wish to write to me? Now *Sardanapalus* is printed; and why then should I declare my willingness that the dedication to me should be prefixed to it?'
Nevertheless I believe that I have justified the confidence you have reposed in me, and that the affair is in order *for the moment*.
Goethe writes to me:

Yes; what did Goethe write to Benecke, breaking a silence of nearly eighteen months, when Gillies had failed to strike a single spark from him at the mention of Byron's name? And how did he write? Stiffly and huffily? Condescendingly and kindly? Would he be touched, or would he be touchy? And was Benecke courting a snub?

[1] Murray Papers. Letter in German from Professor Benecke to Kinnaird; dated from Göttingen, November 25, 1822. The italics are Benecke's.

I can only thank you for your present communication overcome with confusion and surprise. I have followed, in unison with friends from far and near, indeed with all Germany and the whole world, that indomitable character, that inexhaustibly creative, irresistibly impetuous, tender and lovable being. I have attempted to identify myself with him by translations, and to adapt myself to his tenderest feelings no less than to his boldest humour; [and to mention only the latter, nothing but the impossibility of attaining complete clarity about the text could have restrained me from continuing the translation of *English Bards and Scotch Reviewers* which I had begun].

To learn of such sympathy from a man so highly esteemed; to have such a testimony of harmonising sentiments, must be all the more unexpected, as I had never ventured to hope and hardly dared to wish for it.

If you would be kind enough to communicate this to your English friend together with my sincere thanks for his good offices, you would very greatly oblige me.

It is with reluctance that I return the manuscript written in the hand of one so dear to me; and indeed who would willingly deprive himself of the original of a document of such price? Old age, which ultimately begins to have doubts of itself, needs such testimonies, whose stimulating force a younger man might hardly have borne.[1]

For five years Goethe had been writing reviews about Byron; for two years Byron had been writing dedications to Goethe; and it had taken all of six months before the final impetus given by Bancroft's meeting with Byron achieved deliverance of a crumpled scrap of paper into Goethe's hands. The effect of this long-delayed, continually retarded action was extraordinarily dramatic. The ice settling round Goethe's heart melted overnight, and a torrent of emotions – ardent, rapturous, exalted – poured forth. Fifty-two words in Byron's handwriting undid (almost with one stroke of the pen) the incalculable harm and injury his masterpiece had done. That had nearly ruined him in Goethe's eyes; but the personal tribute aroused a dormant passion in the older man which lasted until his death.

Göttingen, Weimar, and indeed all Germany, not to mention foreign visitors, were voluble on the subject of Goethe's vanity. But the feelings which overwhelmed him on receiving Byron's dedication were not due wholly nor even chiefly to self-love. Something stranger was involved: something inexplicable, something extreme. It had been there from the beginning; it had stirred in him powerfully whilst his wife lay dying; it had struck him with blindness on the subject of *Manfred*; it had worked like madness in his brain over *Don Juan*; it was made ecstatically

---

[1] *Briefe*, xxxvi, pp. 204 f. Weimar, November 12, 1822. The passage in square brackets was omitted in Benecke's copy to Kinnaird.

manifest now. Oscillating irrationally between the extremes of attraction and repulsion, Goethe's passion for Byron was to experience other recoils in the years to come; but never again would it reach the point of total estrangement which chance working deviously through Bancroft and Benecke had finally overcome.

It is unlikely that Byron ever received Goethe's declaration of love, although Benecke did his best. Realizing what Goethe expected of him, he copied out the relevant portion of the letter in his reply to Kinnaird, omitting only the passage about *English Bards and Scotch Reviewers*, possibly unwilling to allow that it had defeated Goethe. He transposed the whole into reported speech, which enabled him, by using the third person for the first, to impart a slight shade of formality; and he annotated Goethe's reference to the misgivings of old age with a mark of approval in the margin: 'Very fine', as if he were transcribing an academic exercise; for this sentence went straight to his own elderly heart. Kinnaird for his part was quite as conscious as Benecke that Byron should be made aware of the contents of this remarkable letter, and he set about translating it, writing to Byron on December 17, 1822:

I shall by next Post have a very pleasant communication to make to you from *Goethe*, who is delighted with yr. dedication of *Sardanapalus* to him.[1]

And Byron replied:

I am very glad of old Goethe being pleased, having a great esteem and admiration of that illustrious patriarch of European letters.[2]

Nothing could be more genial and amiable; but what a contrast it presents to Goethe's fervour, which Kinnaird had still not succeeded in rendering into English by January 21, 1823. 'Goethe by the next Post',[3] he promised Byron in a postscript to a letter of that date; but as far as one can tell 'the next Post' never came. The 'good German Scholar' was perhaps ultimately defeated by Goethe's dithyrambic prose in Benecke's reported speech, though he wrestled with it manfully, as can be seen by the rough draft in his handwriting preserved in Albemarle St. It is a gallant attempt, full of erasures and corrections and with some mistakes; but it is incomplete. Kinnaird threw in his hand before the end; Goethe's grief at parting with the manuscript and the mournful reference

[1] Murray Papers.
[2] *Correspondence*, ii, p. 246. Genoa, December 30, 1822.
[3] Murray Papers. Eight letters from Kinnaird to Byron, from January 31 to April 19, 1823, contain no reference to the matter as far as I could discover. I pursued the search no further.

to old age are absent from his page. Otherwise Kinnaird's version conveys Goethe's sentiments fairly accurately, but the emotion behind them is barely discernible; so that even if Byron saw this rendering of the original, he would not have seen far into Goethe's heart. But it is doubtful if he saw it, since there is no acknowledgement and no other mention of it in his published correspondence. This effort of Goethe's to communicate his feelings to Byron failed outright.

Meanwhile a fearful storm was brewing between Byron and Murray, in which Goethe as a dedicatee was again involved, this time as one of the major issues between the poet and the publisher which wrecked the relationship between them. Leigh Hunt and John Hunt, *The Liberal* and the (mislaid) Preface to *The Vision of Judgment* were all bringing matters to a crisis which *Werner* certainly helped to precipitate. Byron, chafing at the delay in its appearance, wrote angrily to Murray on October 24, 1822: 'You have also withheld the publication of *Werner*, etc. *Why?*'[1] If Murray had been merely procrastinating until then, he had now an excellent reason for delaying still further; for the command to prefix to *Werner* the dedication originally intended for *Sardanapalus* had been too emphatic to ignore; but the manuscript (of which no copy had been taken) was not available. It had in fact just started on its way to Göttingen when Byron wrote; for Kinnaird's unconscionable delay in executing Byron's commission to Goethe was no negligible factor in the whole tangled affair. Murray probably did not know where it was; but he knew to whom he had given it, and answered Byron's irate question obliquely: 'Remember Mr Kinnaird has also both dedications to Goethe'.[2] At this time Kinnaird had most of Byron's papers in his possession and was shortly to have them all; and Murray was probably referring to the dedicatory epistle to *Marino Faliero* which he may have handed over at the same time as the inscription to *Sardanapalus*. Byron himself never mentioned a third dedication to Goethe, except for the threat of 'putting another, stating that the former had been omitted by the publisher'.[3] Yet there *was* a third in existence. For when Murray brought out *Werner* on November 22, 1822, with a great splash, giving a dinner and holding a sale which sold thousands of copies, the much sought after volume bore the legend:

To
The Illustrious Goëthe,
By One of His Humblest Admirers,
This Tragedy is dedicated.[4]

---

[1] *Letters and Journals*, vi, p. 129.        [2] Murray Papers; November 5, 1822.
[3] See above, p. 75.                          [4] *Poetry*, vii, p. 302.

Whoever may have composed this tribute (and one cannot help suspecting that it was Murray himself), Byron certainly had no hand in it; for he wrote to Murray a month after publication, but before he had seen a copy:

It was my hope that our concluding transaction should be an amicable one – and I wish that it may be so still. But I perceive by some extracts in a paper that you appear to have omitted, contrary to my repeatedly urged requests, both the *conclusion* to the preface (written last summer and carefully sent to you) referring to the *E.R.* and also the inscription to Goethe. If Mr. Kd. had it, you knew where to find it. You also knew my desire, particularly as you had already omitted it from before *Sardanapalus*, for which I reproved you, and yet you seem to have repeated the same omission. Is this courteous? – is it even *politic*? I repeat to you that *no publisher* has a right to be negligent upon such subjects. . . . Replace at your best speed the inscription to Goethe – and the addition to the preface. . . . Do not force me to do disagreeable things. But in case of your non-attention, I must not only write to Goethe – but publish a statement of what has past between us on such subjects.[1]

Admittedly Byron was speaking without the book; but he was referring throughout to the dedication he had written for *Sardanapalus* and had then not once, but twice and even thrice commanded Murray to prefix to *Werner* instead. Whether his wrath was at all appeased by the desperate step Murray had taken to avert it, history does not relate; for at this point darkness descends and muffles the whole in mystery. The correspondence between Byron and Murray was closing down. Byron wrote again on December 25, 1822, one of his best letters too, still vexed about many things, but frank, disarming, eminently reasonable, full of information and with a little olive-branch in the shape of a joke; but Murray did not answer; indeed the last letter preserved in Albemarle St is dated November 8, 1822; and even a long account of Byron's doings from Missolonghi brought forth no reply. *Werner* was the last first edition of Byron's works published by the House of Murray whilst the poet was alive.

But by no means the last edition. 'Replace at your best speed the inscription to Goethe', Byron had commanded; and unless Kinnaird was the most forsworn of mortals, he must have been urging the same thing. For he also was being subjected to pressure, brought to bear by Professor Benecke, who had concluded the letter quoted above with almost more than tutorial authority:

But now I must urgently request you to see to it that the Dedication, the original of which I enclose herewith, be printed *without the smallest delay* and sent to Goethe. If you wish to do this also through me, I am

---

[1] *Letters and Journals*, vi, pp. 151 and 153. Genoa, December 21, 1822.

quite at your service. And perhaps it would not be out of place to state in a small footnote that the publication has been accidentally delayed.[1]

And Kinnaird replied immediately:

The Dedication will be prefixed to the new edition of *Sardanapalus* together with a note of explanation as to the causes of its not having been inserted in the earlier edition. I shall send three copies to you, one for Goethe, one for yourself & one for the Göttingen library.[2]

Whether owing to Byron's menaces to Murray or to Benecke's insistence, or to a combination of both, the dedication (just as Byron had written it and as Goethe had seen it) was prefixed to the second edition of *Sardanapalus* which appeared separately in 1823, although without the note of explanation promised by Kinnaird. Communications having now ceased between Murray and Byron, it is impossible to tell if Byron ever knew that his orders had finally been obeyed; he never mentioned this edition to anyone else, so that possibly he never saw it. If it were published in order to placate him, this would be more than strange; but one thing at least is certain: it was a very small edition, and is now exceedingly rare. It is not listed by E. H. Coleridge, nor in any other Byron bibliography I have seen. But there is a copy in the British Museum and I have heard of another in Canada. It is not in the Göttingen library, nor in Goethe's library at Weimar, and thereby hangs a tale of gross negligence on the part of Kinnaird. It was never sent to Goethe at all; and he would never have seen the dedication in print had it not been for another intervention on the part of Benecke. But that was still far in the future. For the moment Goethe was completely unaware of the anomalous but highly gratifying fact that two dramas by Byron were circulating simultaneously, each of them bearing an inscription to him.

Even as it was, his elation was extreme. Before returning the manuscript of the inscription to *Sardanapalus*, he had it lithographed and a number of fascimiles made which he distributed among favoured friends, writing rather touchingly to Sulpiz Boisserée:

Lord Byron wished to dedicate his *Sardanapalus* to me, but there were obstacles and delays; nevertheless the manuscript was communicated to me for a short time, and I had it lithographed with all speed. Here is a copy. No one will begrudge an old man the invigorating effect of such a restorative. I have not seen *Werner* yet myself.[3]

[1] Murray Papers, Benecke to Kinnaird, November 25, 1822.

[2] Murray Papers, Kinnaird to Benecke; said by the latter to have been written 'at the end of 1822'. See below, p. 145.

[3] *Briefe*, xxxvi, p. 256. Weimar, January 3, 1823.

G

It was high time that he should, since it had been published nearly six weeks ago; and Goethe began to think so himself as January waned:

I am still waiting in quiet and modest activity for more definite knowledge of the mark of friendship shown me by Lord Byron.[1]

Meanwhile friends both far and near were pestering him for copies of the dedication to *Sardanapalus*, and he had none left.[2] It was an awkward situation altogether, continually calling for explanations:

Lord Byron intended to dedicate his *Sardanapalus* to me, and sent the sheet which was to be prefixed to it to England. I was to be told about it first, there were postponements and delays; then it was decided to prefix it to the second edition of *Sardanapalus*, and the sheet at last found its way to me. Realising the value of such a manuscript, we quickly had a facsimile made, which is all the more valuable, because the dedication will never be printed, and he has, so I hear, dedicated his tragedy *Werner* to me.[3]

Goethe, like Byron, was obviously expecting that (except for the name of the drama) the dedication to *Werner* would be a replica of the dedication to *Sardanapalus*, which he would soon have the gratification of seeing in print. He had a long time to wait before being disillusioned on that score; for, owing no doubt to the break between Murray and Byron, neither the poet nor the publisher sent him a presentation-copy. Murray probably forgot, and Byron was no longer with him in the spirit to jog his memory. So that when *Werner* at last came to hand, on March 24, 1823, it was not even the first edition, but one of Galignani's Paris reprints, presented to him, together with a similar copy of *Sardanapalus*, by Frédéric Soret, a Genevan scientist, tutor to the Duke of Weimar's grandson and one of Goethe's frequent visitors. *Werner* bore the truncated inscription; *Sardanapalus* had none, which was only what Goethe had been led to expect; but he must have felt a stab of acute disappointment at the far less panegyrical language of the eagerly awaited dedication; and he must surely have been disconcerted (to put it mildly) by the omission to honour him with a presentation-copy? But if this were so, he did not allow it to appear, nor to quench his reawakened enthusiasm for Byron. He 'seized upon and swallowed' both dramas and praised them with undiscriminating warmth to Müller as equally admirable. The one bore a visible, the other an invisible dedication to him;

---

[1] *Briefe*, xxxvi, p. 284. Also to Boisserée from Weimar, January 27, 1823.
[2] Cf. ibid, xxxvi, pp. 285 f. To F. L. von Froriep from Weimar, January 27, 1823, asking for another two dozen copies if the plate were still available.
[3] Ibid., xxxvi, p. 300. To C. G. D. Nees von Esenbeck; Weimar, February 3, 1823.

and that was enough to preclude objective criticism. They must be – they were – equal to anything Byron had ever written. Equal? No, superior, as he maintained to Soret. There was decided dramatic progress in these two tragedies; and moreover Byron showed himself to be less sombre and misanthropic now than formerly; he then reverted to his early, favourite and fixed idea, that *Faust* was the *fons et origo* of *Manfred*.[1]

Goethe's feelings of pride and gratitude for the honour done him, deeply rooted (to judge by the letters to Benecke and Boisserée) in humility and self-doubt, gave him no rest. They rose to the surface in his conversations and letters, and they spilled over into a graceful little essay entitled *Dankbare Gegenwart*, published in his journal *Über Kunst und Altertum* at the end of the year 1823. Enumerating the many testimonies of widespread rejoicings and regard which his recovery from a serious illness in February had produced, he took the proffered opportunity to publicize Byron's simultaneous although unrelated act of homage:

Shortly after [a most successful performance of *Tasso*] Lord Byron's *Werner* first came into my hands; and I saw before my very eyes what had already been announced to me, that the peerless poet had dedicated to me one of his most admirable works. Of such a distinction I can only claim to be worthy, because for many years one of my most agreeable occupations has been the faithful and thorough appreciation of this most remarkable contemporary, and the contemplation of that career which indeed I have followed ever since *English Bards and Scotch Reviewers*.[2]

In taking this public stand as one of Byron's earliest and most steadfast admirers, Goethe was betrayed into inaccuracy. He knew little or nothing about Byron until 1816, and his first acquaintance with *English Bards and Scotch Reviewers* was made in 1821. Moreover, had he really forgotten that only three years ago he had been on the brink of declaring himself against the 'peerless poet?' Old men have short memories; nor would one wish at this point that Goethe's had been longer. But, had an American squadron not been lying off Leghorn harbour in May 1822, the instinct warring against Byron might have prevailed; and had no further contact been made between those two dynamic minds, it is possible at least that we might be living in a different world today.

[1] Cf. Eckermann, pp. 531 f. April 13, 1823. Communicated by Soret.
[2] *Werke*, xxxvi, p. 297.

# CHAPTER III

# Communications (1823-1824)

## a. THE FIRST MISSIVE

A CURIOUS feature of the situation which had now developed between Goethe and Byron was their obvious reluctance to address each other directly. Even the sight of the inscription to *Sardanapalus* in Byron's own hand had failed to produce a personal letter of thanks from Goethe; and it seems doubtful whether Byron on his side would have put pen to paper even if he had had something more to go on than 'Goethe by the next Post'. Partly, as can be seen in his letters to Kinnaird, the language-bar appeared very formidable to him; and the threat to Murray: 'I must not only write to Goethe' sounds as if this were an almost impossible feat. But, since translators from the one language into the other were readily available as he very well knew, the root cause probably lay deeper: in Goethe's advanced old age. It was one thing to admire and exalt or even to taunt and to tease the venerable 'patriarch of European letters' from a distance; but anything like intimacy was quite out of the question, and hardly crossed his mind. As for Goethe, he may well have been hindered by the diffidence which deep emotions inspire. There was nothing to show that these were reciprocated; and the only acknowledgement of the messages he had sent through Benecke and Kinnaird was a rather cooler dedication than the one he had accepted with such tell-tale warmth. So that one way and another, both remained shy of entering into a correspondence; and they might never have done so at all, had it not been for young Charles Sterling.

That fortunate youth, son of the British Consul at Genoa where Byron was residing from September 1822 until the following July, had evidently endeared himself to the poet, who had good-naturedly promoted his desire to become acquainted with Goethe during his forthcoming visit to Germany. When he reached Weimar in the early summer of 1823, Sterling was therefore the bearer of a note of introduction in Byron's own hand. It was the merest scrawl, but manna from heaven to the household on the Frauenplan; and Ottilie von Goethe, who unlike her father-in-law had remained faithful to the poet throughout, managed to appropriate it. With the result that it is now lost, or at least lost

86

to sight, since it is not among Byron's published letters. Perhaps some descendant of the wilful 'British Consul at Weimar' is cherishing it still. The fact that Goethe surrendered it, even to Ottilie, is striking. Only a few months earlier he had most unwillingly parted with a manuscript 'written in the hand of one so dear to me', and had actually had it lithographed first; and now he allowed a genuine specimen to be wheedled away from him. True, it was only a formal note, whereas the other had been an expression of homage; and the note after all would remain under his own roof; but still . . . Had the inscription to *Werner* slightly cooled his ardour? Or was it one of those acts of generosity in a moment of gladness we are later so apt to regret? Certainly the sudden appearance of Sterling was nothing short of an event in Goethe's life; and the visitor was made welcome. He seems, although on very slight evidence, to have been an engaging young man. In his rough draft of his Memoir for Medwin, Goethe called him 'a dear young man'. In the more impersonal and stilted finished product he altered this to the chilling testimonial: 'a young man pleasing in his person and pure in his morals'; but, although far from impugning Sterling's moral worth, I suggest that it was mitigated by a good deal of personal charm; and even had he been totally devoid of it, he was Mercury, Messenger of the Gods:

My Lord

I am happy to acquaint Your Lordship that I have been introduced to Mr de Goëthe and found him in a perfect state of health. During the short conversation which passed between us, he expressed his gratitude towards Your Lordship for having honor'd him with the dedication of *Werner*. He enquired particularly whether I thought it likely that you would visit Weimar, signifying at the same time, the high esteem in which Your Lordship is held by himself & all his enlightened countrymen. I beg to return many thanks for the valuable Memorandum, by which, I may say, Your Lordship procured me the acquaintance of the 'illustrious Goëthe'.

The kindness and good will you honord me with, have rendered your memory very agreeable to me, my Lord; and it is with gratitude as well as profound respect that

I have the honor to be

My Lord

Your Lordship's

Most Obedient Humble Servt.

CHARLES STERLING.[1]

An idyllic series of dissolving views presents itself to the mind's eye. Byron in Genoa winning young Sterling's heart by his

[1] Murray Papers. Weimar, June 5, 1823.

kindness; Goethe in Weimar unbending towards the emissary; talking to him about Byron and the inscription to *Werner*, throwing out a tentative invitation and sending flattering messages; Sterling in his lodgings devotedly and faithfully passing them on. And Byron? But here the idyll vanishes to be replaced by a different scene. Just at the time when Sterling's letter reached him, possibly indeed on the same day, Byron was writing urgently to Trelawny:

You must have heard that I am going to Greece. Why do you not come to me? I want your aid, and am exceedingly anxious to see you. Pray come, for I am at last determined to go to Greece; it is the only place I was ever contented in. I am serious, and did not write before, as I might have given you a journey for nothing; they all say I can be of use in Greece. I do not know how, nor do they; but at all events let us go.[1]

'Let us go'; but not to Weimar; let us go to Greece; Goethe's figure wavers, for Trelawny was in the foreground now. There was no reply to the 'dear young man'; no counter-message to Goethe; it was all hustle and bustle and preparations for departure; whilst Goethe in Weimar was meditating a step which must surely bring them closer together?

My Lord

The enclosed was remitted to me from the part of Mr de Goethe with a request to forward it to Your Lordship. I regret that my present task has not fallen to a more worthy person who could have added a suitable translation. Being aware that Your Lordship is not acquainted with the German language, I take the liberty of recommending Mr Noldenhawer [? or Moldenhawer], formerly my master, as the only person in Genoa capable of doing some degree of justice to the original. Your Lordship's 'homme d'affaires' may easily find him out by applying to Mr Barchi.

Monsieur de Göthe is now at Marienbad where he intends to remain till the end of August. The court is removed to Eisenach for a few weeks, so that for the present this celebrated little spot is dull and lonely.

I have the honor to be, with profound respect
      My Lord
         Your Lordship's
            Most faithful Humble Servant
               CHARLES STERLING.[2]

Young Charles might be moping, but it was anything but dull and lonely for Goethe in Marienbad just then, surrounded as he was by lovely woods and hills and in the midst of the fashionable, the great and the gay. New life was pouring into his veins, reviving

[1] *Letters and Journals*, vi, p. 224. Genoa, June 15, 1823.
[2] Murray Papers. Weimar, July 1, 1823.

and rejuvenating him and completely obliterating all traces of the alarming illness of the February before. He was now seventy-four, but desperately in love, having given his heart and being about to offer his hand to Ulrike von Levetzov, aged just nineteen. A direct refusal was gracefully avoided by the tact and diplomacy of the girl's mother; and Goethe's last overwhelming passion beat itself out in poetry. So that it was not exactly dull for him in Marienbad whilst Sterling wrote those lines. And it was the reverse of dull and lonely on board the *Hercules* when Byron read them. He was just about to set sail for Argostoli when, at the last moment, an insured 'packet of some sort or another' arrived from Germany, which Charles Barry, Byron's banker and devoted slave, contrived should reach him in Leghorn harbour where the *Hercules* had been forced to put in owing to contrary winds. For the second time in this story homage from Goethe overtook Byron quite by chance in Leghorn. Bancroft was the intermediary on the first occasion; and now it was Charles Sterling, dutifully forwarding a poem addressed by Germany's greatest poet to the warrior-poet of England. But happily or unhappily Byron was no longer within reach of N or M oldenhawer, or anyone else who could interpret it. Trelawny? Well, he was evidently present when Shelley translated and repeated passages of *Faust* to Byron, in order as he said to impregnate Byron's brain with them. But the bold buccaneer himself needed the services of a Lausanne bookseller to

. . . translate for me passages from the works of Schiller, Kant, Goëthe, and others, and write comments on their paradoxical, mystical and metaphysical theories.[1]

He *may* have been the author of a feeble and inaccurate version in Albemarle St in an unidentified hand; but this seems unlikely; for he made no mention of the arrival of the missive from Germany in his *Recollections* nor in his *Records*, and neither did anyone else except Byron himself, who acknowledged the packet to Barry and the poem to Goethe. It was outside the sphere of interest of those on board the *Hercules*. Pietro Gamba, Teresa's charming, unlucky and far from practical brother, hated the Austrians far too much to have any truck with their language, and Hamilton Browne, an ardent Philhellenist who had learnt both Italian and Romaic, was in all probability ignorant of German. The two conspiratorial Greeks, Vitali and Prince Schilizzi, were entirely absorbed in intrigue. Captain Scott preferred the bottle to poetry; and poor Dr Bruno had not yet had time even to master the art of medicine.

---

[1] E. J. Trelawny, *Recollections of the Last Days of Shelley and Byron*, ed. Morpurgo London, 1952, p. 1.

Lega Zambelli, it is true, was called Byron's secretary; but as this title was an 'Italianism for steward or chief servant' according to his master, hopes in that direction do not run high. The 'learned Fletcher' spoke no language but his own; and as for Byron's devoted gondolier and Trelawny's negro groom, they were quite as likely to prove Germanists as Moretti the bull-dog or Lion the Newfoundland. And even if one and all had been 'good German Scholars', there was hardly time and certainly no inclination to wrestle with a poem in that tongue. So that Byron, having glanced through Sterling's letter, looked at the lines covering a sheet of paper, and perhaps recognized the word 'Muse', but understood 'neither word nor letter' of what they were trying to tell him:

> Ein freundlich Wort kommt eines nach dem andern,
> Von Süden her und bringt uns frohe Stunden;
> Es ruft uns auf zum Edelsten zu wandern,
> Nicht ist der Geist, doch ist der Fuss gebunden.
>
> Wie soll ich dem, den ich so lang begleitet,
> Nun etwas Traulichs in die Ferne sagen?
> Ihm, der sich selbst im Innersten bestreitet,
> Stark angewohnt, das tiefste Weh zu tragen.
>
> Wohl sey ihm doch wenn er sich selbst empfindet!
> Er wage selbst sich hochbeglückt zu nennen,
> Wenn Musenkraft die Schmerzen überwindet;
> Und wie ich ihn erkannt mög' er sich kennen.[1]
>
> .    .    .    .
>
> One friendly word pursues another hither,
> Sent from the South, bringing us hours most sweet;
> Noblest of men, his presence lures us thither:
> Fain is the spirit, fettered are the feet.
>
> What words of cheer can reach him in the distance,
> Whom for so long I've watched, nor e'er forgot?
> Who, striving with his inmost self's resistance,
> Strongly inured, has borne the saddest lot.
>
> Himself esteeming, may he find relief,
> And dare to call himself most blest of men,
> When poetry's power conquers his heart's deep grief,
> And may he know himself (as I do) then!

This was a very strange communication to receive at that moment; and all the stranger if Goethe's later statement is accurate, according to which the poem had been prompted partly

---

[1] Medwin, Appendix, pp. xiv f. Dated June 22, 1823, from Weimar. I have corrected some printing mistakes. Medwin's translation (which Robertson calls 'hardly a translation at all') is on pp. 348 f.

by the note Sterling had brought but chiefly by the rumour that Byron was going to Greece. Sterling's covering note makes that assertion doubly unlikely, and it is permissible to deduce that Goethe was mistaken. Otherwise it is almost incomprehensible that the poem should contain no reference of any sort to the spirit-stirring occasion which was said to have inspired it. The South from which Byron's words winged their way to Goethe was Italy and not Greece; and the poem which just caught Byron as he left Italy for ever reads like a missive from the moon, being completely out of touch with the real situation. It is not, and in the circumstances it could not be, a great poem. It is hardly even poetry at all; but rather a versified exhortation, addressed to the author of *Manfred* in the same tones and almost in the same words which Goethe-Antonio had used to Goethe-Tasso years and years ago: bidding him to know himself and find surcease from his sorrows by recourse to his Muse. Kindly, sympathetic and slightly moralizing, it forms a striking contrast to the highly-wrought fervour of the letter to Benecke; but the contrast with Byron's actual intentions and emotional resurgence is more striking still; and in the unlikely event that Trelawny did achieve a translation of sorts, Byron may have smiled at the soothing sermon the 'old fox' was preaching from his lair, and have told himself that the poem was hardly more applicable to him now than the tale of the murder in Florence had been before. Spiritually speaking the two men were poles apart as each prepared to meet a new crisis in his life: Goethe starting off for Marienbad to put his fate to the test with Ulrike von Levetzov, and Byron setting sail for Greece because 'they all say I can be of use'. Yet even at that harassing and harrowing moment when burning his boats behind him, Byron, realizing from Sterling's letter that a signal compliment was intended, honoured it in the spirit in which it was made. He descended to his little aft cabin and wrote an answer whilst all the commotion of departure (the yelling of orders, the clanking of chains, the thudding of feet and the flapping of shrouds) reverberated above:

Illustrious Sir, – I cannot thank you as you ought to be thanked for the lines which my young friend, Mr Sterling, sent me of yours; and it would but ill become me to pretend to exchange verses with him who, for fifty years, has been the undisputed sovereign of European literature. You must therefore accept my most sincere acknowledgments in prose – and in hasty prose too; for I am at present on my voyage to Greece once more, and surrounded by hurry and bustle, which hardly allow a moment even to gratitude and admiration to express themselves.

I sailed from Genoa some days ago, was driven back by a gale of wind, and have since sailed again and arrived here, 'Leghorn', this morning, to receive on board some Greek passengers for their struggling country.

Here also I found your lines and Mr Sterling's letter; and I could not have had a more favourable omen, a more agreeable surprise, than a word of Goethe, written by his own hand.

I am returning to Greece, to see if I can be of any little use there: if ever I come back, I will pay a visit to Weimar, to offer the sincere homage of one of the many millions of your admirers. I have the honour to be, ever and most respectfully, y[our]

Obliged adm[irer] and se[rvant],
NOEL BYRON.[1]

No one could have done better; hardly a man in ten thousand could have done as well as to produce in the grand manner on the spur of the moment such an admirable piece of prose. Like the early dedicatory letter to *Marino Faliero*, it is a genuine effort at communication, although in a very different tone. It is (in striking contrast to Goethe's verses) completely appropriate both to the situation in which Byron found himself and to his view of the relationship existing between them. Dignified, modest, deferential, it had only one failing. It was not (and could not be) an answer to 'the lines . . . the verses . . . the word of Goethe' which Byron could not read. It was sent through Sterling, and Goethe received it enclosed in a letter from his son on August 11, 1823. He commented in his diary: 'Contemplation of the most extraordinary coincidence';[2] and he was certainly not exaggerating; for never perhaps did contrary winds so much belie their nature. Yet what had they accomplished? A favourable omen for Byron? Desire fulfilled for Goethe? No such violent upsurge of emotion was evident as had overtaken Goethe on reading the dedication to *Sardanapalus*. Byron's obvious preoccupation with Greece and its liberation rather than with Goethe and Weimar may have struck a chill. But he sat down next day, copied out the letter with his own hand and sent the copy to August, who wrote to his father that this attention had delighted young Sterling, adding on his own account: 'It is indeed a splendid letter, on which you can certainly pride yourself'.[3]

Goethe could take pride in it undoubtedly, and was to show that he did so in the future; but if his instinct told him when he read it that Byron did not and never would reciprocate his own feelings, that instinct was sound. This becomes almost painfully clear in the longest as well as the last recorded conversation Byron ever held about Goethe. It was at Metaxata in Cephalonia; and

---

[1] *Letters and Journals*, vi, pp. 237 f. From Leghorn; dated July 24, 1823, in error for July 23.
[2] *Tagebücher*, ix, p. 92. August 11, 1823.
[3] Ibid., ix, p. 373. August 24, 1823.

once more a former student of Göttingen and a pupil of Benecke's must be invoked, the future historian George Finlay (1799–1875) who, abandoning Roman jurisprudence in favour of Greek liberation, had come hotfoot from Göttingen to Cephalonia, from scholarly *colloquia* with Professor Benecke to more enlivening conversations with Lord Byron:

The next time we met was out riding. Lord Byron told me he had been struck at first by my resemblance to Shelley. . . . We then conversed about Germany and its literature, and I found, to my astonishment, Lord Byron knew nothing of the language, though he was perfectly acquainted with its literature; with Goethe in particular, and with every passage of *Faust*. He said nothing could be more sublime than the words of the Spirit of the Earth to Faust, 'Thou resemblest the spirit of thy imagination, not me'. I involuntarily repeated it in German, and he said, 'Yes, those are the words'. The scene of the monkeys had made a considerable impression on him, and I remember, on my saying I suppose Goethe meant to represent men transformed into monkeys, he exclaimed, 'Suppose no such thing – suppose them veritable monkeys, and the satire is finer and deeper'. After a few words on *Wilhelm Meister*, I asked if he had read the *Wahlverwandtschaften*. He said, he did not recollect the hard word, but inquired the signification of it. – I gave some stupid translation, as the *Choice Relationships*. Lord Byron said, 'Yes, yes, the *Affinities of Choice* – I recollect reading a translation, which I should think was not a very good one, for some parts seemed to border on the unintelligible'. I replied, that I thought some parts of the original bordered on it likewise, though, perhaps, they were not within its limits.

'The review of Goethe's *Aus meinem Leben* in the *Edinburgh*', he said, 'was harsh and unfeeling. The literature of Europe is under obligations to Goethe, which entitled him to more respect; but often less ability is required to misrepresent and ridicule than to understand genius.'

I told Lord Byron I had seen the dedication of *Sardanapalus* on its way to Goethe before it had been printed, and the letter Goethe had written to the gentleman who had forwarded it, in which he mentioned that he had once commenced a translation of the *English Bards and Scotch Reviewers*. Lord Byron pulled up his horse, and exclaimed, with eagerness, 'He had, had he? and what did the old gentleman mean by that?' I said I supposed he was struck by such an extraordinary specimen of early genius; but that he had abandoned his design, finding that he could not understand some passages without assistance. Lord Byron: 'No, that is not the reason: you don't understand the tricks of authorship, but I can let you into the secret; there was more of the devil in me than in Goethe, and he was content to borrow my weapons against the *Review*, though I had wished to suppress the work. I remember another anecdote of Goethe. On the publication of *Manfred*, Goethe gave translations of those passages which he considered bore the greatest resemblance to *Faust*, to show my plagiarisms.' I said, 'I am sure, my Lord, you have no fear of being thought a plagiarist.' He replied, 'No, not much, though they seem to be trying hard to prove me one, in England.'[1]

Shelley had obviously 'impregnated Byron's brain with *Faust*' to some purpose. Byron now admired it unreservedly; and yet, as Stroganov had also noted, there was something about the 'old gentleman' which tickled his sense of humour. His tenacious memory is no more apparent with regard to *The Edinburgh Review* than his continued malicious amusement on that score, flashing out in a mischievous comment on Goethe's attempted translation of *English Bards and Scotch Reviewers*. And here one feels inclined to pick a quarrel both with fate and with young George Finlay. Taking his eyes off the clock for once, Professor Benecke had committed what was tantamount to a breach of confidence in showing to his pupil Goethe's self-revelatory letter, although perhaps it would be too much to expect a Professor of German and English Literature to keep such a document to himself. But since he had been guilty of this indiscretion, it seems peculiarly perverse that Byron should not have had the full benefit of it, and that Finlay should have picked out the one irrelevant fact in Goethe's moving declaration of love: his modest efforts (for modest indeed they were) to translate a satire Byron had vainly tried to suppress. Benecke had realized that *English Bards and Scotch Reviewers* had nothing to do with the case he was presenting to Kinnaird and had omitted that particular passage. Finlay passed it on, thus provoking Byron's hilarity; whereas, had the real import of the letter been communicated to him, he would have reacted very differently, and something about his own feelings might have emerged. Be that as it may, fate, scurvily enough, made a feint of presenting a last chance to acquaint Byron with the strength of Goethe's passion for him. He knew both through Bancroft and through Sterling that he was esteemed and admired; but he had not the slightest inkling of the real state of affairs. Finlay should have had; and yet, whilst fate laughed up her sleeve, he proved as incapable of communicating the vital essence of that letter as Kinnaird had been of translating it. The opportunity was irretrievably lost, a mischance much more to be regretted than the misfiring of Goethe's poem which was utterly devoid of any revealing emotion. Even the signal compliment it represented seems to have slipped Byron's memory on this October day when riding out with George Finlay, for he never thought to mention it in this long and leisurely exchange of views and news about Goethe.

But he had not forgotten the review of *Manfred* with its sug-

[1] K. Elze, *Lord Byron*, English Translation, London, 1872; pp. 480 ff. Letter from George Finlay to Leicester Stanhope from Tripolitza, June 1824.

gestion of plagiarism; and 'my plagiarisms' were the last words Byron ever uttered about Goethe, completing a scattered series of remarks, now grave, now gay, penetrated with gratitude and admiration and shot through with mirth, in which sometimes there lurked a protest: 'my plagiarisms'; and then silence which remained unbroken until total silence fell.

## b. THE LAST MESSAGE

In the autumn of 1823, when Byron in faraway Greece was impressing George Finlay with his knowledge of *Faust* and his great admiration for it, Goethe was undergoing the experience of reading *Cain*. It had appeared in 1821, during the *Don Juan* ice-age, and he had ignored it. Making good that deficiency now, he found himself overwhelmed by admiration and overcome by awe. This further revelation of Byron's mind marked a turning-point in Goethe's critical attitude towards a genius whose personality had hitherto preoccupied him more than his works. *Cain* increased his literary opinion of Byron a hundredfold, drawing from him the spontaneous tribute: 'Byron alone I admit to a place by my side'.[1] He then read *The Island* and *Heaven and Earth*, the latter increasing his enthusiasm still further:

About Byron's *Cain* and *Heaven and Earth*. He discussed the latter piece incomparably, with much verve and humour. It was much more comprehensible than the first, which was too profound in thought and too bitter, although sublime, bold and soul-stirring. There was nothing more blasphemous, by the way, than the old dogmatic theology itself, which evoked a wrathful, raging, unjust and party-spirited God.[1]

Intellectually, spiritually and emotionally, Goethe was in fundamental agreement with Byron's attitude to Old Testament doctrine which was at that time Church dogma too. The sympathy he felt in this connection was unalloyed; what is more, it was deep, basic and indestructible. It urged him on to testify in print and to range himself unequivocally with Byron against the embattled hosts of orthodoxy. Yet, as he stated in his review, the deeper he penetrated into the poet's mind, the greater the difficulty he experienced in recreating the work for himself, let alone for others; and he might have abandoned the task as beyond his powers, if he had not been encouraged by an article in *Le Moniteur Universel*, defending Byron against the refutations of Fabre d'Olivet. Chancellor Müller translated it into German for him, and Goethe printed a long extract from it, in which the

---

[1] *Gespräche*, ii, p. 308. Chancellor Müller. October 2, 1823.

author justified Byron's conception of Eve after the Fall and the curse she pronounced on Cain in his drama, concluding with the sentence:

It was for a powerful genius like Lord Byron to paint this picture in all its terrible truth; in this way he had to deal with it, or not at all.[1]

Applying this judgment to *Cain* as a whole, Goethe proceeded to an analysis of the drama, revealing the structure of the poem and the tragic problem in a fashion which showed how truly he had comprehended them, and in a way that would have gladdened Byron's heart. But he died without knowing either how much '*Donny Johnny*' had horrified Goethe, or what a conquest he had made with *Cain*. It was completed by *Heaven and Earth* and *The Vision of Judgment*. On February 12 and 13, 1824, captivated by that brilliant and apocalyptic poem, Goethe went through it several times, looking up unfamiliar words and deeply pondering the vision behind the breath-taking magnificence, the verve and the wit. The more he pondered, the greater the vision grew.'Yes', he sighed to Müller after yet another analysis of *Cain* and *Heaven and Earth*, 'one can understand very well how so great a genius after such magnificent productions should feel weary of the world, and should seize passionately on the events in Greece merely as a new pastime'.[2] A pastime? It looks as if Goethe really thought so then, to judge by a letter he wrote to Charles Sterling a few days later. Byron had sailed away over the sea; and now the 'dear young man' was going too, leaving Germany for Italy and snapping that slender personal link which, at least in the German poet's imagination, he had forged between Byron and himself. A sudden pang assailed Goethe as he realized what he was losing in the person of Charles Sterling; and he sat down to write a farewell letter to the young man who seems (perhaps from modesty) to have gone without calling to say good-bye:

I should have much liked, my dear Mr Sterling, to have taken leave of you by word of mouth and wished you well on your journey personally. I could then also have repeated the thanks which I owe you for paving the way to a closer relationship with Lord Byron, whom I esteem more than I can say. I regard this as one of the fairest gains of my life.

Keep us in your memory! And when you reach Genoa and have an opportunity to give news of yourself to that remarkable man, tell him also about me and mine, and the inexhaustible reverence, admiration and love which we feel for him. Speak out and tell him that we should

---

[1] Cf. *Le Moniteur Universel*, No. 303, pp. 1277 f. October 1823. The whole passage is quoted by Robertson, op. cit., pp. 74 ff.
[2] *Gespräche*, ii, p. 329. Chancellor Müller. March 8, 1824.

look upon any of us as most fortunate who might happen to meet him, wherever it might be, on this globe.[1]

This letter is not only startling because of its impassioned tone, its urgency, its lack of that stiffness and restraint which characterized Goethe's manners and prose in later years. It is remarkable in a different way, in its implicit assumption that Byron would soon weary of his Greek 'pastime' and return to Genoa where he would be accessible to Sterling. Indeed, but for his remark to Müller a few days before, one would wager that he had forgotten all about the expedition to Greece; and did one not know for a fact that Goethe had received Byron's letter from Leghorn, one would deduce that it had gone astray. For this message is no kind of answer to Byron's communication. It displays a most curious indifference to a situation which was occupying the imagination of the whole civilized world. It even ignored the sentence: 'if ever I come back', which ought surely to have aroused some apprehensions. Was this love? No, it was passion, oblivious of everything but its own need to arouse a response, a hopeless passion, and a last hopeless effort to convey it. One can hardly imagine young Sterling telling his Lordship in so many words that his Excellency loved him; but even if he had written straight off to that effect, the message would not have reached Byron in time. And what could it have meant to him if it had? On the very same day when Goethe was pouring his heart out to Sterling, Byron was writing to Kinnaird from Missolonghi:

Dear Douglas, – I write without much certainty that the letter will reach you, for the plague has broken out this morning in the town, and of course precautions will be taken in the islands, and elsewhere. . . . What the event may be cannot of course be foreseen. . . . I shall be the more anxious to hear from you as the communication will probably be interrupted for some time to come. Whatever may [happen] to me, believe me that I ever am, and was, and will be (as long as I am at all),
    Ever yours very faithfully and affectionately,
                              NOEL BYRON.[2]

Though he was spared the plague, Byron had a bare month to live and a strong premonition of death when he wrote those lines to Kinnaird; lines just as urgent, quite as moving and at least as deeply felt as Goethe's to Sterling. Each was communicating his feelings to a far distant friend and hoping against hope for an answer. Neither was to receive one, because Byron died too soon; and Goethe's declaration, had it reached Byron as he lay *in extremis* at Missolonghi, would have been tossed aside in favour of the last letter from Hobhouse which he never rallied to read:

---

[1] *Briefe*, xxxviii, p. 79. Weimar, March 13, 1824.
[2] *Correspondence*, ii, pp. 289 f. Missolonghi, March 13, 1824.

I can assure you here that the Greeks look upon your Avatar as a perfect godsend; one of them said to me in so many words, '*It is Providence who sent that man to our help*'. . . . Your present endeavour is certainly the most glorious ever undertaken by man. . . . Go on and prosper. . . .[1]

\*        \*        \*

In the whole strange story of Goethe's obsession with Byron, nothing is so strange from the purely human point of view as his failure to follow the English poet in spirit on the last adventure of his life. Yet it would be a mistake to conclude from Goethe's remissness in this respect, that his feelings for Byron lacked reality. On the contrary, they formed the great emotional pre-occupation of his declining years and endured long after his passion for Ulrike von Levetzov had died down. Yet even after he had surrendered to *Cain*, going all the way with Byron along that road, memories of the disturbing brilliance of *Don Juan* intruded and preoccupied him. Five days before the news of Byron's death reached Weimar, he instituted a comparison between Torquato Tasso and Byron, to whom he gave the palm as far as intellect, knowledge of the world and creative power went:

'One cannot', he added, 'compare these two poets with each other without the one annihilating the other. Byron is the burning bramble which reduces the holy cedar of Lebanon to ashes. The great epic of the Italian has maintained its fame through centuries; but the whole of *Jerusalem Liberated* could be poisoned by a single line from *Don Juan*.[2]

Goethe was alluding to the parable in *Judges*, in which the bramble (according to the Authorized Version) threatens to devour the cedars of Lebanon by fire if the trees who wish to anoint him as their king do not put their trust in him. Luther used the word *Dornbusch*: yet (according to Eckermann) Goethe preferred the less impressive *Dornstrauch*. Robertson and others when quoting this passage in English have rendered it by 'burning bush'. This immediately recalls the tremendous moment in Moses' life when the Lord spoke to him out of the burning bush; and it is difficult to quarrel with a translation so much in line with Goethe's ambivalent opinion of the author of *Don Juan*, *Cain*, *Heaven and Earth* and *The Vision of Judgment*: a devastating fire devouring holy things; an awe-inspiring portent signifying the proximity of God. He was to harmonize those conflicting views later by means of a mythological symbol; but when speaking of

---

[1] *Correspondence*, pp. 297 and 299. London, March 15, 1824.
[2] Eckermann, p. 557. Dated May 18, 1824, but almost certainly added to another conversation which took place after Byron's death was known in Weimar. See below, p. 103, footnote.

*Jerusalem Liberated,* it was the annihilating power of Byron's laughter that was uppermost in his mind. Nevertheless Byron's apocalyptic writings had raised his status to an unprecedented height in Goethe's eyes; and he surveyed the manifestations of that fiercely flaming spirit with something like awe; little realizing that, when he spoke those words, it had burnt itself out.

Yet that is a misleading way of saying that Byron was dead; for his spirit was burning as fiercely as ever in his writings and in Goethe's mind, otherwise there would be no Part II to this book. It is the measure of a vitality few indeed have possessed in a comparable degree that his effect upon Goethe increased prodigiously after his death, inspiring a great elegiac rhapsody and expanding into cosmology. But quite as strange as this is the fact that death did not deprive Byron of the active initiative in the personal relationship, which continued to develop after he had gone, almost as if he were now desirous of a closer intimacy. This is the reason why the question which naturally arises now: 'What would have been the outcome if they had ever met in the flesh?' must wait for an answer until the whole tale is told. For they were to meet in the spirit again and again, often round unexpected corners. It might be thought that Goethe had by now run through the whole gamut of emotions Byron could inspire; but he was still to be disconcerted and dismayed, delighted and exasperated, overcome with gladness, heart-stricken, downcast and uplifted again. It was a cycle that could only end with his death.

H

3. Portrait of Goethe. Drawing by Schwerdgeburth.

# PART II

## POST MORTEM (1824–1832)

# CHAPTER IV

# Retrospects (1824-1825)

## a. OBITUARIES

GOETHE entered the death of Byron retrospectively in his diary for April 19, 1824, but when the news reached Weimar on May 23, he made no comment. Indeed had he been left to his own devices, he might have allowed weeks or even months to elapse before mentioning the subject to anyone. For it was increasingly his practice to be silent about personal sorrows and bereavements until he could speak of them with equanimity. But the matter was brought up two days later by Friedrich Wilhelm Riemer, one of the less attractive persons in Goethe's *entourage*. He had been August's tutor at one time; but there had been a serious quarrel with his difficult pupil, and Riemer had been banished from the house for a considerable period. He was now back in favour again; and happening to call when Goethe was enjoying an interesting conversation about geology with Soret, he interrupted them with an untimely reference to the sad event. He should have known better and he deserved a good snubbing for his pains; nor could anyone administer snubs with more deadly accuracy than Goethe. But he refrained, embarking (said Soret) on a brilliant summary of Byron's works, and concluding philosophically:

As for the rest, although he has died young, the domain of letters has lost nothing by that as far as the extension of its territory is concerned. Byron could go no further; he had attained the maximum of his powers. What he might have produced subsequently would doubtless still have been beautiful and admirable, but it would have done more for the reader's entertainment than for himself. It would not have extended the limits of the field in which his genius could develop. He had attained the furthest bourne of his imagination in that inconceivable production *The Vision of Judgment*.[1]

Goethe may have been right, and can never be proved to have been wrong; but this method of writing *finis* to Byron's poetical powers strikes cold to the heart. It was in line with Goethe's hard-won philosophy that whatever is, is right; but he would

---

[1] *Gespräche*, ii, p. 345. May 25, 1824. Soret. Eckermann (pp. 556 f.) gives the same account, but dates it May 18, before Byron's death was known in Weimar. He runs it together with the conversation about Tasso and the burning bramble which seems to have occurred on the earlier date.

never have applied it to Byron's death had he been in sympathy with its cause:

He said of Byron's death, that it had occurred at exactly the right time. His Greek enterprise had something impure about it, and could never have ended well.

'It is undoubtedly a misfortune that minds so rich in ideas should be so set on realising their ideals and bringing them into real life. That simply will not do. The ideal and ordinary reality must be rigorously kept apart.'[1]

Goethe's epitaph on Byron would seem to have been 'No loss to literature, and a good riddance to life'; but in reality his first statement was due to an instinctive reaction, almost automatic with him by then, to cover up a wound; and the second was prompted by his deep distrust of revolutions in any shape or form, which also accounts for his silence on the subject of Greece both in the 'Leghorn' poem, supposing him to have been aware of the facts, and in the letter to Sterling, when he certainly was. He had tried to believe that Byron's undertaking had been merely a pastime; but the moment had come when that explanation would no longer serve, and he was brought face to face with a vital factor in Byron's make-up to which he was innately antagonistic. Misanthropy and immorality were both to be deplored; but quite as deplorable and considerably more dangerous were the liberal doctrines and the revolutionary ardour which Byron had manifested by going to Greece. The world as a whole has been inclined to see in Byron's death at Missolonghi something comparable to Cawdor's in *Macbeth*:

> nothing in his life
> Became him like the leaving it; he died
> As one that had been studied in his death,
> To throw away the dearest thing he owed
> As 'twere a careless trifle.

Goethe held a diametrically opposite opinion. It seemed to him a lamentable end, a symptom of the disruptive forces he disliked and feared so much in the political world. They had destroyed Byron; and for some time after the first shock of the news Goethe found it hard to forgive either the man or the movement for that. 'The fairest star in the poetry of the century had set'; and all hopes of a personal meeting were blighted; grief and anger struggled for supremacy in his mind.

With feelings so torn, he cannot have been overjoyed when Medwin approached him through Soret for a Memoir on his relations with Byron; but, in a first rough draft written on June

---

[1] *Gespräche*, ii, p. 350. Chancellor Müller. June 13, 1824.

15, 1824, the bitterness welling up in his heart found an outlet in a savage attack on the English nation:

> The English nation has no cause at all to reproach Lord Byron for his shortcomings; when he is at fault, he is at fault as an Englishman, as the undisciplined heir to wealth, pedantically educated and with no moral training, inclined to contradiction, delighting to be in opposition, rejoicing in censoriousness, and first maligning his own people, king and commons, then finally, losing all hold on himself, maligning without measure or object the whole world. These bad habits, which have gradually grown on him are national and domestic; and it will always remain a wonder that he remained such a good man and as a poet raised himself above all his contemporaries.[1]

It was a cathartic notion to sketch the rake's progress of a rebel, who never had a chance because he was an Englishman. It enabled Goethe to say straight out how deplorable he thought Byron's politics, and at the same time to lay the whole blame on the shoulders of the English nation. Having cleared the air in this way, he proceeded to a short, straightforward but not very impressive account of the history of the relationship between them. This was followed a month later, when Goethe's anger with the English had somewhat subsided, by the full-dress obituary which Medwin reproduced in the appendix to his book, much disfigured by printing-mistakes, and of which he gave a rather garbled English translation in the body of the work. It is a strange and pathetic document. The rough draft was in the first person; the completed version began in the third, moving on loftily to the royal plural. Involved and wordy, pompous and stiff, it dwells complacently and yet nostalgically on the few hard facts behind the complex, contradictory and piercing emotions which Byron inspired in Goethe; and the muffled mournfulness towards the end has a certain poignancy:

> The desire has been expressed to procure some information about the relationship which existed between Lord Noel Byron, unhappily too early deceased, and Herr von Goethe. The following brief account may be given.
>
> The German poet who, up to his present advanced age, has striven to appreciate scrupulously and dispassionately the merits of his predecessors and contemporaries, having always regarded this as the surest means of self-development, could not but become aware of the great talent of the noble Lord soon after his first appearance; and he has also unremittingly continued to follow the progress of his remarkable achievements and incessant activity.
>
> In doing this it was easy to see that the universal recognition of his

---

[1] *Werke*, xlii, i, pp. 427 f. It was towards the end of this short tribute that Goethe wrote: 'The fairest star in the poetry of the century has set.' Otherwise it is not very interesting.

poetical merit increased in direct proportion with the rapid growth in volume and significance of his productions. The pleasure and interest which these have awakened among us here would have been complete, had not the gifted poet by his passionate life and inner discord blighted to a certain extent both for himself and his friends his brilliant and unbounded productivity and marred the delightful enjoyment of his high destiny.

But his German admirer, not misled by this, followed his strange life and poetic activity in all its eccentricity which was all the more conspicuous because it is surely unparalleled in past centuries and we were therefore completely without the means to calculate whither such a career might lead.

Meanwhile the efforts of the German poet did not remain unknown to the Englishman, who gave unequivocal proofs of this in his poems, as well as by many friendly greetings sent through travellers.

There then followed, surprisingly, also through the good offices of a friend, the original of a dedication of the tragedy of *Sardanapalus*, couched in the most flattering terms, with the kind enquiry if it might be printed in front of the work in question.

The German poet who, at his advanced age, knew himself and the value of his achievements, could only contemplate humbly and gratefully the words of that dedication as the expression of an eminent and magnanimous mind, inexhaustible in creating its own objects. Nor did he feel disappointed when, on account of manifold delays, *Sardanapalus* appeared without the preface, but was happy in the possession of a lithographed facsimile as a most precious memento of it.

But the noble Lord did not relinquish his purpose of showing a significant kindness to his German contemporary and fellow-poet; and the tragedy of *Werner* bears upon it a highly-prized memorial.

After this, it will surely be realised that the aged poet, experiencing so much goodwill, rare enough on this earth, shown him quite unexpectedly by so highly celebrated a man, also prepared to express clearly and forcibly with what veneration he was penetrated for his unsurpassed contemporary, and with what sympathetic feelings he regarded him. But the task turned out to be too great, and appeared ever greater the nearer it was approached. For what can one say of a mortal whose merits cannot be exhausted by thought or speech?

When therefore Mr Sterling, a young man pleasing in his person and pure in his morals, made his way directly from Genoa to Weimar in the spring of 1823 and brought with him a small piece of paper with a few words of introduction in the handwriting of the honoured poet; and when, soon after that, it was rumoured that the noble Lord was about to employ his great mind and his manifold powers on deeds dangerous and sublime beyond the sea, hesitation was no longer possible, and the following poem was hastily written.

.     .     .     .     .     .     .     .

It reached Genoa, but found him no longer there; the admirable friend had already set sail and was believed by everyone to be far on his way; but delayed by storms he put into Leghorn, where what had been so cordially sent was just in time to reach him; he replied to it at the very moment of his departure on July 24, 1823 in words fraught with pure and noble feelings, a most precious testimony to a valuable relationship, which will be preserved by the possessor with his most highly cherished documents.

Greatly as such a missive rejoiced and touched us, inevitably arousing the fairest hopes for the future, it has now acquired by the untimely death of the high-hearted writer the greatest and most poignant value, since it intensifies for us alas! in particular the universal grief of the whole civilised and poetical world; for we had been allowed to hope that we should be able to welcome personally after his great purpose had been achieved this splendid spirit, this happily-won friend and this most humane of victors.

But now we are uplifted by the conviction that his nation will suddenly awaken to sobriety from the transports of rage and censorious vituperation in which part of it has indulged against him; and that it will unite in comprehending that all the husks and dross of the individual and his age, through which and out of which even the best men have to work their way, were only temporary, transient and evanescent; whereas the astonishing fame to which he has now and for future ages raised his native land will remain boundless in its glory and incalculable in its consequences. We are certain that this nation, which can boast of so many great names, will place him, transfigured, amongst those, in honouring whom it at all times honours itself.[1]

Unwieldy though this statement is, and sounding too almost as if amplified by a loud-speaker, it is an organic whole, reproducing the course of Goethe's increasing regard for Byron, undeterred even by that 'inner discord' which he still lamented somewhat on the lines of his reviews and the 'Leghorn' verses. The poem was there for all to see; but Goethe was careful to omit any mention of the reviews. He had realized in time where that might lead when sketching out the rough draft:

I have often warmly expressed my sentiments towards him to others, but have not given any public expression to them; only in some numbers of *Kunst und Altertum* a few passages will be found translated, and a few conjectural remarks on the personality of the poet. The index at the end of the fourth volume gives the reference to these.[2]

Medwin had probably asked Soret whether there were anything already printed that he could quote; and, in the very act of supplying the information, a timely recollection of the Florentine murder story stayed Goethe's hand; he would also rather darken counsel if necessary than appear to be at one with the hateful English in their outcry against the immorality of *Don Juan*. He

---

[1] *Werke*, xlii, i, pp. 100 ff. Cf. also Medwin, Appendix, pp. x ff., and for his English translation, pp. 343 ff. The text of the poem is given where I have placed the omission-marks.

[2] Ibid , xlii, i, p 428

therefore wrote discouragingly to Soret (who would pass it on to Medwin) when sending him the completed Memoir:

Of *Manfred, Cain, Don Juan*, I have translated but little, and only expressed my thoughts about them in a few brief words. These things are scattered through the four volumes of *Kunst und Altertum*.[1]

This is purposely misleading; the review of *Cain* is a long, serious and thoughtful article, which in other circumstances Goethe would have been glad enough to acknowledge. But to draw attention to one was to draw attention to all; whereas who would take the trouble to hunt through four volumes (no mention of an index now) for 'a few brief words' scattered here and there? No hint of this aspect of Goethe's interest in Byron was therefore given in the Memoir, which errs altogether, especially at first, on the side of dignified vagueness. Thus the 'unequivocal proofs' in Byron's poetry that he was aware of Goethe's is an oblique reference to *Manfred* and *Faust*; and 'the many friendly greetings brought by travellers' sadly need confirmation. They may have been created by wishful thinking, a day-dream induced by Sterling's visit, or they may have existed in reality; the travellers remain anonymous and unidentifiable. But the story of the dedication to *Sardanapalus* and *Werner* is factually accurate as far as Goethe knew; and his mention of the lithographed facsimile of the *Sardanapalus* inscription is a veiled assurance that he could produce proof of it. It is also clear from what follows that Goethe was feeling, if not remorse, then certainly some compunction that he had failed during Byron's life-time to give adequate expression to his gratitude, veneration and sympathy in a public manner. He was now doing his best to make amends; and he even brought himself to refer with becoming respect and admiration to 'deeds dangerous and sublime beyond the sea'; but it is a curious and noteworthy fact that he went out of his way to avoid any mention of Greece. A warmer and slightly more natural tone prevails from the moment of Sterling's entry on the scene; but undoubtedly the most stirring part of the whole is the eloquent address to the English nation. It has been called 'Goethe's famous impertinence'; but what epithet would have been strong enough if the opening paragraph of the rough draft had been used instead? This was published posthumously and therefore made no great stir; but it is crucial for Goethe's attitude to Byron from now onwards. He achieved a partial solution of the conflict which Byron's revolutionary and rebellious tendencies induced in his mind, by directing his anger against us; as a nation we are therefore partly responsible for the final result.

[1] *Briefe*, xxxviii, p 197 July 14, 1824

## b. DIALOGUE WITH THE DEAD

Thomas Medwin's *Conversations of Lord Byron: noted during a Residence with his Lordship at Pisa, during the years* 1821 *and* 1822 appeared in London at the end of October 1824, and Goethe was reading the book on November 18, when he alluded in his diary to 'the very beautiful poems' it contained. French and German translations were already to hand; but as the French only gave prose renderings of the poems, Goethe must have been using either the original or the German version, which retained the poems in English. He may have chosen his own language in order to master the contents without loss of time, and discover if there were (as he hoped) any allusions to himself of the same kind as those which had filled him with such pride in the inscription to *Sardanapalus* and the letter from Leghorn. The reader should now be in a state of some trepidation supposing him to have a heart in his breast; for, if such allusions there were, would they not almost certainly be cancelled out by that mocking laughter which Ticknor, Stroganov, Bancroft and Finlay had all heard in turn? Happily Medwin, mindful perhaps of Goethe's collaboration, seems to have exercised some editorial discretion; or possibly Shelley's unqualified enthusiasm for Goethe had its effect upon Byron; at all events, although the German poet was to sustain some unpleasant shocks, lack of reverence on Byron's part was not amongst them. But on the whole it was to prove a disturbing experience; and all the more so because of the inept, if not actually fraudulent, medium through whom Goethe was about to hold a dialogue with the dead. Medwin was not the man to evoke the spirit of Byron, nor even the charm of his personality and conversation which Mary Shelley (no indulgent critic) felt stealing over her again on reading Moore's *Life* and finding in it:

... *our* Lord Byron – the fascinating, faulty, philosophical being – daring the world, docile to a private circle, impetuous and indolent, gloomy, and yet more gay than any other. I live with him again in these pages – getting reconciled (as I used in his lifetime) to those waywardnesses which annoyed me when he was away, through the delightful tone of his conversation and manners.[1]

Shelley himself described Byron's serious conversation as 'a sort of enchantment', and left a poetical record of it in *Julian and Maddalo*:

> Our talk grew somewhat serious, as may be
> Talk interrupted with such raillery
> As mocks itself, because it cannot scorn
> The thoughts it would extinguish: – 'twas forlorn,

[1] Smiles, op cit., ii, p. 319. To John Murray, January 19, 1830.

Yet pleasing; such as once, so poets tell
The devils held within the dales of hell,
Concerning God, freewill, and destiny.
Of all that Earth has been, or yet may be;
All that vain men imagine or believe,
Or hope can paint, or suffering can achieve,
We descanted. . . .

This glimpse of what Byron's conversation could be like when Shelley was there to enkindle him is all the more tantalizing because Shelley's name and sometimes even Shelley's presence are mentioned in the *Conversations*, and frequently in connection with Goethe. For it was during this period at Pisa (1821–22) that he was translating parts of *Faust* and expounding them to Byron. How totally different the latter's comments would have sounded, had Shelley and not Medwin recorded them for posterity. Medwin was only capable of producing *his* Byron, in some sort a reflection of himself and also a speaking witness to the fact which Hobhouse extolled and Parry deplored, that the poet always adapted himself to his company, be it never so trifling. The result is not unlike the mangled and garbled messages purporting to come from the dead at spiritualistic *séances*; and there is also something of the same discomfort in listening. For between the covers of a book much discredited and yet faithful after its fashion, Byron can be heard chattering away inconsequently and irresponsibly; and Goethe raising his voice in muffled and measured tones towards the end: Byron, totally unconcerned as to whether or not his voice would carry beyond the grave; Goethe deliberately addressing posterity with all the weight due to the fame of both. A ghost babbling lightly about a living man who was tensely listening for his own name; and then lifting up his voice in mourning for the heedless and unmindful ghost. This is a sufficiently eerie situation to satisfy even the 'Vampyre crew' at Geneva; and the passage of the years has made it more uncanny still; for both poets are now in their graves, so that it has become a dialogue between the dead, in which each is speaking past the other, as they so often did in life.

To imagine Goethe hunting through Medwin's *Conversations* for references to himself is not to go beyond the limits of legitimate deduction; but lip-reading must often be resorted to when listening-in to his comments; for with one important exception he made no direct allusion to the passages personal to himself. This does not mean that thoughts will be attributed to him which he never entertained, nor even that many words will be put into his mouth which he is never known to have uttered. There must, it is true, be some guess-work; and where this is the case, the expressions used are bound to be sadly inadequate; but this is a disadvantage which Goethe shares with Medwin's Byron; and the following account of what happened in his mind when faced with the spirit evoked by Medwin is factually accurate in the main and cannot be very wide of the mark in detail. He was probably already vaguely dissatisfied and distressed by the general tone of Byron's disclosures to Medwin when he came to the following passage:

I was convinced something very unpleasant hung over me last night: I expected to hear that somebody I knew was dead; – so it turns out! Poor Polidori is gone! When he was my physician, he was always talking of Prussic acid, oil of amber, blowing into veins, suffocating by charcoal and compounding poisons; but for a different purpose to what the Pontic Monarch did, for he has prescribed a dose for himself that would have killed fifty Mithridates', – a dose whose effect, Murray says, was so instantaneous that he went off without a spasm or struggle. It seems that disappointment was the cause of this rash act.[1]

Poor Polidori indeed! Ever since the faraway days of *Werther*, Goethe had professed to despise all suicides, although in his heart he well knew the *tedium vitae* to which they succumbed; and he wrote movingly and sympathetically on the subject to his old friend Zelter, whose son had taken his own life. But for the rank and file, and especially for those who were said to have followed in Werther's footsteps, he had nothing but bitter contempt, expressing this so cynically to Benjamin Constant that the Frenchman commented: 'C'est le moins bonhomme que je connaisse.'[2] Lord Bristol, Bishop of Derry, would probably have subscribed to that opinion. Little knowing the measure of his adversary, the English prelate had actually taken Goethe to task in 1797 for having written *Werther*, an immoral and damnable work, inciting to self-destruction. What about the great ones of the earth? Goethe had retorted furiously. They send hundreds and thousands to their death and then sing *Te Deums*. And what about the clergy? he thundered, making a direct assault on the dumbfounded bishop. Their sermons on hell-fire have landed many a poor wretch in the mad-house; and their orthodox doctrines, a denial of all sense and reason, have unsettled the minds of many more who, lost in a labyrinth of doubt, can envisage no issue but death. And *he* was to be blamed forsooth for ridding the world of a dozen blockheads and ne'er-do-wells whose limited minds had misunderstood his meaning, and who in any case were better dead?[3]

---

[1] Medwin, p. 119.
[2] *Gespräche*, i, p. 331. February 16, 1804.
[3] Cf. Eckermann, pp. 741 f. March 17, 1830.

Probably, thought Goethe now, this young man called Polidori was just such another; and what 'disappointment' could possibly be urged in defence of this obviously pathological specimen?

He had entertained too sanguine hopes of literary fame, owing to the success of his *Vampyre*, which, in consequence of its being attributed to me, was got up as a melo-drame at Paris. The foundation of the story *was* mine; but I was forced to disown the publication, lest the world should suppose that I had vanity enough, or was egotist enough, to write in that ridiculous manner about myself. . . . Perhaps Polidori had strictly no right to appropriate my story to himself; but it was hardly worth it. . . .[1]

'Hardly worth it' – 'the strangest production of this strange man . . . his best work'; and it had been written, if not invented, by someone else. It must have been Byron's spirit behind it which had impressed Goethe so much; but even then, would he have called it his best work if it had not been for the subject? There was an unholy fascination about that: the night-side of nature; the night-side of life. Goethe had always felt the pull towards such themes, and had treated vampirism himself in *The Bride of Corinth*; a fearful superstition, but . . .

Who can help being superstitious? Scott believes in second-sight. Rousseau tried whether he was to be d—d or not, by aiming at a tree with a stone; I forget whether he hit or missed. Goethe trusted to the chance of a knife's striking the water, to determine whether he was to prosper in some undertaking. The Italians . . .[2]

How strange that Byron should bring that up; he must have got it from *Dichtung und Wahrheit*; but the incident itself took place years and years ago. Goethe was wandering along the Lahn wishing that he could paint the river sparkling in the sun-shine through the willow-trees along its banks. What a tempting subject; but would he ever make a painter? And then came that urgent, irresistible command, seemingly from the depths of his being, to put it to the test: to throw the pocket-knife he was holding in his left hand straight into the river. If he saw it strike the water, his wish would be granted; if not . . . But the oracle was characteristically ambiguous; for though he saw the water spouting up like a fountain, the willow-trees hindered him from seeing the knife plunge in.[3] So Byron had read *Dichtung und Wahrheit*? But no, that could not be; for here he was confessing to almost total ignorance of German, although he retained childish memories of Gessner's *Abel* which he had read at school. Gessner's

---

[1] Medwin, pp. 119 ff.
[2] Ibid., p. 122.
[3] *Dichtung und Wahrheit*, Part III, Book 13, second paragraph.

*Abel* and Byron's *Cain*! Could there be a greater contrast? The one communicating idyllic charm, the other alight with burning spiritual vision . . . It was sad to think that Byron had never seen Goethe's review of *Cain*, and had never known how deeply his German fellow-poet venerated him for that work and how well he understood it, even advancing in its favour the selfsame arguments Byron was now using to Medwin: 'I always thought *Cain* a fine subject, and when I took it up I determined to treat it strictly after the Mosaic account'.[1] Word for word almost what Goethe had written. 'He holds to the letter of the Biblical tradition';[2] and here was Byron repeating it: '*Au reste*, I have adhered closely to the Old Testament, and I defy anyone to question my moral.' Yes, and those critics who were crying out against blasphemy would do well to see where the real blasphemy lay: in the old dogmatic theology with its sacrilegious notions about God. But the English as a race were incapable of that, as witness the attitude of this person called Hobhouse who

. . . has denounced *Cain* as irreligious, and has penned me a most furious epistle, urging me not to publish it, as I value my reputation or his friendship.

A fine friend to have; but at least Sir Walter Scott thought differently, and so did a certain Shelley . . . now where had Goethe heard that name before? In a rather curious context too . . . Wait, it was coming back . . . He was that silly and sensitive young man who had figured in the *Letter from Geneva* prefixed to *The Vampyre*. Goethe had thought at the time that he was an odd friend for Byron to have. However he certainly did justice to *Cain*; but how they all harped on Milton as a kind of touch-stone, including Byron himself:

Johnson, who would have been glad of an opportunity of throwing another stone at Milton, redeems him from any censure for putting impiety and even blasphemy into the mouth of his infernal spirits. By what rule, then, am I to have all the blame? What would the Methodists at home say to Goethe's *Faust*?

And why should Goethe care what they said, or any of the hypocritical English, from the Bishop of Derry downwards?

His devil not only talks very familiarly *of* Heaven, but very familiarly *in* Heaven. What would they think of the colloquies of Mephistopheles and his pupil, or the more daring language of the prologue, which no one will ever venture to translate?

Shelley was even then putting that scene into memorable

[1] Cf. Medwin, pp. 150 ff., for Byron's defence of *Cain*.
[2] See below, p. 183.

English verse, partly for Byron's benefit, who evidently believed that it would never be published; and his declaration recurred to Goethe's mind when Lord Leveson-Gower's translation of *Faust* appeared in 1829 without the Prologue:

It is not the difficulty of the translation which will have hindered the noble Lord, but religious, or rather High Church scruples; perhaps not his own, but those of his aristocratic friends. Nowhere are there so many hypocrites and so much sanctimoniousness as in England.[1]

Luckily, Germany was very different, as Byron seemed to realize:

And yet this play is not only tolerated and admired, as every thing he wrote must be, but acted in Germany. And are the Germans a less moral people than we are? I doubt it much.

And well may he doubt it, thought Goethe; an honest, sober and solid people, not to be compared for a moment with the race of hypocritical humbugs maligning Byron in England. And although Byron was wrong in thinking that *Faust* had been performed in Germany, that was not on account of its subject, since the subject . . .

*Faust* itself is not so fine a subject as *Cain*. It is a grand mystery. The mark that was put upon Cain is a sublime and shadowy act: Goethe would have made more of it than I have done.

Goethe's pulses stirred. That the poet who had written that sublime drama should pay him such a high compliment was wonderful enough; but even more precious were the proofs he was giving of his vital interest in Goethe and his deep knowledge of *Faust*; no wonder that this was so apparent in *Manfred*, as Goethe had realized at once. Of course the English would call it plagiarism; but . . .

The Germans, and I believe Goethe himself, consider that I have taken great liberties with *Faust*. All I know of that drama is from a sorry French translation, from an occasional reading or two into English of parts of it by Monk Lewis when at Diodati, and from the Hartz mountain-scene, that Shelley versified the other day. Nothing I envy him so much as to be able to read that astonishing production in the original.[2]

This was a body-blow. 'A sorry French translation?' That could only mean the long prose quotations that irritating woman Madame de Staël had given in *De l'Allemagne*; and Byron was right; it was indeed a sorry affair. As Goethe had grumbled to

[1] *Gespräche*, ii, p. 590. May 1829, F. Förster.
[2] Medwin, p. 170.

Riemer at the time, she was incapable of giving accurate impressions of his works, because she did not understand them'[1] 'An occasional reading or two into English?' Was that really all Byron had known about *Faust* when he was writing *Manfred*? But then Goethe must have been mistaken about the relationship between the two poems; he had thought for instance that the conjuring up of Astarte before Manfred in the Hall of Arimanes was taken from the apparition of Gretchen to Faust on the Brocken; and it now appeared that Byron had only become acquainted with the 'Hartz mountain-scene' in 1821 or 1822 owing to a versification by Shelley . . . Hm . . . Shelley, who had nearly fainted at the gruesome vision of a woman with eyes in her breasts; he might be suitable enough as an interpreter when it came to the spectre of Gretchen with a blood-red gash round her throat. Better certainly than Madame de Staël. But how unfortunate it was that Byron should have heard about Goethe's assumption made in all good faith that Byron had 'taken great liberties with *Faust*'. Not that he had said that, nor even thought it; and as to originality . . .

As to originality, Goethe has too much sense to pretend that he is not under obligations to authors, ancient and modern; – who is not? You tell me the plot is almost entirely Calderon's. The fête, the scholar, the argument about the *Logos*, the selling himself to the fiend, and afterwards denying his power; his disguise of the plumed cavalier; the enchanted mirror, – are all from Cyprian. That *Magico Prodigioso* must be worth reading, and nobody seems to know any thing about it but you and Shelley. Then the vision is not unlike that of Marlowe's in his *Faustus*. The bed-scene is from *Cymbeline*; the song or serenade, a translation of Ophelia's in *Hamlet*; and, more than all, the prologue is from *Job*, which is the first drama in the world, and perhaps the oldest poem. I had an idea of writing a *Job*, but I found it too sublime. There is no poetry to be compared with it.[2]

*          *          *

'I knew next to nothing of Goethe's *Faust* when I was writing *Manfred*', declared Byron, speaking through Medwin. 'Can he say the same of Calderon's *Magico Prodigioso*, Marlowe's *Faustus*, Shakespeare's *Cymbeline* and *Hamlet*, and above all of the Book of Job?'

'I have for the most part not even read all those fine things Lord Byron mentions', replied Goethe heatedly through the mouth of Eckermann; 'still less were they in my thoughts when I was writing *Faust*. But Lord Byron is only great when he is writing poetry; as soon as he reflects, he is a child'.[3]

[1] *Gespräche*, i, pp. 722 f. May 19, 1814.          [2] Medwin, pp. 170 f.
[3] Eckermann, p. 139. Dated [? inaccurately] January 18, 1825. Two separate conversations were probably fused under this date; for the 'plagiarism' passage is given by Chancellor Müller on December 17, 1824.

I

At the time of speaking (1824) Goethe had undoubtedly read 'all those fine things', with the possible exception of *Cymbeline*; but Eckermann need not be taken too literally as far as the tense is concerned; and Goethe did not know Marlowe's *Faustus* in 1808 when *Faust I* appeared. But he had been well acquainted with Calderon ever since 1802; and it seems unlikely that *El Magico Prodigioso* escaped his notice at the time when he was completing *Faust I*. But his irritation is more important at the moment than his accuracy; although we should never have known how deeply he resented Byron's dismemberment of his *Faust* had it not been for the temerity of Eckermann. The temerity, and perhaps something else? Johann Peter Eckermann (1792–1854) had come into Goethe's life in June 1823 and had been immediately made aware of the spell cast by Byron over the German poet. He had been urged and later almost commanded to learn English in order to be able to read in the original the works of a poet 'whose personality is of an eminence such as has never been before and will hardly come again'.[1] Perhaps this was not very good news for a would-be poet to hear, especially as Goethe serenely disregarded or (worse still) discouraged Eckermann's own poetical aspirations. Whatever the reason, there was certainly some malice behind his deliberate introduction of Byron's dissection of *Faust*; and this led Goethe in a moment of pardonable vexation to claim even greater ignorance of authors who might have been plundered for *Faust* than Byron had done when defending the originality of *Manfred*. Actually long lists of 'sources' and influences have been made out in both cases; for like all writers they were under many obligations to other authors as Byron realized; but Goethe's petulant use of the word 'child' (confirmed by Müller who was also present) shows that he had not 'too much sense' to take the slur on his originality calmly. So that his thoughts when he first came across that passage in Medwin's *Conversations* will have been at least as vehement as those expressed to Müller and Eckermann somewhat later:

Byron only judges excellently and clearly about what he perceives, reflection is not his *forte*; his judgments and combinations are then often those of a child.

He is far too patient about the reproaches of plagiarism, only undertaking skirmishes in his defence, instead of bringing up the great guns to annihilate his opponents.

Does not everything achieved by the past and the present belong to the poet by right? Why should he fear to take flowers where he finds them? Only by assimilating the treasures of others does one attain to greatness. Have I not appropriated *Job* and a song from Shakespeare

[1] Eckermann, p. 55. October 19, 1823.

for my Mephistopheles? Byron was for the most part only unconsciously a great poet.[1]

That is why he does not know how to defend himself against similar absurd attacks made against him by his own nation. He should have expressed himself more forcibly against them.

'What is there is mine', he should have said, 'and it is perfectly indifferent whether I have taken it from life or from a book; the only thing that matters is whether I have used it right!' Walter Scott used a scene of my *Egmont*, and he had the right to do it, and as he did it sensibly, he is to be praised. In the same way he imitated the character of my Mignon in one of his novels; but whether that was done as wisely is another matter. . . . In the same way my Mephistopheles sings a song from Shakespeare, and why not? Why should I trouble to invent one of my own, when Shakespeare's was so apt and said exactly what I wanted? If therefore the exposition of my *Faust* has some similarity with *Job*, that's quite right too, and I should be praised rather than blamed for it.[2]

But was Byron blaming him? Had he not simply said that Goethe, like everyone else, was under obligations to other authors? As far as the *casus belli* went, both poets, the 'childish' and the wise one, were in complete theoretical agreement on the subject of plagiarism in the abstract, Byron expressing his opinion pithily as a truism, Goethe proclaiming it with angry eloquence. Nor did either blame the other for taking his subjects where he found them; Goethe on the contrary commended Byron highly for borrowing from him; but both believed that blame was implied when it came to the mention of *their* sources. Byron was restive on the score of the liberties he was supposed to have taken with *Faust*; and Goethe was incensed by the list of obligations he was presumed to be under, amongst which *El Magico Prodigioso* loomed so misleadingly large. Both he and Calderon, there was no denying that, were under deep debts to magical tradition; but that was a very different thing from asserting that he had taken his plot almost entirely from *El Magico Prodigioso*, on the strength of a handful of parallels, some of them far-fetched and others non-existent. And yet, and yet . . . did something tell Goethe that 'very interesting lectures' might be held on the similarities and dissimilarities between the German and Spanish dramas? But that was nonsense, of course; the whole passage was nonsense; Byron's judgments and combinations were those of a child.

On second thoughts, however, it was Medwin and not Byron who had drawn those preposterous parallels between *El Magico Prodigioso* and *Faust*; for Byron did not know the Spaniard's play, though Shelley did. Shelley . . . how ubiquitous that man was;

---

[1] *Gespräche*, ii, pp. 369 f. Chancellor Müller.
[2] Eckermann, pp. 139 f.

probably at the bottom of this if all were known. And if Goethe thought that, he was right in a way. For Shelley was reading and translating scenes from both dramas at the time and talking animatedly about the resemblance between them:

> Have you read Calderon's *Magico Prodigioso*? I find a striking similarity between *Faust* and this drama and if I were to acknowledge Coleridge's distinction, should say Goëthe was the *greatest* philosopher, and Calderon the *greatest* poet. *Cyprian* evidently furnished the *germ* of *Faust*, as *Faust* may furnish the germ of other poems; although it is as different from it in structure and in plan as the acorn from the oak.[1]

Let someone like Medwin hear something like this, and he will follow it up in his own way; for it certainly looks as if the *tu quoque* argument of Byron's which annoyed Goethe so much derived ultimately from Shelley whose mind swayed the whole circle on all questions of poetry not excluding Byron:

> . . . on calling on him one morning, he produced *The Deformed Transformed*. Handing it to Shelley, as he was in the habit of doing his daily compositions, he said:
> 'Shelley, I have been writing a *Faustish* kind of drama: tell me what you think of it.'
> After reading it attentively, Shelley returned it.
> 'Well,' said Lord Byron, 'how do you like it?'
> 'Least,' replied he, 'of any thing I ever saw of yours. It is a bad imitation of *Faust*; and besides, there are two entire lines of Southey's in it.'
> Lord Byron changed colour immediately, and asked hastily what lines? Shelley repeated,
> > ' "And water shall see thee,
> > And fear thee, and flee thee,"
> They are in *The Curse of Kehama*.'
> His Lordship, without making a single observation, instantly threw the poem into the fire.[2]

Either Shelley or Medwin was at fault here, for there are no such lines in *The Curse of Kehama*;[3] but Byron could not know that, and the mere supposition was enough to discompose him altogether. There was war to the knife between him and Southey; and he must have remembered with dismay his conclusion to the first canto of *Don Juan*, where he had deliberately quoted from the despised Poet Laureate adding the gibe:

> The four first rhymes are Southey's every line:
> For God's sake, reader! take them not for mine.[4]

[1] *The Letters of Percy Bysshe Shelley*, ed. Ingpen, 2 vols., London, 1915; ii, p. 954. Shelley to J. Gisborne from Pisa, April 10, 1822.
[2] Medwin, pp. 183 f.        [3] Cf. *Poetry*, v, p. 469.        [4] *Poetry*, vi, p. 80.

And now the joke had rebounded; no wonder that he flung the manuscript straight into the fire. It was enough to put him out of love with *The Deformed Transformed* for ever. It was also more than enough to put Goethe out of love with Shelley and to turn him into a potential champion of the ill-treated drama. For he would be able to read it and he was going to read it. Byron had re-written it from memory (unless he had another copy) and Medwin had seen it announced for publication two years later. A bad imitation of *Faust* indeed? And who was Shelley to be so sure? Let Goethe judge for himself. The judgment was to be decidedly in Byron's favour:

Lord Byron's transformed devil is a continuation of my Mephisto-pheles, and quite right too! Had he attempted to evade him from some whim to be original, he would certainly have made a worse one.[1]

So much for Shelley; and it heartened Goethe to think that if *Faust* had played a far more insignificant part in *Manfred* than he had assumed to be the case, Byron had nevertheless written a '*Faustish* kind of drama', and proclaimed it as such. What a disaster that insufferable Shelley had nearly brought about with his nonsensical criticism; no judge of poetry obviously; for he had actually taken that glorious ode, *The Burial of Sir John Moore*, to be a rough sketch of Campbell's. If that was his idea of a rough sketch, Goethe was sorry for him:

The ode on the death of General Moore is one of Byron's most beautiful poems. Shelley must have been a poor creature not to have felt that; altogether Byron seems to have been much too kind to him. . . . I shall feast on this splendid poem of Byron's for a whole month, and ask for no other fare.[2]

He could not live alone, and that is why, in spite of all his eccen-tricities, he was very indulgent towards his associates. One evening he read the magnificent poem on the death of General Moore out loud, and his noble friends did not know what to make of it. That did not affect him in the least; he put it back in his pocket. As a poet he really behaved like a saint. Anyone else would have sent them to the devil![3]

How Byron could put up with Shelley amazed Goethe; and as he skimmed the pages, always on the alert for his own name, his sense of outrage at what Medwin called the 'sort of suicide' so nearly consummated by burning *The Deformed Transformed* con-tinued until it was overlaid by an uneasy premonition that some-thing worse was on the way. For Byron was commenting satirically

[1] Eckermann, p. 140. Dated January 18, 1825.

[2] Cf. Medwin, pp. 133 ff., and *Gespräche*, ii, p. 367. Chancellor Müller, November 20, 1824. As will be remembered, the poem was really by Wolfe.

[3] Eckerman, p. 150. February 24, 1825.

on a certain scandalous novel purporting to give the history of his life and adventures; and this could only be *Glenarvon*, by now a very sore subject with Goethe, whose nerves tautened at the phrase: 'and the Germans think it is not a caricature', whilst his eyes raced over the page:

One of my foreign biographers has tacked name, place, and circumstance to the Florence fable, and gives me a principal instead of a subordinate part in a certain tragical history therein narrated. Unfortunately for my biographers, I was never at Florence for more than a few days in my life. Hence, however, it has been alleged that murder is my instinct; and to make innocence my prey, part of my nature.[1]

He wiped his forehead. The 'foreign biographer' was someone else; for Goethe had 'tacked' no name to that thrice-accursèd tale. Yet, if Byron had seen his review of *Manfred*, he must be bracketing Goethe together with those others who took him for a murderer and worse. But that was old history now; it was long enough since Goethe had known better. Why look back? Because Byron was forcing him to do so, imposing this retrospect upon him, destroying his peace of mind. It all hinged now on whether or not Byron had ever known that Goethe had taken *Glenarvon* seriously:

You tell me that Baron Lutzerode had been asking you for some authentic particulars of my life, to affix to his translation of *Cain*, and thus contradict the German stories circulated about me, and which, I understand, even Goethe believes.[2]

'Even Goethe'; so Byron knew; knew when he had written the letter from Leghorn; but could he have known when he was writing the dedication to *Sardanapalus*? Impossible to credit that ... and yet it seemed to be true:

I mean to dedicate *Werner* to Goethe. I look upon him as the greatest genius that the age has produced. I desired Murray to inscribe his name to a former work; but he pretends my letter containing the order came too late. – It would have been more worthy of him than this.[3]

'The expression of a magnanimous mind': Goethe had used that phrase about the dedication in his Memoir for this very book; and he rejoiced now that he had done so; it was even more appropriate than he had realized. Byron was magnanimity itself. Anyone else would have sent Goethe to the devil. And how *could* he have credited that tale, when he had always felt as if there were a mysterious affinity between himself and Byron? It was strangely poignant now to find on the printed page before him that Byron had felt the same:

[1] Medwin, pp. 273 f.        [2] Ibid., p. 277.        [3] Ibid., p. 329.

I have a great curiosity about every thing relating to Goethe, and please myself by thinking there is some analogy between our characters and writings. . . .[1]

Between their writings . . . perhaps analogy *was* the right word for the poetical link connecting *Manfred* with *Faust*? Between their characters? Yes; Goethe could tell a tale about that: the dark side, the wild side, the pull towards death; he shared all that with Byron; but it was in subjection now, whereas Byron had surrendered. And Goethe? 'Forward over graves'; that was his motto, and that his reward. No wonder that sometimes defeat seemed greater than victory and less bitter in the mouth; as it did now, at this moment, with Byron's voice in his ears:

So much interest do I take in him, that I offered to give £100 to any person who would translate his *Memoirs*, for my own reading. Shelley has sometimes explained part of them to me. He seems to be very superstitious, and is a believer in astrology, – or rather was, for he was very young when he wrote the first part of his Life. I would give the world to read *Faust* in the original. I have been urging Shelley to translate it. . . .

Shelley again! intervening, expounding and misleading! Far from being very young when he wrote the first part of *Dichtung und Wahrheit*, Goethe was sixty if a day; and surely even Shelley might have realized that the horoscope of his nativity given in the opening paragraph was meant to be taken symbolically and not literally? Goethe would have given the world too, if Byron could have read *Faust* in the original; any translation by Shelley . . .

. . . but he said that the translator of *Wallenstein* was the only person living who could venture to attempt it; – that he had written to Coleridge, but in vain. For a man to translate it, he must think as *he* does.

So Shelley at least knew his limitations, thought Goethe grimly, who was never to know how magnificently that despised young man was translating *The Prologue in Heaven*. Polidori and Medwin between them had not taught Goethe to love Shelley; but what had Medwin taught him to think about Byron? He hardly knew himself on that first occasion when he was racing through the text with only one end in view; and having finished he must have felt that he had at times been suffering the proverbial fate of eavesdroppers. Polidori and *The Vampyre*; *Manfred*, *Faust* and *El Magico Prodigioso*; *Glenarvon* and the murder-myth: he would far rather have heard nothing at all about any of them; and he must try to put them out of his mind. They mostly repre-

[1] Cf. Medwin, pp. 329 ff.

sented mistakes of his own, misunderstandings, misstatements, misjudgments; and it was too late now to do anything about them ... Too late ... He would never meet Byron in this world; never be able to tell him all he had felt on receiving the dedication to *Sardanapalus* and the letter from Leghorn; nor what he had been feeling now as he listened to Byron's tributes to his genius and enthusiastic praise of his masterpiece. Well, he had done what he could belatedly by his Memoir for this book:

The high admiration in which Lord Byron was held in Germany may be appreciated by the following communication, and tribute to his memory, which I have just received from the illustrious and venerable Goethe, who, at the advanced age of seventy-five, retains all the warmth of his feelings, and fire of his immortal genius.[1]

That day Goethe probably read no more; although he may have glanced through the Appendix which contained his own Memoir in German, and winced at the printing mistakes. It also seems likely that he went on next day to the memorable *Account of Lord Byron's Residence in Greece*, reprinted from *The Westminster Review*; for he said to Chancellor Müller on November 20 that, had Byron lived, he would have become for Greece another Lycurgus or Solon.[2] This is high praise and a hopeful sign; but it is the only reference he ever made to a monograph which told a tale of uncomplaining fortitude, statesmanship, wisdom and greatness, entirely cancelling out the triviality and general jejuneness of most of the conversations as recorded by Medwin. But Goethe was still antagonistic to the cause for which Byron gave his life. On receipt from the Duke of Weimar of an account of the last days at Missolonghi, he confessed that he was deeply moved at the thought of so admirable a being dying so young, and went on to express horror at the fog-infested swamps and the fearful conditions generally, but he uttered no word that could be construed as approbation for the venture as such,[3] and he continued to ignore everything in the Appendix to the *Conversations* which had reference to Greece. That being so, there was little enough in the body of the book, barring some poems and the few passages expressive of Byron's veneration for himself, to counteract the sad sense of disenchantment inevitably produced when once the bewildering sensations aroused by the first reading yielded to a more critical approach:

I am reading them now for the second time. I would not have missed them, but they leave a painful impression. What a lot of gossip, often about some wretched trifle; what touchiness about every fatuous judg-

---

[1] Medwin, p. 343          [2] *Gespräche*, ii, p 367
[3] Cf *Briefe*, xxxix, pp 22 f  To Karl August from Weimar, November 25, 1824

ment of the journalists; and what a disorderly life with dogs and monkeys and peacocks; everything without order or connection.[1]

Medwinitis had set in, a peculiarly insidious disease, from which Goethe was not the only sufferer; but he was certainly unique in catching it on the top of an attack of Graecophobia brought on by Byron's death. It was a serious complication, but never really critical; for his deep-seated ineradicable passion was stronger than the germs of disillusionment and distaste:

My relationship with Lord Byron was certainly a most delicate and tender one, based on an early felt and carefully tended admiration for his great poetical gifts. In the course of the years it was also happily increased by reciprocal goodwill, which encouraged the fairest hopes, cut off by a cruel fate.

My grief is too deep to permit expression for any external reason; only if the Muse herself should force me, I would have to obey her.[2]

It was decidedly not the Muse who had forced him to produce that stilted and muted Memoir; on the contrary, it was Medwin; and it was Medwin too who, by printing the passage about the 'sources' of *Faust*, had provoked the outburst about Byron's childishness. That epithet has clung and has been repeated *ad nauseam* ever since Matthew Arnold trumpeted it abroad as the last word of wisdom on the subject of Byron, maintaining that it represented Goethe's considered opinion and final judgment. It was neither; and it should no more be taken seriously than Byron's equally petulant and equally pardonable exclamation: 'The devil may take both Faustuses, German and English – I have taken neither.'

## c. MEDWINITIS

The irritation produced in Goethe by Medwin's *Conversations of Lord Byron* had one entirely unforeseen and unforeseeable result: a literary pearl in the shape of Eckermann's *Conversations with Goethe*. Byron's recklessness in exposing himself to Medwin was a word to the wise, a warning reminder of the host of diarists and letter-writers in Goethe's vicinity who would certainly make literary capital of their reminiscences after his death. Their nature being an unknown quantity, this seemed to call for an authoritative version of his conversations, presented as Medwin had presented Byron's, but recorded with greater discretion and in an entirely different tone. The conversations themselves would be of a weightier calibre, significant and serious, accurately reported (for he intended to check them personally) and truly revealing his life

---

[1] *Gespräche*, ii, p 369. December 17, 1824. Chancellor Müller.
[2] *Briefe*, xxxix, p. 49. To Josef Max from Weimar, December 18, 1824.

and thoughts. It was in this fashion that Eckermann's fascinating book came into being; and even though it was continued, expanded and completed without the poet's guiding hand, it remained true to his intentions. Though Goethe was no Socrates, and quite as surely Eckermann was no Plato, the creative poetical gift which the Master rather cruelly discounted in his disciple disengaged the Platonic personality of the poet in his old age: serene, benign, wise and lovable, absolutely real, yet with the added charm of a work of art. But it is neither art nor nature, this last gift of Goethe's to posterity, in which he himself consciously collaborated by sitting for his portrait in words; it is something between the two, and reads at times as if James Boswell were trying his hand at writing a *Symposium*. This is not to impugn Eckermann's essential trustworthiness, nor even on the whole his verbal accuracy (literal accuracy is a different matter); it is rather to illuminate the manner in which these conversation-pieces were composed; and the painter Johann Wilhelm Zahn (1800–71) who was present during a dinner-party in 1827 when Eckermann was taking notes gives a side-light on his method. Goethe was supported by Ottilie and her younger sister Ulrike (another household pet), by Chancellor Müller his financial adviser and trustee, by Riemer his literary coadjutor and executor, by Meyer his art-expert, by Vogel his physician and by Eckermann his Boswell:

Those living lexicons sat round him, and he appealed to them as occasion arose, for he did not choose to burden himself with book-learning. Riemer represented literature, Meyer the history of art, and Eckermann unwound himself like an endless coil of quotations on any and every subject. In between he listened to the words of the Master with bated breath, and appeared to be memorising them on the spot as if they were oracular decrees. Meyer on the other hand . . . gazed upon the face of the friend of his youth with a touching expression which betrayed as much tenderness as admiration.[1]

Nothing could be more unlike this atmosphere saturated with love and worship than the free and easy aura surrounding Byron's confidences, reflections and mystifications poured out pell-mell to Medwin and adding yet another link to the chain of fatality forged by his too easy intimacy and lack of reserve. Yet when George Finlay met him in Greece, he noticed that the poet was reticent to a fault on serious subjects and afraid of being carried away by his feelings:

Lord Byron uttered this [tribute to the Turks] in an unemphatical, and rather affectedly monotonous tone. I afterwards observed, that he

[1] *Gespräche*, ii, pp. 506 f. September 7, 1827.

adopted this tone not unfrequently, whenever he uttered any thing which diverged from the commonest style of conversation. Whenever he commenced a sentence which showed that the subject had engaged his mind, and that his thoughts were sublime, he checked himself, and finished a broken sentence, either with an indifferent smile, or with this annoying tone. I thought he had adopted it to conceal his feelings, when he feared to trust his tongue with the sentiments of his heart. Often, it was evident, he did it to avoid betraying the author, or rather the poet.[1]

This recalls Tom Moore's engaging anecdote of his visit to Venice:

Happening to remark, in looking up at the clouds, which were still bright in the west, that 'what had struck me in Italian sunsets was that peculiarly rosy hue – ' I had hardly pronounced the word 'rosy', when Lord Byron, clapping his hand on my mouth, said, with a laugh, 'Come, d—n it, Tom, *don't* be poetical.[2]

Memories of Goethe discoursing sublimely about the sunset to Sulpiz Boisserée arise. They help to explain not only the striking inferiority of Medwin's records to those of Eckermann, but the general difference in level between all the conversations reported of Byron and those repeated by Goethe's intimates and awe-stricken visitors. Granted that Medwin was a feeble enough medium, that Leigh Hunt was jaundiced and venomous, that Lady Blessington was *très snob, presque cad* and that Trelawny was eaten up with envy; even so the tone of the subjects which Byron chose to discuss, or allowed his interlocutors to introduce with the single exception of Shelley, bear out Finlay's observation. Byron might, and very often did, talk for effect; but the effect he aimed at was that of a man of fashion; and moreover after his exile, he seems on the whole to have ceased from imposing his personality unduly, and to have presented by preference his affable, concili-atory, informal and gossiping side to visitors. Whereas Goethe never scrupled to bring the whole force of his terrific personality to bear when it suited him, whether it suited others or not.

Eckermann presents him in one light, and not only Eckermann; but from the beginning, and notably in his middle years, he could and did horrify others, quite apart from the complaints of egoism, stiffness, formality and cold-heartedness so constantly raised. He was always dominant and often formidable. He could be as gentle as a summer breeze, or boisterous and rough and fearfully rude; stupefyingly silent or irresistibly eloquent; oppressively solemn and too much on his dignity, or inordinately garrulous and painfully hilarious. A divine glory shone from him at times, transporting the onlookers; but it was nervous work when he came to a social

<hr>

[1] Elze, op. cit., p. 480.
[2] Moore, p. 412.

gathering in a bad temper and began to stride up and down the room. As long as he was silent, no one else dared to utter; and woe betide those who laughed out of turn; Goethe was quite capable of reducing them to tears. Yet when he unwittingly brought Grillparzer almost to this pass by his coldness and stiffness, he was angelically warm-hearted and kind; although, when the spirit so moved him, he would ignore or snub, or bait such old familiar friends as Wieland and Müller almost past endurance.

Long and loud were the laments and complaints which Goethe's less engaging behaviour produced, but they only went to swell the chorus raised in honour of his greatness, which neither hostile nor indifferent observers ever sought to belittle. Whereas the contrary desire was active in Byron's case from the days of his exile onwards if not before. He himself was one of the prime movers in this; for he had no mind to play the lion after his disaster, and rarely (if ever) uttered the lion's roar. The 'puissant and splendid personality' displayed in his works was so well cloaked by frivolity and persiflage in daily life that it escaped the notice of the Medwins, the Hunts, the Lady Blessingtons and the Trelawnys of this world:

It would require a person of his own wonderful capacity to draw his character, and even he could not perform this task otherwise than by continuing the history of what passed in his mind; for his character was as versatile as his genius. . . . All that can be hoped is, that, after a number of the ephemeral sketches of Lord Byron have been published, and ample information concerning him obtained, some master hand will undertake the task of drawing his portrait. If anything like justice be done to Lord Byron, his character will then appear far more extra-ordinary than any his imagination has produced, and not less wonderful than those sublime and inimitable sketches created and painted by the fanciful pen of Shakespeare.[1]

Failing that master hand, one can only lament that it was part of Byron's destiny to fall among thieves, just as it was Goethe's good fortune to escape them. But Byron's ill-luck with memoir-writers went even further. 'Don't attempt to defend me', he implored Tom Moore during the separation-scandal; 'who can bear refutation?'[2] He was fated to bear it in bulk after his death in Teresa Guiccioli's compilation *Lord Byron jugé par les témoins de sa vie*. This painstaking and praiseworthy effort to show her hero in his 'true light', made by a writer who knew Byron at least as intimately as Eckermann knew Goethe and worshipped him quite as devoutly, somehow never cut any ice as regards his virtues; but it was all-too effective in rousing the ire (not to say the bile) of

[1] Elze, op. cit., p. 488. Colonel Leicester Stanhope.
[2] *Letters and Journals*, iii, p. 267 February 29, 1816.

Mrs Beecher Stowe and producing the pandemonium she let loose on the subject of Byron and Augusta. Something similar had happened once before with Goethe and Bettina von Arnim, with Byron and Lady Caroline Lamb. The two poets had much in common as far as women were concerned; and there was also a striking temperamental resemblance between Bettina and Caro. Both were fantastic, poetical, spoilt and romantic creatures with an itch for exhibitionism and a streak of nymphomania, and both flung themselves at their chosen idols with the same recklessness. The idols behaved slightly differently; for not only was Goethe considerably older than Bettina, and she was never his mistress, but he was also in love at the time with Marianne von Willemer; whereas Byron and Caroline were very young and it looked at first like a *grande passion* on both sides. But both he and Goethe began by encouraging the adoration and responding to the affection lavished upon them and then cooled off when the pace became too hot and the woman in question a nuisance; and both finally broke with their extravagant poursuivants in a decidedly callous manner. The result in print was an ecstatic and enchanting mingling of poetry and truth in *Goethes Briefwechsel mit einem Kind*, positively deifying Goethe, and the hysterical chanting of a comminatory hymn 'bemonstering' Byron in *Glenarvon*. In view of all this combined with the admirable reticence of Charlotte von Stein, that deeply disillusioned Egeria, one can only conclude that it was just Byron's luck to light upon Medwin, and like Goethe's good management to single out Eckermann.

On the other hand he was decidedly unfortunate in his written sources for Byron's life. At the dawn of his interest he had been bamboozled by *Glenarvon*, and now he found himself faced by the speaking likeness presented by Medwin:

Great talents are rare [he almost moaned], and it is seldom that they recognise themselves; but powerful, unconscious action and thought have highly pleasing as well as unpleasant consequences, and in such conflicts a great life passes away. Medwin's *Conversations* give remarkable and sad examples of this.[1]

'Great talents ... a great life'; at least Medwin had not dwarfed Byron's image in Goethe's mind; but there were 'unpleasant consequences' to be faced, and Goethe faced them in a long conversation with Eckermann, dated by the latter February 24, 1825. He had an eager and sympathetic listener, especially on the subject of Byron's failings, and there were a great many of them to consider; but the conversation opened with high praise

---

[1] *Werke*, xli, 2, p. 154. Probably the beginning of a review for *Über Kunst und Altertum*.

for *Marino Faliero*, which Goethe had been reading the evening before, happily still in ignorance of the dedicatory epistle to himself biding its time in Albemarle St. He began by saying that if he were still the director of the Weimar theatre he would produce this play, although it would have to be shortened. Eckermann reminded him that Byron was not in favour of writing for the stage; and Goethe rather unwillingly conceded that he might not be as capable as a Houwald of hitting the popular taste. But what a dramatist he was! Unequalled in his powers of invention, unrivalled in the way he untied a dramatic knot, always beyond expectation and better than one could possibly foresee. Eckermann deftly instanced the prowess of Shakespeare in this field with special reference to Falstaff, and gently insinuated that to bracket them together was almost too high a compliment to Byron. It was probably Eckermann who thereupon introduced the topic of Byron's adherence to the three unities, that exploded dramatic bugbear. Goethe could not but laugh at Byron's tame submission in this respect, he who in his person had never subjected himself to any discipline nor acknowledged any laws. But, although like everyone else he had misunderstood the reason for these rules, they were a salutary corrective to a temperament always at war with limitations. Would that he had been able to restrain himself in the moral sphere as he had done in his art! His inability to do this was his ruin; and it could truly be said of him that his unbridled temperament had brought him to the grave. Goethe was now firmly astride his anti-revolutionary hobby-horse which equated *Zügellosigkeit* (libertinism or libertinage) with liberalism; and he launched out into a description of Byron's life as essentially that of a political fugitive. It began with *English Bards and Scotch Reviewers*, he told Eckermann, which turned all the great men of letters against him, so that he was forced to retreat slightly in order to exist at all. It continued with ruthless political opposition to the existing government and those attacks on church and state which drove him out of England and would have ended by hounding him out of Europe. Wherever he was, he felt confined, and despite the most unlimited personal freedom the world oppressed him as if it were a prison-house. His going to Greece was no voluntary decision; he was driven to it because he was at loggerheads with the world.

He was utterly in the dark about himself, living passionately from day to day, neither knowing nor caring what he did. Permitting everything to himself and approving of nothing in others, he inevitably incurred his own displeasure, and roused the world up against him. His open break with tradition and patriotism was not only the personal ruin of so admirable a being, but his revolutionary ideas and the continual mental agitation they involved hindered the proper development of his talent; for his eternal opposition and disapprobation were highly detrimental even to his best works.

A few weeks earlier Goethe had been reading Byron's parliamentary speeches which strengthened his notion of the speaker as a thorn in the flesh of the body politic; for he obviously had no conception of the function of the opposition in our constitutional system; nor was he aware of the power of the Whig party, even though it was out of office when Byron was making *inter alia* his humane and eloquent protest in the Lords against the Nottingham Frame-breaking Bill. Somewhat later Goethe came to the conclusion that, if only Byron had been able to rid himself of his subversive views by repeatedly airing them in Parliament, he would have been a far purer poet; but as it was, a great deal of his negative activity in literature and in life could aptly be described as suppressed parliamentary speeches.[1] It *is* an apt description; but the word negative is not, and difficult to justify in view of Byron's statement to Medwin:

Perhaps, if I had never travelled, – never left my own country young, – my views would have been more limited. They extend to the good of mankind in general – of the world at large. Perhaps the prostrate situation of Portugal and Spain – the tyranny of the Turks in Greece – the oppressions of the Austrian Government at Venice – the mental debasement of the Papal States (not to mention Ireland) – tended to inspire me with a love of liberty. No Italian could have rejoiced more than I, to have seen a Constitution established on this side of the Alps. I felt for Romagna as if she had been my own country, and would have risked my life and fortune for her, as I may yet for the Greeks. I am become a citizen of the world.[2]

Whereat Goethe:

. . . all active opposition aims at what is negative, and what is negative is nothing. If I call the bad bad, what is gained by that? But if I actually call the good bad, much harm is the result. He who wishes to have a salutary effect must never abuse anything, and simply ignore what is wrong, doing only what is right. For it is not important to pull anything down, but to build something up, something in which humanity can take pure pleasure.[3]

Goethe's blindness to the positive side of Byron's revolutionary ardour, his tacit denial that humanity could take any pleasure in the establishment of free constitutions for the peoples of Europe

[1] Eckerman, p. 168. December 25, 1825.
[2] Medwin, pp. 282 f.
[3] Cf. Eckerman, pp. 145 ff., for the full text of the conversation of February 24, 1825.

is daunting enough. 'Safety first for the *status quo*' will always have many adherents; but to deduce from it that Byron's passionate political idealism, the one great disinterested factor in his life, was his spiritual no less than his bodily ruin is a serious misreading of his character and life. It is true that the hostility made manifest during the separation-scandal had a strong political bias behind it; it is also true that many passages in Medwin's *Conversations* show Byron involved in Carbonari activities and suffering for it; but Goethe's belief that his exile and subsequent fate were entirely due to political causes was a pure delusion. The great central fact of Byron's dislocated existence, the separation from his wife, was the real cause of his self-imposed exile and the insuperable obstacle to his return. Byron was quite as voluble to Medwin on that unhappy topic as he was about the Carbonari, and far more open to criticism for the manner in which he broached it. Goethe passed that by, although he reprobated in general terms the licentiousness of his life in England, on which Byron harped with tedious complacency, and the details of which were certainly reminiscent of a most disorderly existence:

The skull goblet; a new order established at Newstead. Julia Alpinula. Skulls from the field of Morat. Lord B.'s contempt for academic honours; his bear; the ourang-outang. A lady in masquerade. Mrs L. G.'s depravity. Singular occurrence. Comparison of English and Italian profligacy. Fashionable pastimes; Hell in St James's Street; chicken-hazard. Scrope Davies and Lord B.'s pistols. . . .[1]

This kind of thing was not calculated to win Goethe's favour; but it did not discompose him half so much as Byron's revolutionary spirit; and he had an answer to it, ascribing all his moral lapses and levities to the count of the society he was born into rather than to his own. And it was a solution which (as he had already realized when planning his Memoir for Medwin) could be applied to everything else he disliked in Byron:

Lord Byron [he now told Eckermann] is to be regarded as a man, as an Englishman and as a great talent. His good qualities derive in the main from the man; his bad from the fact that he was an Englishman and a peer of England; and his talent was incommensurable.

All Englishmen as such are without the power to reflect; dissipation and party-spirit prevent quiet mental development. But they are great as practical men.

That is why Lord Byron could never attain to self-knowledge, and why his reflections are altogether wide of the mark. . . .

Byron's high rank as an English peer was very disadvantageous to him; for if every talent is hindered by the outside world, how much

---

[1] Medwin, p. xiii. From the table of contents.

more is that the case for one of such high birth and great wealth! A certain middle state is much more conducive to talent; and this is why all great artists and poets are found in the middle classes. Byron's inclination towards the unlimited would have been far less dangerous to him, had he been of lower birth and lesser wealth. As it was, he had it in his power to put every whim into execution, and that involved him in innumerable affrays. And further, how could rank impress one who was of such high rank himself, and impose respect upon him? He said whatever he felt, and that brought him into irreconcilable conflict with the world.

One sees with surprise how great a part of the life of a rich Englishman of rank is spent in seductions and duels. Lord Byron himself tells us that his father seduced three women.[1] How could he be a steady son after that?

He lived, one might almost say, like a primitive man; and with his way of behaving, the necessity of self-defence must have been daily present to him. Hence his eternal pistol-shooting. He must have expected to be called out at any moment.

To blame everything on the English peerage was a happy way out; and it gave Goethe great satisfaction to assure Eckermann that all the extravagances of Byron's life and mind were due to the unfortunate fact that he had been born an Englishman, worse still, a rich Englishman, and worst of all an Englishman of noble birth. That was his misfortune as a man; but as a poet:

... whatever he produces is crowned with success, and one can truly say that in his case inspiration takes the place of reflection. To write poetry was an absolute necessity to him; and then everything that proceeded from him as a human being, and in particular what came from his heart, was admirable. He came by his things as women by pretty children: they take no thought about it and have no idea how it comes to pass. He is a great talent, a born talent, and I have never met genuine poetical power greater than in him. In his apprehension of externals and in clear perception of past conditions he is quite as great as Shakespeare. But as a pure individuality Shakespeare transcends him.

Goethe had talked himself back into a high state of enthusiasm; and having found a scape-goat in the English aristocracy he was able to rationalize if not yet to reconcile his conflicting opinions about Byron, which had been greatly intensified by Medwin's book and propelled in a new direction. During the long diatribe on Byron's disastrous revolutionary tendencies, there is no mention of gloom and hypochondria, those spectres of the past. They are indeed almost totally to seek in Medwin's *Conversations* where, except when talking about liberty and even sometimes then,

[1] Cf. Medwin, p. 59: 'He ran out three fortunes, and married or ran away with three women.'

K

Byron makes a cheerful impression on the whole, and in the main a shallow one. But the suppressed parliamentary speeches bulk fairly large; with the result that Goethe found himself insensibly shifting his ground and taking up the standpoint that political subversiveness had been the destructive element in Byron's life and works, whereas personal bitterness and despair had been blamed until now. Goethe might and must condemn this element; but Byron himself could escape judgment; he was the victim of the sins of his nation and not of his own.

In this frame of mind it was inevitable that Goethe should contradict himself flatly when one of Byron's obnoxious country-men voiced in his presence several of those very criticisms he had made to his intimates on hearing of the poet's death and after reading the *Conversations*. Consistency is a virtue more favoured by little minds than by great ones; and it was decidedly no moment for rigid consistency when Sir William Congreve (1772–1828), the inventor of the once famous Congreve rockets, took it upon himself to belittle Byron:

CONGREVE: . . . Byron has doubtless interested you a good deal. But you will allow that, though he died very young, he nevertheless died too old for his fame.

GOETHE: I cannot altogether agree with you there. Even his last works, where he allowed himself to be carried away too much by his ardour, are impregnated with his genius. It is clear that he was writing in the heat of the moment and extremely rapidly. Those works are, if you like, beautiful extravagances, but sublime extravagances.

CONGREVE: Oh yes, he was always in too much of a hurry.

GOETHE: Not always. His *Doge of Venice* must have cost him long studies. He lived for three years in that city, and one sees that he took the trouble to study the locality thoroughly. *Sardanapalus* is full of carefully thought-out beauties, and I could mention other works in which one sees that thought has bodied forth the fantasies of the imagination. As you see, we Germans are much interested in Byron's poetry; Byron is one of our favourites. We see in him only the great poet, leaving it to England to search out grievances against his person, which are no concern of ours.

CONGREVE: But you like Walter Scott too, I suppose?

GOETHE: We like him too. Our ladies, who make the fame of authors, are divided between Scottists and Byronists. These last are those who are stout-hearted and fiery-spirited. The others prefer Scott.

CONGREVE: I still think that Byron has rather lost than gained by writing too much. That is a misfortune for distinguished people. They expend themselves in one or two efforts, and after that they produce nothing new.

GOETHE: As far as Byron is concerned, your criticism arises from the fact that he never rested. He wrote incessantly, and was therefore forced to copy his forms or to see his faculties diminish. If he had allowed himself those moments of relaxation which the intellect requires as much as the physical man, then he would have risen to greater and more sublime heights than ever. What makes him most admirable in my eyes is that with such a genius he had so true a judgment and such penetrating observation.[1]

It is a pleasure to watch Goethe eating his words with every appearance of relish rather than sell the pass to an Englishman. And Soret who had heard Goethe declare that Byron had reached the limit of his poetical powers when he died, must have been highly entertained as he listened to him now, assuring Congreve that only a little rest was needed, and Byron would have attained to greater and more sublime heights than ever. Only unconsciously a great poet? No indeed; thought bodied forth the fantasies of his imagination. A childish thinker? Far from it: a soaring genius gifted in addition with true judgment and penetrating observation. Great men can be inconsistent, it is true; but there was never any question, when Byron's shortcomings were mooted by the English, on which side Goethe would be. Not one inch of ground was to be yielded to Congreve on this occasion, even though it meant making a strategic withdrawal from positions Goethe had been occupying ever since Byron's death.

## d. ANTIDOTE

Sir William Congreve had been sent to the rightabout, but the basic conflict with Byron's spirit remained unresolved. It had originally been an off-shoot of the inner warfare waged against the Faustian side of Goethe's own nature, and wore a double aspect. On the one hand, Faustianism carried to this excess was an element profoundly to be deplored; on the other, it was like being young again to meet it in *The Corsair*, *Lara* and *Manfred* and thus to experience once more the wild, tormenting ecstatic emotions of *Werther* and the *Urfaust*. With the appearance of *Don Juan* however, the focus shifted; something more dangerous than deep despair underlay its derisive laughter. In fact it looked like nihilism, which great humour, whether savage and satirical or sunny and serene, seems to hold in solution. Goethe withdrew, almost as if he were retreating before the evil eye, making motions of repudiation. But he was helplessly magnetized by Byron's personality; one gesture of homage, and hostility went overboard to make way for unconditional surrender to the spirit animating *Cain*. But hardly had that conflict come to rest, before the realization of an element in Byron's spiritual make-up even more disturbing than incurable melancholy or murderous mirth rose

[1] *Gespräche*, ii, pp. 380 f. April 28, 1825. Communicated by Soret in French.

up to confound him, and the struggle was resumed. He could not give up Byron; but his passionate liberalism would have been a stumbling-block to Goethe wherever, whenever and however manifested. That it should have come to a head in Greece was a cruel complication. For Goethe's Hellenism was penetrated through and through with the romantic fervour inspired by visions of a golden age, and was the very antithesis of Philhellenism. Ever since he had attained to years of poetical discretion, Greece had represented for him an absolute ideal of perfect beauty, simplicity and serenity, radiantly remote from the brawling banality of modern life. He had broken down over the *Helena*-act he was writing for *Faust II* in 1800, because he could not bring himself to desecrate that wonderful world by exposing it in the person of Helen to contact and contamination with Northern medievalism embodied in Faust. Even in the interests of tradition and even under the guise of poetical symbolism, the juxtaposition revolted him. And it was perhaps in order to keep his ideals and illusions intact that he had stubbornly refrained from visiting Greece in person. 'The ideal and reality must be kept rigorously apart.' But Byron had recklessly attempted to unite them; a poet, the greatest poet of the age, spreading the revolution in Greece; bringing Greece into the news! And because it was Byron, he was shattering Goethe's dream. How could it maintain itself in face of this violent irruption? The light that never was on sea or land was dispelled by the garish light of common day; the marble statues of the gods dislimned before the onslaught of a rabble in arms. Loveliness, stateliness and grace were being shouted down by liberation and revolt. Moreover to the honour of Goethe's heart (that supposedly ossified organ) the sorrowful anger he felt at Byron's death greatly aggravated his distaste for the cause. The whole undertaking was 'impure'.

Only a few months later he was taking a different tone, and this was due to William Parry of all unlikely persons. Not very much is known about this self-styled 'Major of Lord Byron's Brigade'; and what little information there is does not much redound to his credit. He had been a fire-master in the navy and then a clerk in Woolwich Arsenal, where he somehow acquired the reputation of being General Congreve's right-hand man and an expert manufacturer of Congreve rockets. Had Goethe read his *Last Days of Lord Byron* when arguing with Congreve, he would have let off some rockets himself. The reputed artillery expert was long and eagerly awaited at Missolonghi; and when he finally arrived in February 1824, Byron wrote in high spirits:

. . . amongst other fire-brands, our fire-master Parry (just landed) has disembarked an elect blacksmith, entrusted with three hundred and twenty-two Greek Testaments.[1]

According to hostile reporters, this was all that Parry ever did; for neither had he any of the promised rockets with him, nor could he manufacture them with the materials available. Whether this were due to his own incompetence or not, it was a bitter blow to the whole garrison, and a poor advertisement for Parry, whose stock was very low when Trelawny came to Missolonghi after Byron's death:

The fire-master was a rough burly fellow, never quite sober, but he was no fool, and had a fund of pot-house stories which he told in appropriately slang language; he was a mimic, and amused Byron by burlesquing Jeremy Bentham and other members of the Greek committee. Besides these accomplishments, he professed a thorough knowledge of the art of fortification, and said he was the inventor of shells and fire-balls that would destroy the Ottoman fleet and the garrison of Lepanto. All he did, however, was to talk and drink. He was three months in Greece, returned to England, talked the committee out of £400 for his services, and drank himself into a madhouse.[2]

It is always as well to have confirmation of any of Trelawny's tales, and confirmation of Parry's end is to be found in a manuscript note bound up with a copy of his book on Byron in the London Library:

The author of this book became insane, and was, after a long residence in other institutions, received into this, where he was some time afterwards visited by his son, who gave me the particulars of the patient's history, as recorded in the case book; he also was kind enough to send me this work.

W. C. BEGLEY<br>Hanwell, June 2, 1842.

Intemperate, quarrelsome and officious, Parry may have been; but he was certainly 'no fool', or he could never have persuaded the Greek Committee to part with £400 for services reputedly worthless. They did not appear quite in that light to Leicester Stanhope, who disliked him personally,[3] so that he was perhaps a rather better proposition than Trelawny made out; but he was obviously not fitted to deal with the desperate situation at Missolonghi, through which (presumptuously, boastfully and ineffectively) he attempted to bluster his way. He was heartily disliked by everybody but Byron; and yet, to judge by his book, he was far

---

[1] *Letters and Journals*, v, p. 314. To Charles Hancock from Missolonghi, February 5, 1824.

[2] Trelawny, op. cit., pp. 171 f.

[3] Cf. L. Stanhope, *Greece in 1823 and 1824*, London, 1824, pp. 113, 115 f., 128 and 294 f.

from unlikeable and mentally the reverse of despicable, facts which have given rise to the supposition that someone else wrote it for him. But if he had been the mere pot-house buffoon Trelawny describes, could he ever have obtained Byron's trust and even Byron's affection? In the fearful emotional and intellectual isolation at Missolonghi, he seems to have clung to Parry as to the only human being within reach; and if the latter's bluff manners and crude jokes relieved some of the misery of his mind, this should be accounted to the fire-master for righteousness. But, far more important than that was the genuine and dogged devotion Byron inspired in him which is reflected in his remarkable book with its shrewd, sensitive and even penetrating portrait of Byron as Parry knew him at Missolonghi:

I felt, from the moment I first saw him, a very great respect for him, mingled with something like pity. There was a restlessness about him which I could not comprehend, and he seemed, at times, weary both of himself and others. It was plain, that his wishes for the welfare of Greece went beyond his means of serving her; and he appeared surrounded with difficulties, without a steady friend near him capable of giving him a judicious opinion. . . . The respect I had for him, with his condescension and kindness to me, gave him immediately something of that power over my mind which the late emperor Napoleon is said to have had over his soldiers. . . . I soon perceived, not only that Lord Byron had no friend in Greece, but that he was surrounded by persons whom he neither loved nor trusted. Beyond the walls of his own apartment, where he seemed to derive amusement from his books, and from his dog, Lion; and pleasure from the attachment of his servants, particularly from the attentions of Tita, he had neither security nor repose . . . it was evident to me, from the very commencement of our acquaintance, that he felt himself deceived and abandoned, I had almost said betrayed. He might put a good face on the matter to others, because he would not be thought Quixotic or enthusiastic; he might even be, as in fact he sometimes was, the first to laugh at his own difficulties, to prevent others laughing at his folly; but in his heart, he felt that he was forlorn and forsaken.[1]

The idle trifler depicted by Medwin begins to disintegrate. Parry proceeded to show him up as an imposter:

His conversation with me was generally serious, and when it related to Greece, almost despairing. The reader will find the Lord Byron whom I knew, a very different man from the Lord Byron of Captain Medwin. . . . I speak of him as I found him, not as he has been represented; but the manly reality will not, I think, turn out to his Lordship's disadvantage . . . with other companions he indulged in whims and pranks; with them also he talked on a variety of frivolous things greatly to his own disadvantage. . . . In such conversations were those stories

[1] W. Parry, *The Last Days of Lord Byron*, London, 1825, pp. 23 ff.

collected, which, since his death, have been circulated so much to the disadvantage of his memory. Never did the words of a man, uttered in the hour of confidence and mirth . . . so rise up in judgment against him. I have heard him so often indulge in language similar to that which is reported by Mr Medwin, that what he has stated appears to wear an air of truth.[1]

If Parry had written those words expressly for Goethe, they could hardly have been better chosen, accounting as they do convincingly for 'the Lord Byron of Captain Medwin', and yet showing what a travesty of his real self that personage was. Goethe, who had already expressed his derogatory opinion of the English nobility very forcibly to Eckermann, now found to his extreme gratification that Parry, who had observed Byron closely, also put the whole blame for the poet's failings on to the shoulders of his peers; and what is more in terms almost identical with those he had used himself:

To all plain men, such as I am, it will probably appear as it did to me, that the exalted birth, and consequent neglected moral training of Lord Byron were his greatest misfortunes. He never conquered the mischievous prejudices, and the more mischievous mental habits which they led to. He was a nobleman, an only son, and a spoiled, neglected child. He had to suffer from all these circumstances, and derived a considerable share of his unhappiness from each. To almost everything that could nurture vice in the human heart he was early and unfortunately long exposed. He was of a rank above control; possessed money and was an orphan; then came fame, not gradually and hardly earned, but at once and overwhelming; and bestowed probably for what he had thrown off in some bright and delightful moments. He was so felicitous in his language, so quick in thought, that writing was to him not labour but pleasure. He was not only a poet, but, like other young noblemen, he was, for several years, a man of what is called fashion, and *ton*, and the opinions which he then imbibed, and the habits he then formed, he never afterwards got rid of. He deferred to them in his conversation and his manners, long after he had learnt to despise them in his heart. Naturally, like most men of very exalted genius, he was contemplative, and loved solitude rather than society. At least, in all our conversations, his Lordship was serious and reflecting, though wonderfully quick, acute, and discerning. With his other companions he was, as I have said, light, volatile, and trifling. He was still the man of fashion . . . and his companions being unable to comprehend his more exalted thoughts, he let himself down to their level, and again became an unthinking, talking trifler. To use, perhaps, a homely proverb, he 'howled with the wolves', and has been represented as vain, overmastering, gasconading, violent, unreflecting, capricious and heartless, because these are too much the characteristics of the class to which he belonged, and who reported of him. His noble and

[1] Parry, op. cit., pp. 28 and 258 f.

devoted enthusiasm in the cause of liberty; his courage, endearing him even to the rude Suliotes; his generosity, which never allowed him to leave one want or woe unrelieved he could mitigate; the humanity which made him sacrifice time and money and ease to soothe the sorrows of the unhappy prisoners, have all at times been forgotten, and he has been held up to the censure of the world by heartless and pretended friends, who were quite unable to appreciate all the nobleness of his character.[1]

As an antidote to Medwinitis, this passage is powerfully effective, and all the more so in Goethe's case because it was a complete justification of his own beliefs. So complete indeed as to be almost uncanny when one reflects that a master-mind like Goethe's should have entertained and expressed exactly the same opinions of Byron as a fire-master in the British Navy. Goethe was so much impressed by this passage, that he put the whole into German and sent it to Zelter, urging him to get hold of the book in translation if possible, since nothing could raise one better to a clear and lofty standpoint from which to view Byron. Everything else that had been said about him hitherto sank down and vanished away like mists in the valley.[2] He also praised the book warmly to Chancellor Müller, agreeing with the author in attributing Byron's death to his vexation and anger at the fearful mismanagement of affairs in Greece; and he confessed to Eckermann that Parry had shown Byron to be far nearer perfection and much clearer about himself and his intentions than anything that had been written about him so far, drawing highly flattering conclusions about the author:

'Major Parry himself', continued Goethe, 'must also have been a very remarkable, indeed a high-minded man, to comprehend his friend so truly and to represent him so consummately. One particular observation in his book is especially precious and welcome. It is worthy of an ancient Greek, indeed of Plutarch himself:

"Unfortunately, his enemies, and those who have spoken against him with most zeal and talent, have been taken from the middling classes. Possessing and praising the virtues he wanted, and overlooking or incapable of feeling those he possessed, they have most unfairly and unjustly censured him for not being like themselves; and for wanting that species of self-command, and that conformity to the national model, which are only the results of a situation he was unfortunately never placed in."

'Now, what do you think of that?' said Goethe; 'one does not hear something like that every day, does one?'[3]

---

[1] Parry, op. cit., pp. 260 ff. Cf. above, pp. 130 f.

[2] *Briefe*, xxxix, p. 215. June 6, 1825.

[3] Eckermann, pp. 160 f. June 11, 1825. Cf. also Parry, op. cit., pp. 263 f. Goethe paraphrased the passage in German. I have given the original text.

It is perhaps rather less than Plutarchian, but it is shrewd; and it was a shrewd blow too at those English philistines considered by Goethe to be such moral humbugs. But apart from this, and from the significant fact that Goethe and Parry saw eye to eye about Byron, there is a quality in the fire-master's book which justified the German poet's high opinion, something sterling and memorable. In fact it was not altogether unworthy of the part it was destined to play in world-literature by accomplishing a miracle which not even Byron himself could have performed without Parry: it won Goethe over to the cause of Greece. Possibly Pietro Gamba's *Narrative of Lord Byron's Last Journey to Greece*, read a few months previously, may have slightly softened his heart; but it was 'Major Parry of Lord Byron's Brigade' who cured him not only of Medwinitis but of the more virulent Graecophobia, by inoculating him with Philhellenism. Chancellor Müller noted his 'much greater sympathy with the Greeks' and attributed this to Parry; and there is a still surer sign in a strange little poem of the period. Admiration for Byron's expedition to Greece had until now been a minus quantity, indeed something still more negative had been present. But Parry's book inspired Goethe to see the liberation of Greece in a different light, and Byron as its fallen hero:

> Stark von Faust, gewandt im Rat
> Liebt er die Hellenen;
> Edles Wort und schöne Tat
> Füllt sein Aug' mit Tränen.
>
> Liebt den Säbel, liebt das Schwert,
> Freut sich der Gewehre;
> Säh' er, wie sein Herz begehrt,
> Sich vor mutigem Heere!
>
> Lasst ihn der Historia,
> Bändigt euer Sehnen;
> Ewig bleibt ihm Gloria,
> Bleiben uns die Tränen.
>
> .    .    .    .    .
>
> Strong in arm, in counsel skilled,
> For the Greeks – devotion;
> Noble words and deeds fulfilled
> Stir his deep emotion.
>
> Loves the sabre, loves the glaive,
> Looks on arms with yearning;
> Ah, to lead an army brave –
> For that his heart is yearning.

Leave him to the storied page,
And restrain your grieving;
Glory his immortal gage,
Tears for us he's leaving.

Coming from Goethe, this odd little ditty is almost revolutionary
in tone; but a much greater revolution was taking place in his
mind. Urged on by Eckermann, he had finally decided in March
1825, to complete the second part of *Faust* of which a scheme and
some fragments were in existence. The longest of these was the
beginning of the *Helena*-act which he had shrunk from continuing
in 1800 because it meant bringing Helen into the presence of
Faust, although he had later roughed out a plan for this central
episode. Even now he hesitated, and turning his attention to the
final outcome of the drama, he made sure of the fifth act. Then
he came back to Helen and began to read everything about
Greece he could lay his hands on, in order to recapture the impetus
which had dictated some four hundred lines a quarter of a century
ago. It was whilst he was employed in this fashion that Parry's
book came out. The disaster at Missolonghi began to take on
another aspect. Helen and Faust and Greece and Byron melted
and merged in Goethe's mind; and he suddenly realized that there
was a part for Byron to play in the *Helena*-act, a part already
shadowed forth in the haunting little poem Parry had inspired.
So strangely do circumstances co-operate in the production of
works of art. The 'rough burly fellow' called Parry, never quite
sober and now headed for Hanwell, had amused Byron at Missolonghi by burlesquing the members of the Greek Committee.
But it was decreed that he should also enact another part, that of
midwife to Euphorion, a sprite-like, flame-like, Byronic being of
whom Goethe's Muse was delivered by a masculine Mrs Gamp.

CHAPTER V

# Full Circle (1826-1832)

## a. AN OLD SHEET OF PAPER

WITH the conflict resolved at last, Goethe's grief at Byron's death was finding poetical expression and emotional sublimation in the fate and figure of Euphorion, and the elegiac mood which he had sternly suppressed until now was allowed freer access to his mind:

> He told me that Byron's was a most extraordinary spirit, and that there was a life in his works which guaranteed their immortality. 'Alas', he added, 'little did I think, when I wrote him some verses of encouragement, that they were to be verses of farewell.'[1]

Preoccupied with the vital essence of that extraordinary spirit and with his own deep sense of loss, he must also have pondered the curiously unequal relationship which had always existed between them, in which the vitalizing influence came from Byron and the emotional response, now as in the past, was Goethe's alone. This was the core of the situation he was representing in the *Helena*-act, and it received the strangest confirmation when, on March 26, 1826, a package arrived addressed to him in the now familiar handwriting of Professor Benecke. He opened the parcel and there fluttered out, like a ghost from the past, a well-known scrap of paper covered with Byron's handwriting. It was the manuscript dedication to *Sardanapalus* returning to him after many years. How long, one wonders, did Goethe gaze at that lost and precious relic before even looking at the letter in English from Douglas Kinnaird which accompanied it and the explanation in German by Professor Benecke? It may have been minutes; it may have been hours; for time stood still; but this is what Kinnaird had written:

PALL MALL EAST,
February 24, 1826.

Dear Sir,

I had the honor some few years since to be the channell of communicating to you, at the request of my deceased Friend Lord Byron, a tribute which his Lordship was anxious to pay to your Genius and

---

[1] *Gespräche*, ii, p. 405. October 4, 1825. Communicated by Alessandro Poerio in Italian.

141

high literary Fame, in the Dedication to you of his Tragedy of *Sardanapalus* –

The melancholy task is now imposed upon me by Mr Hobhouse, the distinguished Friend and Executor of the illustrious Poet, to invite you to add your name to those of a Committee of Gentlemen, who propose to carry into effect the national wish for erecting a suitable monument to the memory of our departed countryman – That list will contain the names of none who are not distinguished by literary honors, or by the good fortune of having been personally acquainted with the late Lord Byron – I avail myself of the friendly offices of my old Friend and Instructor, Professor Benecke, to insure the arrival of this letter into your hands, and I shall be much flatter'd to receive thro' the same channell, the expression of your sentiments upon the proposal submitted to you.

I have the honor to be
Dear Sir,
Your most obedt. Servant,
DOUGLAS KINNAIRD.[1]

It was a gratifying and flattering proposal and Goethe felt highly honoured by it; but far purer was the joy with which he regarded 'the old sheet of paper in Lord Byron's handwriting' as Benecke described it in his covering note, adding doubtfully that 'it may still have some value for you' and almost apologizing for the liberty he was taking in enclosing it. Kinnaird had kept off the delicate subject altogether; for neither of them had any conception of what the sight of that old sheet of paper would mean to Goethe:

At dinner today Goethe was extremely happy and affectionate. He had received during the day-time a document by which he set great store, namely the dedication of *Sardanapalus* in Lord Byron's handwriting. He showed it to us at dessert and at the same time kept on teasing Ottilie to give him back Byron's letter from Genoa. 'For you see, my dear child', he said, 'I have now got everything together connected with my relationship with Lord Byron; even this remarkable document reached me today, marvellous to relate, and the only thing now lacking is that letter.'[2]

But 'Byron's amiable admirer' refused to part with it, airily suggesting instead that Goethe should surrender the manuscript dedication to her, so that both could be kept together; and they went on bickering amicably in this strain until the ladies retired. Left alone with Eckermann, Goethe fetched a red portfolio from his study and displayed its contents to his disciple:

---

[1] A. Brandl, *Goethes Verhältniss zu Byron*, Goethe-Jahrbuch, Frankfort am Main, 1899; xx, pp. 25 f. Benecke's letter to Goethe is dated from Göttingen, March 23, 1826.
[2] Eckermann, p. 177. March 26, 1826.

'Look', he said, 'I've put everything together here which bears on my relationship with Lord Byron. Here is his letter from Leghorn, this is a copy of his dedication, this is my poem, and here is what I wrote for Medwin's *Conversations*; and now only the letter from Genoa is lacking; but she won't give it up.'[1]

It was a meagre enough collection; but it represented 'one of the fairest gains' of Goethe's life and he treasured it accordingly, regretting deeply (but too late) that he had ever allowed that one little note to fall into Ottilie's fragile but prehensile hands. However the *Sardanapalus* dedication was safe; and there was also the very agreeable proposal made by Kinnaird to ponder:

His spirit was quite full of Byron on this occasion, and he poured out a thousand interesting utterances about him, his works and his talent.

'The English', he said among other things, 'may think of Byron what they like, but so much is certain: they can produce no other poet who could be compared with him. He is different from all the others and for the most part greater.'[1]

A week later he wrote to Kinnaird and Benecke, to the former accepting the proposal in cordial and dignified terms:

The honourable and kind proposal of your highly esteemed Committee to include me in the circle which has been formed to erect a monument to the admirable being whose life has been too early cut short, has inspired me with the warmest feelings; for no one certainly has felt more warmly and cherished more faithfully a high regard for his extraordinary personality than I have.

I therefore accept, my dear Sir, most gratefully the offer that has been made to me, and ask you to express my deep respect to the estimable men who are directing the undertaking, and to inform me from time to time of its further and doubtless rapid progress; for I should not like, as a participator, to be behindhand in my obligations.[2]

To Benecke he wrote more expansively, and very emphatically on the subject of the dedication, which he did not mention to Kinnaird:

The letter you have again sent me has given me no small pleasure; I accept most gratefully in the enclosed the invitation of the estimable Committee, and at the same time I beg you to contribute the sum of £20 for me; for I should wish to omit no proof of how highly I prize the spirit of that man which has all-too early wasted and consumed away the most remarkable personality that could possibly be born.

The dedication of *Sardanapalus* is of the utmost value to me. Although I cannot ascribe the favour of such a document to my own merits, it yet remains very remarkable that a younger man should have revered so enthusiastically in his predecessor an aspiration felt irresistibly in himself.

[1] Eckerman, pp. 177 f. Date as above.
[2] *Briefe*, xli, pp. 4 f. April 3, 1826. Original in German.

Accept the thanks I owe you, and keep me in touch with any further developments of this praiseworthy undertaking. For even though the departed has already erected a glorious spiritual monument to himself, it is very right and proper that an actual, permanent memorial should bring him visibly to the memory of posterity. He may have lived his life as many others; but he was gifted, revered, beloved as few.[1]

Certainly beloved as few were ever loved by Goethe, whose mind kept circling round the subject of Byron's interest in himself, causing him about six weeks after he had received the dedication to compile a little list rather misleadingly headed:

### ENGLAND

*Werther* translated speedily, but from the French.
Later *Iphigenie*.
Reprinted by Unger.
At the beginning of the century translation of *Götz von Berlichingen* by Walter Scott.
Interest of Coleridge.
Several attempts to translate *Faust*.
Others, whose names must be looked up.
Retzsch's engravings of *Faust* reproduced.
Lord Byron's interest.
His remarks.
Passages from his writings.
His interest probably aroused by Lewis and Schelle [Shelley!], but only in the most general way.
In . . . there are traces of *Faust*.
Personal relationship brought about by Sterling.
The little collection to be edited and copies to be distributed.[2]

It is possible that Goethe began to compile that list in order to tabulate what he knew about his fame in England, but almost automatically it developed into a series of notes about his standing with Byron. Had the latter's interest been aroused by the available translations? More probably alas! by Lewis and the despised 'Schelle'; but 'only in the most general way'. The omission marks suggest either that Goethe hesitated to commit himself now even to traces of *Faust* in *Manfred*, or that he was uncertain how best to translate *The Deformed Transformed*. In either case it signified that he was waiving his claim to the paternity of *Manfred*, although it is possible that the 'passages from his writings' were those printed earlier 'to show my plagiarisms'. But the *pièce de résistance* of the whole was the 'little collection' in the red portfolio, enriched beyond measure by the latest addition and causing Goethe such pride that he intended to print it for private circulation.

---

[1] *Briefe*, xli, pp. 5 f. Weimar, April 3, 1826.
[2] Brandl, op. cit., p. 29. Dated Weimar, May 8, 1826.

Meanwhile Professor Benecke was far indeed from sharing Goethe's delight at the arrival of Byron's dedication to *Sardanapalus*. On the contrary he was outraged at such an embittering reminder of Kinnaird's broken promise of four years ago. He had probably often fumed at the unconscionable delay in ratifying it; and the reappearance of the document still in manuscript was decidedly the last straw, confirming his darkest suspicions that it had never been printed at all. It was just as well that he had kept Goethe in ignorance of Kinnaird's positive assurance, raising no false hopes in that exalted quarter; but the moment had now come to call his perjured pupil to task:

My dear Friend [he wrote to Kinnaird in considerably cooler tones than those he had used in 1822],
    I was very glad to see from your letter of March 4 that you had not forgotten me. I carried out the commission to Goethe immediately, and I send herewith his answer to you. I wrote to him that it was by no means the intention to ask him for a financial contribution but that his name alone was desired. At the same time I told him that it had been settled that no contribution should exceed the sum of £20 Sterl. He answered me thereon: 'I beg you to contribute the sum of £20 for me, for I should wish to omit no proof of how highly I prize the spirit of that man which has all-too early wasted and consumed away the most remarkable personality that could possibly be born.'
    Please let me know, if there is anything further that I can do to execute this commission. – But now to another question, which, particularly as it concerns Goethe himself, is of the utmost importance to me. *Did Goethe ever receive a copy of* Sardanapalus *with the dedication prefixed to it?* You wrote to me at the end of the year 1822: 'The Dedication will be prefixed to the new edition of *Sardanapalus* together with a note of explanation' (I had explicitly demanded this) 'as to the cause of its not having been inserted in the earlier edition. I shall send three copies to you, one for Goethe, one for yourself & one for the Göttingen library.'[1]

Bravo Benecke! He may have failed in the past to make a 'good German Scholar' of Douglas Kinnaird; but his tutorial writ still ran; and his correspondent must have felt that he was back *in statu pupillari* as he read on:

Personally I have received *nothing whatsoever*. Did you send Goethe a copy by another hand? – If not, then an omission very disagreeable to me must be made good: how that is to be done I leave to you, but I will willingly lend a hand. You could if you like give anything you may have to send me to Sir Lewis Moeller, Privy Councillor of Legation to the Hanoverian Government in London, addressed to Professor Benecke – for the Göttingen library.

[1] Murray Papers. Dated from Göttingen, April 9, 1826. Original in German except for the quotation from Kinnaird's letter. The italics are Benecke's.

Be kind enough to write me as soon as possible how the matter stands – Farewell.

Your faithful friend,<br>BENECKE.

How was it to be done? That was the problem facing Kinnaird when he went round to Albemarle St to consult with John Murray already destined in his mind to play the part of scape-goat. Bad news awaited him there. The separate edition of *Sardanapalus* to which the dedication had been prefixed in 1823 was now out of print and totally unprocurable. There was, it is true, the 1825 edition bound up with *The Two Foscari* and carrying the inscription to Goethe; but if that were sent, there could be no camouflaging the unforgivable negligence of which Kinnaird had been guilty in 1823. Although Murray was probably as innocent as he was ignorant of this aspect of the affair, still he should have forwarded an author's copy to Goethe himself as he had been directed to do. Both were therefore in a quandary from which they extricated themselves with speed and skill, trusting to luck that the result would pass muster. Three copies of the dedication were printed on separate sheets and gummed into three copies of the first edition of 1821 which included *The Two Foscari* and *Cain* and was luckily still in print. I deduced that this must have happened on reading the following passage in Goethe's letters:

Unless I am mistaken the volume of Lord Byron's tragedies intended for me in 1821 and inscribed to me arrived before your departure. This incited me to reread *Sardanapalus*, *The Two Foscari* and *Cain* with ever increasing astonishment at Byron's wonderful talent.[1]

Now as this was obviously the first edition from which the inscription had been omitted, the dedication could only have been inserted later; and sure enough, on examining the copy in the Göttingen University Library, dated 1821 and bearing the legend in Kinnaird's handwriting on the fly-leaf: 'From the Honble Douglas Kinnaird to the Göttingen Library', I saw at once that

the dedicatory sheet had been gummed in separately, although neatly and inconspicuously enough to escape the notice of the

[1] *Briefe*, xli, p. 103. To Chancellor Müller from Weimar, August 3, 1826.

unwitting. Certainly neither Goethe nor Benecke had the slightest suspicion that any trick had been played; and Benecke clearly believed the account of the matter which Kinnaird gave him, for he wrote to Goethe when sending him his copy:

Only after I had expressed a suspicion on the subject was the discovery made that the bookseller Murray had totally forgotten to send off the book which I now enclose. Your Excellency will therefore overlook what is due absolutely and entirely to the negligence of the bookseller and accept with friendly remembrance of him who is gone even this belated proof of the homage which Lord Byron felt impelled to offer to the first of living poets.[1]

Benecke's efforts to exonerate Kinnaird sound oddly enough as if he were exculpating Byron, who was obviously blameless, and whose belated proof of homage, seen at last in print, overwhelmed Goethe completely:

The things you have so kindly forwarded to me in the past have always been important [he told Benecke]; this last is astonishing and as flattering as it is saddening. Strange thoughts arise in me when I think that this incomprehensible being should have assigned *Sardanapalus* in particular to me, since I have always preferred it to all his other plays. The levity of the king, the charm of the Greek girl, the strange and wonderful bond between those two persons banish the hypochondriacal ghosts with which the admirable poet was wont to oppress his friends; they only appear now and again as if they were stepping from the clouds.

But I must beware of speaking of the beauties of this piece; one can never exhaust a production of that kind by pondering over it; it is a new experience every time one reads it.

I felt that again on this occasion. But how keenly I wished that I could have responded by some sign of friendship for the honour done me. It is too late now, and I am in danger of tormenting myself with the question how this copy, marked with his own hand, could have been withheld from me for so long, and how the friendliness thus shown to me could for so long have been kept hidden; and indeed by the inscription to *Werner* have been still further covered up and removed from any attempt at elucidation.

If I on the one hand owe this quite unexpected discovery to you and am in your debt for a tribute which, in these days particularly, is beyond price, you for your part must rest convinced that I realise to the full the value of its happy effect upon me and my circumstances.[2]

Well might Goethe be perplexed and saddened and even tormented by the impenetrable mystery which he sensed behind the mere 'negligence of the bookseller' and which had delayed the arrival of the volume until it was too late to acknowledge it to the

---

[1] Brandl, op. cit., p. 28. Göttingen, July 4, 1826.
[2] *Briefe*, xli, pp. 98 f. Weimar, July 27, 1826.

donor. As he grieved over this fatality, he may also have reproached himself in his heart for delaying his personal thanks
until he should see the dedication in print. 'It is too late now', he
mourned; and, even as he wrote those words, it may have
occurred to him that at least it was not too late to be first in the
field with a public memorial to Byron. The *Helena*-act which
enshrined that monument was nearly finished. What was to
hinder Goethe from publishing it separately with all possible
speed? As an episode it was complete in itself; and as a tribute it
would be well-timed. Moreover, as he had determined not to
publish *Faust II* during his lifetime, that estimable Committee of
Gentlemen in England would almost certainly forestall him; and
as none of them, or indeed anyone else, had loved and revered
Byron half as much as he, it was only fitting that his memorial
should precede theirs. It would be poetical justice too, since it was
owing to English dilatoriness that the precious volume Byron
had destined for him had only now come to hand. The *Helena*-act
went to press on January 29, 1827, and was published the following
Easter under the descriptive sub-title *Classical-Romantical Phantasmagoria*. Thorwaldsen's statue of Byron, commissioned by the
Committee of Gentlemen, was finished in 1834 and refused by the
Dean and Chapter of Westminster Abbey in that same year, a
circumstance which would have added fuel to the flames of
Goethe's Anglophobia had he lived to know of it. Ten years later,
the succeeding Dean repeated the refusal; and after lying for
some time in a shed on a wharf by the Thames, the statue was
finally erected in the Library of Trinity College, Cambridge, in
1845. Goethe's In Memoriam therefore led the way by nearly
twenty years, and no one will begrudge him that precedence,
whilst some may feel that the applause Byron received on the
first occasion when the *Helena*-act was read out loud in public was
the greatest tribute he and Goethe have ever called forth:

Just a week ago today I read Goethe's *Helena* to the Literary
Society . . . we assemble during the summer months in a lovely garden
and hold our readings in a hall whose doors and windows stand wide
open to the balmy evening air. And as twilight was falling and I came
to the hymn in praise of Byron, the nightingales began to sing so
loudly outside the windows that I could hardly make myself heard.[1]

Perhaps Byron would have begged the nightingales not to be
poetical; but, if Eckermann repeated this story to Goethe (which
I fear he did not), the German poet would have been charmed;
and it is strange indeed to think in this connection that William

---

[1] H. H. Houben, *J. P. Eckermann. Sein Leben für Goethe*, 2 vols. Leipzig, 1925–28;
I, p. 308. K. E. v. Holtei to Eckermann, Berlin, June 18, 1827.

Parry had any hand in the *Helena*-act and that Professor Benecke was responsible for its premature publication. But, though he was the proximate cause that it was applauded by the Berlin nightingales in the summer of 1827, no one but Byron could have induced Goethe to break the seven seals under which, as he put it in 1831, the second part of *Faust* was to lie until his death. 'Only when I am no longer in a position to do so', he added, 'may others lay hands on it'.[1] Yet he detached the central act of his great dramatic mystery and exhibited it to the world in honour of the poet whom he placed above all living poets and most of the dead. The greatest of German poets and the greatest admirer Byron ever had thus repaid an hundredfold the dedication to *Sardanapalus*.

The spurious copy Goethe received from Benecke had justified the labours spent on it by Murray and Kinnaird; amongst which, in spite of Goethe's assertion that it was marked by Byron's own hand, I am far from suggesting that forgery played any deliberate part. Murray had been instructed by Byron himself in 1822 to send a copy to Goethe 'from the author'. Either he or Kinnaird wrote that message on the fly-leaf, and Goethe believed that it was in Byron's handwriting. This seems the obvious explanation, but it is incapable of proof, for the book in question has disappeared from Goethe's library. It was catalogued by his librarian Kräuter at the time; but it is not to be found in Schüddekopf's later card-index; and the Weimar authorities are of the opinion that it vanished very shortly after Goethe's death. If they are right, then I for one am morally certain that Ottilie abstracted it. Be that as it may, though the mysterious volume itself has disappeared, its counterpart is in Göttingen, bearing witness to the fact that the book which so deeply affected Goethe's mind and heart had been faked up to deceive him. Yet in a deeper sense Murray and Kinnaird were at long last bringing the truth to light. It was the edition now in Goethe's hand for which the dedication had originally been intended, and the instructions Byron had given all those years ago had finally been carried out. The wheel was slowly turning.

About six weeks after Goethe's letter to Benecke, Prince Pückler Muskau called to pay his respects. He was almost as spectacular a figure in the cosmopolitan scene as Byron himself; be-glamoured by the East, worshipped by women, he combined the qualities of a Don Juan and an intrepid traveller with lively literary talents and a genius for landscape-gardening; and wherever he went he left a sensational trail in his wake. As one would expect, this dashing prince was an enthusiastic admirer of Byron;

---

[1] *Gespräche*, ii, p. 767. August 25, 1831. F. Förster.

and he was delighted to discover that Goethe shared not only that emotion but also his Anglophobia:

He then spoke of Byron very lovingly, almost like a father about his son, which was very agreeable to me on account of my own high enthusiasm for this great poet. Amongst other things he contradicted the absurd statement that *Manfred* was an imitation of *Faust*; but he said that it was certainly very interesting that Byron should have used unconsciously the same mask for Mephistopheles as Goethe had done, although he had given him quite a different part to play. He regretted greatly never to have known him personally and he censured the English nation severely and no doubt with the greatest justice for judging their great compatriot so pettily, and in general for having understood him so little.[1]

The lesson Goethe had learnt from Medwin's *Conversations* was clearly bearing fruit. Byron's 'childishness' about Calderon had shown him how misleading such external resemblances can be, and what a degree of poetic injustice can be done by making too much of them. He even minimized his influence on *The Deformed Transformed* by using the word 'unconsciously', whereas he had Byron's own word for it that it was 'a *Faustish* kind of drama'; and indeed the resemblance between the devil in Byron's play and Mephisto is close enough to justify the epithet. Goethe's awareness of this combined with his absorption in Euphorion, the child of Helen and Faust, and therefore in a double sense his own spiritual offspring, accounts for the impression Pückler Muskau received of a father's love for a son; otherwise, even during the period when he believed that he had fathered *Manfred*, Goethe's feelings for Byron were more passionate than paternal; and it was not with a father's pride that he displayed to Grillparzer a week or two later his 'correspondence with Lord Byron', reverently wrapped up in a piece of silk;[2] nor was it discernible when, at about the same time, the grandson of Karl August, then a child of eight, was honoured in a similar way:

. . . one day my teacher Soret took me to call on Goethe who received us in his study. Goethe was always uniformly and consistently friendly and kind to me and proved himself the same on this day too by taking out of a writing-desk near the stove two books to show me, one of them wrapped up in an Indian cloth. It was *Sardanapalus* which Goethe had probably received shortly before from the author, and which bore the proud yet humble inscription: 'To his liege lord'.[3]

---

[1] *Gespräche*, ii, p. 451. September 14, 1826.
[2] Ibid., ii, pp. 458 f. October 2, 1826.
[3] *Ibid.*, ii, p. 871. Communicated by the Grand Duke Karl Alexander of Weimar in 1899 on the occasion of the 150th anniversary of Goethe's birth. The other 'book' was the manuscript of *Götz von Berlichingen*.

Thus towards the end of the *annus mirabilis* which saw the completion of the *Helena*-act, the old poet of Weimar and its future ruler gazed together at a dedication which, after many vicissitudes, had at last found its way in print:

To
## THE ILLUSTRIOUS GOËTHE.

Little Karl Alexander spelt it out slowly, for it was written in English and he was reading it for the first time. Goethe knew it by heart, but he read it again:

A Stranger presumes to offer the homage of a literary vassal to his liege lord, the first of existing writers – who has created the literature of his own country and illustrated that of Europe. – The unworthy production which the author ventures to inscribe to him is entitled SARDANAPALUS.

## b. 'COUNT STRONGSTROGANOFF'

Goethe's peace of mind (if his mind ever were quite at peace about Byron) came within an ace of being wrecked when Byron's 'Count Strongstroganoff' visited him, probably in the summer of 1827.[1] But who *was* this mysterious Russian, and how far can his account of the meeting with Goethe be trusted? Biedermann, the first editor of Goethe's *Conversations*, maintained a marked reserve about the document which, he said, existed only in a fragmentary copy about which he could obtain no information whatsoever. He omitted to say how the copy came into his hands, whether it were in manuscript or in print, and whether it were written in Russian or German, in which language he published it. He was equally in the dark about the date of the interview it described; but from internal evidence it was obviously after Byron's death in 1824; and as *Faust II* was represented by Goethe as being in its final stages, it must have been well after 1825. As far as the narrator of the account is concerned, there are three Count Stroganovs to choose from, all members of the same family, although only two of them satisfy the conditions. The one chosen by Beutler, the latest editor of the *Conversations*, is Count Grigori Alexandrovitch Stroganov (1770–1857), a famous and distinguished diplomat who attempted to call on Goethe in February 1823, when the latter was too ill to see him. His age is against him. He was nearer fifty than forty and at the height of his diplomatic career when Byron, rising thirty, was painting Venice red. The relationship described by 'Strongstroganoff' as having existed between two equally dissipated young men, the Russian being by

[1] See above, pp. 52 f.

several years the junior, makes Beutler's attribution impossible. Grigori's eldest son, Count Sergei Grigorevitch Stroganov (1794–1882) was the right age and would do very well; but the second son, Count Alexander Grigorevitch Stroganov (1796–1891) would do even better; and Biedermann had it on the authority of Bartenev, editor of *Russian Archives*, that Alexander, accompanied by his younger brother Alexei, did in fact visit Goethe in Weimar.[1] Now Alexei figures largely in the account; and although (unlike his two elder brothers) he will be sought for in vain in Russian encyclopædias and biographical dictionaries, his existence is vouched for by Durylin, who says that he was in the Ministry for Foreign Affairs in the 1820s.[2] It all seems to fit in, except for the entries in Goethe's diary. He noted a morning visit from a 'Count Stroganoff' on July 30, 1823; he dispatched a case of minerals to 'Count Alexander Stroganoff' the following August, and was repaid in kind by Count Alexander in September 1827.[3] Goethe never mentioned Alexei; 'Strongstroganoff' never mentioned minerals; the visit (certainly later than 1823) was not paid in the morning; and was represented as the first ever made. Editorial ignorance of the source of the document combined with Goethe's silence about a most extraordinary visit, which none of the many said to be present ever mentioned either; the lack of any allusion to such a person as Stroganov in Byron's published letters and journals or in the many reminiscenses published about him would justify extreme scepticism about the whole episode but for the presence of 'Count Strongstroganoff' in *Don Juan*. This might weigh very light in a court of law; but as a poetical piece of confirmatory evidence it is not to be despised, especially when taken in conjunction with the account given by the Russian of his visit to Goethe in Weimar. Whoever he may have been, and whenever the episode took place, and however much it may have been written up retrospectively, it was certainly not invented, It tallies too closely with the actual state of affairs existing between Byron and Goethe which only someone who knew both poets personally could have detected.

The narrator embarked on his visit to Goethe in a thoroughly bad temper and in a hostile frame of mind, being prejudiced against the Germans generally and Goethe in particular, both as a poet and as a man. He himself, he declared superciliously, had never felt any kind of reverence for his writings. They were well enough when they expressed pithy thoughts or communicated gay good spirits or Goethe's deep but disillusioning knowledge of

---

[1] S. Durylin, *Russkie Pisateli u Goethe v Weimar*, in Lituraturnoe Naslyedstvo, 1932, Nos. 4–6, p. 411.      [2] Ibid., p. 415.
[3] Cf. *Tagebücher*, ix, pp. 85 and 89, and xi, pp. 116 f.

5. The family seat of the Stroganovs.

human nature; but those qualities were only present in a few of
the works. Stroganov disliked most of the others intensely; and,
although he praised *Faust*, he condemned the *Wilhelm Meister* saga
root and branch. As for Goethe's technique:

> When he begins to expand, to analyse, to depict and to adorn, then
> the cold and diffuse complacency with which he listens to himself is in
> the highest degree repulsive to me; and so are his bogus patchwork of
> twaddling thoughts and his finicking filigree-work composed of second-
> hand and borrowed emotions.[1]

However, added Stroganov contemptuously, it was just those
characteristics which the Germans most admired. But then, the
Germans! He knew them well enough not to be surprised at that.
For he despised them utterly and regarded with lofty disdain the
whole clan of vociferous Goethe-worshippers. No wonder that he
was simmering with irritation because he had been somehow
manœuvred into paying a visit of state to the great man; he, who
so much disliked German etiquette and ceremony. To add to his
sense of injury, he had been obliged to exchange his comfortable
travelling-clothes for full-dress regalia, a circumstance which was
as little to his fastidious taste as it was delightful to the less sophisticated mind of his younger brother Alexei, sitting beside him
scented and curled as if he were on his way to some lovely lady,
and in such mischievous high spirits that, had he not possessed
impeccable social manners, Stroganov would have trembled for
the consequences. Alexei seems to have been much the younger of
the two, the spitting image probably of his brother in the old days
at Venice when that unregenerate youth 'Strongstroganoff' had
found favour in Byron's eyes. Determined that Goethe should find
no favour in his, Stroganov regarded very critically the gravity of
the servants who received them and the solemn formality of their
master, 'a very well-made man with expressive features', whose
exaggeratedly dignified bearing put Alexei's impeccable manners
to a severe test, whilst his brother mentally contrasted the cere-
monial parade surrounding them (much to its detriment) with
the amiable and elegant tone prevailing at the Russian court and
in all the highest circles of his native land. The arrogance of
Goethe's demeanour was ludicrously incongruous, Stroganov felt,
with the degree of distinction he was showing to them because
they were foreign noblemen. For it was impossible that Goethe
(or any other man) could in reality admire himself so much as to
justify such pride, or on the other hand feel the deference he was
displaying to them, since their rank was their only title to his
esteem and he knew nothing else about them.

[1] Cf. for the whole account given in the text, *Gespräche*, ii, pp 780–791.

There was obviously no pleasing Stroganov and equally not a hope of impressing him. The conversation broached in these inauspicious circumstances he characterized loftily as incredibly trivial. The brothers had been invited to an evening reception at which a large concourse of guests was present; summoned, as the Russian sardonically surmised, in order to regale Goethe's admirers with the spectacle of two such rare birds as a couple of Russians from the Crimea who had read his writings and actually understood them. Unwilling to figure in this guise, Stroganov, gleefully supported by Alexei, retaliated by treating Goethe as if *he* were the remarkable spectacle, and they the sightseers who had come to gape. But it would not do. Goethe saw through the attempt and skilfully kept them in the limelight; with the result that they were bombarded and badgered on all sides with exasperating questions about the habits and customs of their native land. Before very long, the controversial subject of Russian despotism was mooted, and all the topsy-turvy Western notions about serfdom and so on were given an airing. The company was not ill-informed as to facts, Stroganov acknowledged; and Goethe in particular was very well informed; but the point of view was totally and utterly false, since not one of those present had the slightest conception of the patriarchal system on which serfdom was founded. In his efforts to enlighten them, Stroganov incurred the suspicion of being a champion of slavery and felt so much incensed by this that he determined to take it out of Goethe. The poet, it is true, had remained more or less neutral during the outwardly courteous debate; but he had been visibly entertained by it and seemed to be savouring the discomfiture of his foreign guests. It was high time, thought Stroganov, to bring him to book.

Abruptly changing the conversation, he introduced the subject of Goethe's writings, and began to put a series of highly debatable questions about them, a proceeding which threw the assembled company into dire confusion, but which they were powerless to prevent because of the unruffled air and well-bred ease of manner with which Stroganov conducted the examination; whilst Alexei vexed and charmed and disarmed them by his impudence and grace. Together they started those poetico-philosophical hares which Goethe's German admirers were for ever chasing in vain under his ironical and unhelpful gaze. How should one read the *Westöstlicher Divan*? What was the inner meaning of *Faust*? What basic philosophical idea underlay his works? So the probing went on as coolly and unconcernedly as if Goethe were a hundred miles away. Case-hardened to such indiscretions, the poet remained perfectly composed, and uttered an ambiguous phrase or two now and again with a smile; but he left his literary reputation in the hands of a professor from Jena or Leipzig, Stroganov couldn't remember which and had forgotten his name. It was almost certainly Reimer, August von Goethe's luckless tutor, now Professor at the Weimar *Gymnasium* and firmly established as the Master's indispensable hack-collaborator in matters literary as well as the semi-official interpreter of his utterances to *hoi polloi*. Allowing for some exaggeration on Stroganov's part, the man he proceeded to describe is Riemer to the life. This academic personage now shouldered as to the manner born the task of expounding Goethe's works to two benighted foreigners, whilst the poet smiled approval and encouragement. As an externalized piece of defence-mechanism against intrusive strangers Riemer functioned so smoothly, that Stroganov was convinced he was habitually used for that purpose and probably even kept for it. He rose to the present occasion with his wonted volubility, pouring out a turgid stream of learned, philosophical jargon, probably meaningless and certainly unintelligible, unless indeed one had waded through all the heavy tomes and indigestible journals which were the professor's daily fare. Far from being impressed (let alone gravelled) by all this bombast, Stroganov suavely proposed that the orator should speak in French, since he himself was insufficiently familiar with the new enrichment of the German tongue by the technical jargon of the Berlin school of philosophy, not to mention the thousands of barbarously corrupted words taken over recently from Greek and Latin and French.

Presumably incapable of expressing himself in that lovely and lucid language, Riemer solemnly declared that it was impossible to discuss the Master in any other idiom but his own. This proved too much for Goethe, who slipped out of the room; but it gave Stroganov the opportunity he had been working for; and well aware that the subject of this curious controversy was listening at the door, he made use of the opening which Riemer had given him:

I put an end to the argument with the statement that it was impossible to come to an agreement when the disputants held such diametrically opposite views. For, whereas the learned professor was convinced that no foreign nation was capable of judging Goethe's genius and his philosophical and moral influence on the age, I for my part was equally convinced with Lord Byron and his countrymen, that Goethe had been more completely misunderstood by the Germans than by any other nation in the world.

Yes; he had done it; he had introduced Byron's name (dragged him in by the hair of his head, for it is unlikely that Byron ever said any such thing); and now let the 'old fox' come out of his lair, Stroganov was ready for him. Had Goethe, who by this time was back in the room, queried his statement or put one question about Byron, the flood-gates would have been opened and Byron's mocking laughter would have rung through the room. But Goethe held his peace, though the eyes of all present were turned apprehensively towards him. He looked grave, but perfectly serene and ceremoniously invited his assembled guests to follow him in to supper. His attitude towards Stroganov seemed to betray some annoyance at the poor compliment the latter had paid the German people, but his occasional surreptitious glances at the temerarious Count betokened anything but anger. The conversation at table was halting and sporadic, for Stroganov's outrageous statement still seemed to be echoing in the air; and when he took his leave he was convinced that he had offended his host, his fellow-guests and their common patriotism beyond repair. But he was wrong. He had yet to plumb the depths of the national inferiority complex. Every single member of the company whom he met later hastened to assure him that what he had said was only too true, and applied to everyone but the speaker. He, and he alone, should be exempted from the general criticism. Stroganov was still further alienated from the Germans to discover that what would have given mortal offence in Russia, England or France had caused no umbrage in Weimar. He would have thought better of them, he commented acidly, if they had defended even their national failings against a foreigner.

Not yet privy to the state of Goethe's feelings for Byron, he was considerably taken aback to receive a note next morning from his host of the evening before asking for the pleasure of his company on a drive; and an hour later the astonished Count found himself *tête-à-tête* with Goethe in a chaise, for Alexei had not been invited. It was a glorious and exhilarating spring morning; but could that be the only reason for the startling transformation which had occurred in Goethe since the night before? He was no longer the same man. Gone, or very nearly gone, were the signs and symptoms of old age. Even more remarkable, vanished was every vestige of formality and stiffness. Stroganov could hardly believe his eyes as he surveyed the radiant features, the flashing eyes and the seething vitality of his companion, only held in restraint by the manly composure of his advanced years. And the Russian could hardly believe his ears when Goethe, intimate, cordial, almost gallant in his manner, began to congratulate him on the many significant and striking things he had said the evening before. There was flattery in every word and every gesture, and it was impossible to parry these compliments, for his honey-tongued companion was in full swing. He had recognized, he said, in the Count a man of independent mind; and it was the good opinion of such men which he prized above rubies. He was in like case with Voltaire, who desired nothing more ardently than the recognition of those who withheld their applause; and this had struck him forcibly last night on hearing the Russian speak so frankly about public opinion. Here, he had said to himself, is a man of spirit and character whose good opinion would be worth having. Seizing the first pause Goethe made, Stroganov protested with mock-modesty (for it is clear from beginning to end that he yielded to no one in the matter of pride) that he was at a loss to imagine how the opinion of a mere globe-trotter could be of the slightest importance to so great a man who enjoyed worldwide fame.

The answer to this leading question was an impassioned outburst on the nature of fame in general and of Goethe's in particular. Stroganov listened more and more spellbound to this rhapsody and wrote it down as far as possible *verbatim* on his return from the drive, with a view to publishing it after Goethe's death:

Fame, my dear Count, is the most glorious sustenance for the soul: it strengthens and uplifts the spirit, refreshes the emotions, and the weak human heart is fain to regale itself with such fare. But as one treads the road to fame, how soon one learns to despise it! Public opinion deifies men and blasphemes gods. It often belauds the very faults which make us blush, and mocks at the virtues which are our pride. Believe me, fame is almost as wounding as infamy. For thirty years I have wrestled with my disgust for it; and you would understand that, if you could witness even for a few weeks the number of strangers who daily insist on coming to admire me, many of whom (and this applies to nearly all the French and English) have never even read my works, and most of whom do not understand me. The meaning and significance of my life and writings is the triumph of what is purely human. I cling to that, and therefore I enjoy what fortune offers me in the shape of fame; but a sweeter gift by far is the understanding of healthy humanity. I would even rather be contradicted outright by those who realise the purely human significance of art than receive the morbid enthusiasm of our extravagant German poets who stifle me with praises. And therefore I willingly concede up to a point the truth of your statement that Germany has not understood me. There is a spirit of sensual exaltation abroad among the German people which affects me as something alien. Art and philosophy are divorced from life and assume an abstract character; far removed from the well-springs of nature which should fertilise them. I love the genuine intellectual life of my country and I like to stroll through its mazes, but only and always in the company of life and nature. I revere life more highly than art which does but beautify it.

Did Goethe's lips tremble slightly as he concluded this confession in a different tone of voice?

You are right: Byron has completely understood me, and I believe that I understand him. I prize his judgment as highly as he honoured mine; but I have not been so fortunate as to hear his opinion of me in its entirety.

Truth will out. It was not for his *beaux yeux* (as Stroganov had felt all along) that the Russian had been taken for this drive, overpowered with flattery and overwhelmed with confidences. It was because he had lived near the rose and had made it clear the evening before that he knew Byron's opinion of Goethe 'in its entirety'. Shut up with the German poet at such close quarters in the chaise, Stroganov must have wished himself to the devil for ever having introduced the subject; but even more acute must have been his relief that he had not developed it in anger. . . . Give him a moment or two now to collect his thoughts (to bring them back from those far-off days when he and Byron had revelled the nights away in Venice, and he had been so deeply in the poet's counsels) and all would yet be well. . . . Stroganov gained a little time by passing on to Goethe some of the details of Byron's private life which he had learnt at that time, and the German poet listened eagerly, but it was not enough. The Russian had claimed to know what Byron thought about Goethe, and the latter was determined to hear everything that had been said. Stroganov for his part was no longer so eager to oblige him as he had been the night before when he flung down his challenge in public. He now saw to what an extent Goethe was under the spell of Byron, and he himself was insensibly yielding to the charm Goethe was lavishing on him. The tact and good breeding, which had abandoned him at the party, now made it unthinkable that he should come out with the truth to his tensely expectant companion. Not that the unadorned truth was in itself so hurtful. Byron's comments about Goethe were nearly always eulogistic; but the inopportune gaiety which so often accompanied them must at all costs be suppressed. And so it came about that Goethe was regaled with all the flattering things Byron had said about him, whilst Stroganov observed a circumspect silence about the irreverent laughter he had heard. But he did not falsify his recollections altogether. When Goethe had drunk deep enough of Byron's praise, his companion ventured to hint that the English poet's opinions sometimes differed from the German's. Far from taking this amiss, Goethe was greatly stimulated by these divergencies; and he went on talking about Byron for the rest of the day in a most animated fashion, raising and discussing topics (said Stroganov) which he would certainly never dare to canvass with anyone else. The Russian pointed this out to his interlocutor, who did not deny it; but stated that he had hidden everything they were talking about

in the second part of his *Faust*, which his countrymen would
certainly pronounce to be the most boring production of his life.
And sure enough, Stroganov concluded triumphantly, a few years
later he received a copy of that posthumous work together with
an article in a leading German journal to the effect that, just as
the book considered as a material object had survived Goethe's
bodily existence, so too the spirit it enshrined had outlived his
genius. This further proof of the denseness of the Germans delighted Stroganov, who did not live to see the pendulum of
intellectual opinion about *Faust II* swing violently to the opposite
extreme.

'Strongstroganoff' had come and gone, and the danger was
past. He was probably the only man then alive who had both the
knowledge and the nerve to reveal to Goethe what a strong dose
of humour was mixed with Byron's admiration. Goethe was spared
that painful shock on this occasion; and what is more he was
spared from undergoing it publicly because, when it came to the
point, his personality dominated and kept in check the almost
uncontrollable hostility of a tempestuous Russian. But he was
spared a private disclosure for another reason: because of the
transformation Byron's name operated in him, a transformation
floodlighting the hidden recesses of his heart and exposing him
helplessly to his antagonist. This turned a potential enemy into
someone quixotic enough to shrink from wounding the poet's
heart so obviously at his mercy, another transformation brought
about by Byron's name and its never-failing magic for Goethe.

## c. ROUT OF AN ENGLISHMAN

In August 1829 Henry Crabb Robinson (1775–1867) did what
in him lay to dispel the magic and came near to quenching his
own ardour for Goethe instead. Old Crabb (a most endearing
eccentric) knew practically all the literary notabilities both in
England and in Germany and was a doughty Germanophil. He
had spent five years studying in Jena at the beginning of the
century when Wieland, Goethe, Herder and Schiller were all in
their prime, with the result that the names of Goethe and Schiller
ever afterwards peppered the notes and letters scattered broadcast
among his friends. They also intruded without rhyme or reason
into his conversations and were the ruin of his famous breakfast
parties:

There was little to gratify the unintellectual part of man at these
breakfasts, and what there was was not easy to be got at. Your host,
just as you were sitting down to breakfast, found he had forgotten to
make the tea, then he could not find his keys, then he rang the bell to

have them searched for; but long before the servant came he had gone off into 'Schiller-Goethe', and could not the least remember what he had wanted. The more astute of his guests used to breakfast before they came, and then there was much interest in seeing a steady literary man, who did not understand the region, in agonies at having to hear three stories before he got his tea, one again between his milk and his sugar, another between his butter and his toast, and additional zest in making a stealthy inquiry that was sure to intercept the coming delicacies by bringing on Schiller and Goethe.[1]

But, if Goethe was Crabb Robinson's King Charles's Head, there were after all good reasons for it:

Were this my last hour (and that of an octogenarian cannot be far off), I would thank God for permitting me to behold so much of the excellence conferred on individuals. Of woman, I saw the type of her heroic greatness in the person of Mrs Siddons; of her fascinations, in Mrs Jordan and Mdlle Mars; I listened with rapture to the dreamy monologues of Coleridge – 'that old man eloquent'; I travelled with Wordsworth, the greatest of our lyrico-philosophical poets; I relished the wit and pathos of Charles Lamb; I conversed freely with Goethe at his own table, beyond all competition the supreme genius of his age and country. . . . Compared with Goethe, the memory of Schiller, Wieland, Herder, Tieck, the Schlegels, and Schelling has become faint.[2]

Although Robinson never questioned Goethe's greatness, his first impressions were not exactly favourable:

My sense of his greatness was such that, had the opportunity offered, I think I should have been incapable of entering into conversation with him; but as it was, I was allowed to gaze on him in silence. . . . On our entrance he rose, and with rather a cool and distant air beckoned to us to take seats. As he fixed his burning eye on Seume [a poet], who took the lead, I had his profile before me, and this was the case during the whole of our twenty minutes' stay. He was then about fifty-two years of age, and was beginning to be corpulent. He was, I think, one of the most oppressively handsome men I ever saw. . . . The conversation was quite insignificant. My companions talked about themselves – Seume about his youth of adversity and strange adventures. Goethe smiled, with, as I thought, the benignity of condescension. When we were dismissed, and I was in the open air, I felt as if a weight were removed from my breast, and exclaimed, 'Gott sei Dank!'[3]

[1] W. Bagehot, *Literary Studies*, Everyman Series, 2 vols., London, 1916; ii, p. 295.

[2] H. C. Robinson, *Diary, Reminiscences and Correspondence*, ed. Sadler; 3 vols., London, 1869; iii, pp. 463 f. Diary for February 16, 1858.

[3] Ibid., i, pp. 110 f.; 1801. I quote from Sadler for the conversations with Goethe when, as here, neither Biedermann nor Beutler gives the passage. Otherwise I quote from the *Gespräche*, which use the versions from the unpublished diaries, whereas Sadler for the most part gives the less lively and detailed retrospective reminiscences.

Robinson attributed part of his almost panic-stricken awe during his first encounter with Goethe to the striking likeness which he discerned between the German poet and the great tragic actor Kemble, which also impressed Gillies in 1821. But that was not the main reason why wild horses would not have dragged him back into Goethe's presence then; it was that distant, daunting, freezing manner warranted to keep visitors in their place. Three years later, however, on returning to Weimar in 1804, Robinson was agreeably surprised to find the great man considerably more approachable. This was probably because at a visit to the Weimar theatre, Benjamin Constant came up to greet Robinson cordially, and was later seen to whisper his name to Goethe:

On this he turned round and, with a smile as ingratiating as his ordinary expression was cold and repulsive, said: 'Do you know, Mr Robinson, that you have offended me?' – 'How is that possible, your Excellency?' – 'Why! You have visited everyone in Weimar except me.' I felt that I blushed. – And said in the fitting tone: 'You may imagine any cause, your Excellency, but want of reverence.' – He smiled: 'I shall be happy to see you at any time.' – Of course, I left my card next morning – and the next day there came an invitation to dinner – I dined with him several times before I left Weimar – and the acquaintance did not cease on this German residence.[1]

The impression created on this occasion, although still rather overwhelming, was less crushing:

In Goethe I beheld an elderly man of terrific dignity: penetrating and unsupportable eye: a somewhat aquiline nose and most expressive lips, which closed seemed to be making an effort to move as if they could with difficulty keep their hidden treasures from bursting forth. – A firm step ennobling an otherwise too corpulent body; a free and enkindled air, and an ease in his gestures, all which combined the gentleman with the Great Man.[2]

Robinson missed seeing Goethe in 1818 when he was again in Germany; but they kept in touch and the Englishman's well-developed bump of reverence increased with the years; so that when Goethe sent him a set of medals in 1828 stamped with his own features and those of the Duke and Duchess of Weimar (struck as a memorial of the fifty years during which Karl August and Goethe had together ruled the duchy), Old Crabb was so much overcome by this honour that words failed him and he did not acknowledge the gift for several months. In January 1829 however he assured the donor that the delay must on no account be attributed to the want of a due sense of obligation; and indeed

---

[1] *Gespräche*, i, p. 341; March 17, 1804. The title used was *Herr Geheimrat*. Cf. Sadler, i, pp. 186 f.
[2] Ibid., i, p. 343. March/April 1804. Cf. Sadler, ii, p. 430.

his almost tremulous veneration for the German poet had become a part of his nature.

His feelings for Byron were entirely different: tinged with something like contempt and decidedly hostile. Moral considerations apart, it could hardly be otherwise, since he belonged heart and soul to the opposite camp. At a poetical banquet given by Monkhouse at which he was present in the company of Coleridge, Wordsworth, Lamb, Rogers and Moore, the last-named described him chirpily as 'one of the *minora sidera* of this constellation of the Lakes'.[1] Deeply devoted to Wordsworth and personally unacquainted with Byron, Old Crabb felt his hackles rising at the mere sight of him or the mention of his name; and it was completely in character that in later years he considered Lady Byron 'one of the best women of the day';[2] whereas she, when a censorious young girl, had confided to her diary that he was 'clever, but afraid people will not notice it'.[3] They drew together in the fifties about matters religious; and this again was almost inevitable in Robinson's case; for he was so pious that he often regretted what he believed to be a want of religious feeling in his idol Goethe. Great piety is not always conducive to good taste; and Lady Byron (much vexed with Dr Kennedy's account of Byron's arguments against eternal damnation) actually sent Robinson a long, searching and damaging analysis of her husband's belief in predestination, the rock against which she was broken, as she mournfully declared. Her own views on all subjects being rigidly fixed, it was evidently inconceivable to her that Byron's might have changed; nor did she feel any compunction at communicating the torments of a presumably 'lost soul' to a third party by no means enamoured of her dead husband.[4] But that was far in the future. Long before then, Robinson had taken his own line about Byron, stoutly resisting the onslaught upon his emotions from the poetical front:

After dinner I read Lord Byron's *Manfred* to Mrs Becher and Miss Lewis. I had occupied myself during the forenoon in writing a critique on this painful poem, which nevertheless has passages of great beauty. The ladies would have been greatly delighted with it, I dare say, if I had encouraged their admiration.[5]

Goethe was made of sterner stuff. Do what Old Crabb would in August 1829 he could neither dim nor shake nor even slightly discourage the German poet's delight in Byron. During the seven

[1] Cf. Sadler, ii, pp. 247 ff. for Moore's and Lamb's accounts of this banquet, which took place on April 4, 1823.
[2] Ibid., iii, p. 411. Diary for September 13, 1853.
[3] E. C. Mayne, *Life of Lady Byron*, London, 1929, p. 16.
[4] Cf. Sadler, iii, pp. 435 f. Lady Byron to Robinson from Brighton, March 5, 1855.
[5] Ibid., ii, pp. 58 f. Diary for June 22, 1817.

afternoons and evenings which the two men spent together it was Byron, Byron all the time; and, in the light of Stroganov's experience, one can hardly fail to see Byron's influence behind Goethe's excessive warmth of manner, which quite disconcerted Robinson who kept on remembering the very different reception he had met with in 1801:

*Then* he never honoured me with a look after the first haughty bow, *now* he was all courtesy. . . . On leaving him the first evening, he kissed me three times. (I was always before disgusted with man's kisses.) Voigt never saw him do so much to any other.[1]

I was oppressed by the cordial reception and as the cordiality increased during two most interesting conversations, the sense of unworthiness is but increased and now disturbs the otherwise delightful feelings which several hours' conversation has produced.[2]

Like Stroganov, Old Crabb probably felt in his bones that this excessive geniality must have an ulterior motive; and his personal diffidence was increased by Ottilie who set out to charm him and (like her father-in-law) rather overdid it:

Goethe calls her a Crazy Angel and I can already feel the force of the Epithet – her reception of me was odd; I hope not persiflage. – She had waited for me twelve years! yet it was cordial – and she spoke so much about my coming again, reading English etc. that I cannot but hope she spoke as she felt.[3]

She certainly spoke as she felt, being a true-blue Anglomaniac; and Goethe's affection for his visitor was partly no doubt for old times' sake. He also 'ardently enjoyed' the news of his own extended reputation in England; but over and above all this was the heaven-sent opportunity to talk at length about Byron with a well-informed compatriot; and to break a lance for the English poet should the well-informed compatriot prove ill-disposed towards his countryman. Robinson was certainly not well-disposed to Byron; but, unwilling to quarrel with Goethe, he made manful efforts to change the subject by introducing the names of other contemporary poets who, in his opinion, were infinitely superior to Byron. It was all in vain. Goethe had never read Burns' *Vision* and seemed more than content to remain in ignorance of it, in spite of its strong resemblance to his own *Zueignung*. The mention of Charles Lamb produced nothing more encouraging than the question: 'Did he not write some pretty verses about his own name?' Believing that Coleridge at least would break down this bland indifference, Robinson proceeded to read aloud to his

---

[1] Cf. Sadler, ii, pp. 430 and 432; 1829.
[2] *Gespräche*, ii, pp. 603 f. August 2, 1829.
[3] Ibid., ii, p. 605. Same date. Robinson gave the German for 'Crazy Angel': *Verrückter Engel*.

M

perfectly acquiescent host *Love* and *Fire, Famine and Slaughter*. Goethe damned them with faint praise; but was in raptures when poor Old Crabb was coaxed into reading the last part of *Heaven and Earth* out loud as well. This was fortunately one of the only two works of Byron which the reader really liked; the other (and about this too Goethe was tremendously enthusiastic) being the first two acts of *The Deformed Transformed*. Here therefore was at least some common ground; but Robinson naturally felt that, if Goethe would but consent to listen to John Milton, he would think the less of Byron ever after. He therefore inflicted *Samson Agonistes* on his revered friend. Nothing if not obliging, Goethe praised it highly, gave proof of intelligent interest and made several apt comments; but Byron's prestige did not suffer in the least:

> The only thing that a little disturbed my enjoyment of his company was his excessive admiration of Lord Byron. – I read to him Milton's *Samson Agonistes* – he was ignorant of it – professed to admire it; praised it; said he would read it again – but he did not praise him with the hearty warmth with which he enjoyed *Heaven and Earth*.[1]

This confidential communication to some Leipzig friends after Robinson had left Weimar shows that Goethe had not succeeded in throwing any dust into his would-be teacher's eyes; but he had been sufficiently impressed to attempt to throw some dust into his own:

> He drew my attention finally to Milton's *Samson Agonistes*, and read it with me. It is interesting to make the acquaintance of Lord Byron's predecessor here; he is as grandiose and comprehensive as the latter; but, to be sure, the descendant presses on to limitless horizons and is wildly varied, whereas the other appears simple and stately.[2]

A decade earlier, or even less, this would certainly have meant that Goethe much preferred Milton; for stateliness and simplicity had been his highest ideals ever since he had fallen under the spell of classical antiquity. But now, in his old age, he was gravitating back to the 'limitless horizons' of his youth, partly inspired by Byron; and certainly the second part of *Faust* is as 'wildly varied' as anything Byron ever wrote. So that, even had Goethe possessed a more sensitive ear for English verse, he might not have judged very differently; as it was, Milton, considered as a rival to Byron, fell decidedly flat and was allowed at most to be a precursor.

'He reverted again to Lord Byron . . . his admiration was excessive – his remarks all eulogistic'; these were the cries from the

---

[1] W. von Biedermann, *Goethes Gespräche*, 2nd ed., 5 vols., Leipzig, 1909–11; v, p. 169. August 27, 1829.

[2] *Briefe*, xlvi ,p. 54. To Zelter from Weimar, August 20, 1829.

depths from which Old Crabb earnestly endeavoured to point out
to Goethe spots on the Byronic sun. Goethe benignly pretended to
see them, but never really looked; and the utmost Robinson could
wring from him was the concession that the idea of selling one's
soul in order to 'gratify such an appetite' as Manfred's passion for
Astarte was not poetical. As Manfred never surrendered his soul
but remained passionately master of it from beginning to end, this
one concession shows how carelessly Robinson had read the poem.
Goethe remembered it rather better; for he cancelled out his
concession by 'falling back' on the indomitable spirit of Manfred,
who was not defeated even at the last. One's heart bleeds for Old
Crabb but it goes out to Goethe for his unwavering allegiance.
Nor was he content with mere passive resistance; he advanced to
the attack; and the Englishman was well and truly routed when it
came to *The Vision of Judgment*. Goethe had known this poem
intimately since 1824 and admired it beyond bounds; indeed it
seems almost certain that when, in 1825, he set out to save the
soul of Faust in a highly ironical battle-scene between Mephisto
and the angels,[1] he was under the influence of Byron who had
performed the same good office for George III in an equally
ironical fashion. He now persuaded Robinson to read the poem
out loud to him and poured out a torrent of praise into the wincing
ears of his visitor. 'He enjoyed it like a child', said the latter
despairingly; for he had hoped for better things from Goethe than
a volley of ecstatic exclamations: 'Fantastic! what a nerve!
heavenly! unsurpassable!' Robinson was completely taken aback;
but Byron would have recognized the 'analogy' between Goethe
and himself of which he had spoken to Medwin. Goethe's response
to the poem which he characterized as 'the sublime of hatred'
reveals the reality and the depth of the bond between them and
the turbulent layers of consciousness beneath. But there was
consciousness too on Goethe's side of something else: of his own
great age and approaching death. He repeated slowly and emphatically the whole of stanza ten, dwelling on the last two lines
('conscious that his own age was eighty'), and thinking perhaps of
the 'sepulchral melodrame' that awaited him:

Of all

    The fools who flocked to swell or see the show,
Who cared about the corpse? The funeral
    Made the attraction, and the black the woe,
There throbbed not there a thought which pierced the pall;
    And when the gorgeous coffin was laid low,
It seemed the mockery of hell to fold
The rottenness of eighty years in gold.[2]

---

[1] Act V, *Grablegung*.                    [2] *Poetry*, iv, p. 490.

Crabb Robinson broke into whatever macabre and piercing thoughts these lines aroused by stating that stanzas thirteen, fourteen and fifteen were favourites with him. Goethe 'concurred in the suggested praise'; and he could hardly fail to do so, since they contained a passionate protest against the belief in eternal damnation:

> 'God save the king!' It is a large economy
>   In God to save the like; but if he will
> Be saving, all the better; for not one am I
>   Of those who think damnation better still;
> I hardly know too if not quite alone am I
>   In this small hope of bettering future ill
> By circumscribing, with some slight restriction,
> The eternity of Hell's hot jurisdiction.
>
> I know this is unpopular; I know
>   'Tis blasphemous; I know one may be damned
> For hoping no one else may e'er be so;
>   I know my cathecism; I know we're crammed
> With the best doctrines till we quite o'erflow;
>   I know that all save England's Church have shammed,
> And that the other twice two hundred churches
> And synagogues have made a *damned* bad purchase.
>
> God help us all! God help me too! I am,
>   God knows, as helpless as the Devil can wish,
> And not a whit more difficult to damn,
>   Than is to bring to land a late-hooked fish,
> Or to the butcher to purvey a lamb;
>   Not that I'm fit for such a noble dish,
> As one day will be that immortal fry
> Of almost everybody born to die.[1]

Goethe, who had set out determined to undermine the disastrous belief in eternal damnation in his version of the Faust-legend, and whose outburst to the Bishop of Derry showed how hotly he resented the attitude of 'England's Church', responded with every fibre of his being to the savage laughter of the dead man, fiercely attacking a doctrine which Goethe had ironically smiled away. It was a significant moment in the joint history of these two minds, this meeting here at the world's end in absolute harmony and accord. And it is significant in another way to find that Goethe singled out Byron's description of Satan as peculiarly sublime without any prompting from Robinson:

[1] *Poetry*, iv, p. 492.

But bringing up the rear of this bright host
  A Spirit of a different aspect waved
His wings, like thunder-clouds above some coast
  Whose barren beach with frequent wrecks is paved;
His brow was like the deep when tempest-tossed;
  Fierce and unfathomable thoughts engraved
Eternal wrath on his immortal face,
And *where* he gazed a gloom pervaded space.[1]

The sombre majesty of this evocation was not within Goethe's scope. Incapable of giving (or unwilling to give) those great proportions to the spirit of evil which Dante, Marlowe, Milton and Byron felt to be essential, he had even made his Mephistopheles a devil of slighter stature than his legendary original in the folk-book. But he applauded the sublimity of Byron's delineation, breaking out into delighted laughter later on when Southey appeared, and relishing the ironical conclusion to the full. 'Byron has surpassed himself', he informed Crabb Robinson; 'such a one never existed before, nor ever will again'. And never again will *The Vision of Judgment* live through such an exalted hour.

Old Crabb smiled wryly when he read some years later in Goethe's correspondence with Zelter that he had behaved in Weimar in 1829 as a sort of missionary on behalf of English poetry. As a missionary, he had not been a striking success, having failed outright to dethrone Byron and put Milton in his place; but his failure went even deeper than that:

> He was not aware that I had not the courage to name the poet to whom I was and am most attached – Wordsworth; for I knew that there were too many dissonances of character between them. As Southey remarked to me, 'How many sympathies, how many dispathies do I feel with Goethe!'[2]

Not only had Crabb Robinson been defeated in his efforts to weaken Goethe's sympathy for Byron, he had actually done something towards dispelling his dispathy for *Don Juan*. The Englishman's oblique disparagement of his idol's poetry goaded him into giving Byron's masterpiece another trial; and he spent the evening of August 16 after his visitor had left him reading the thirteenth and fourteenth cantos of that 'most immoral' work; and lo and behold it was 'not without renewed admiration for that extraordinary poetic mind'.[3] Dealing as they do with Newstead Abbey, these two cantos are outstandingly beautiful and brilliant and might well arouse his admiration; but only an Englishman

---

[1] *Poetry*, iv, p. 495.
[2] Sadler, ii, p. 439. Written some time after 1834.
[3] *Tagebücher*, xii, p. 113. August 16, 1829.

could have brought him to read them; anything however was
possible when an Englishman tried to belittle Byron to Goethe:

> Goethe's love for Byron amounts to a passion [wrote the sculptor
> David who was modelling his bust at the time]. One day he was moved
> from his impassive calm by a compatriot of the English poet who had
> dared to blaspheme against the author of *Childe Harold*.[1]

## d. A BYRON MANUSCRIPT

Having paid Byron a public poetical tribute, and in a series of
encounters with Crabb Robinson having with the utmost geniality
worsted English captiousness about his idol, Goethe may have
felt that there was now nothing left to do, and that his passion for
Byron would together with his declining years go down like sunset
or melt like a rainbow, to borrow a phrase from his favourite poet.
But before the wheel could come full circle, there was one more
revolution to be made. The truth about Byron's feelings for Goethe
had been only half-told in the dedications to *Sardanapalus* and
*Werner*, in the letter from Leghorn, in Medwin's *Conversations*, and
in Stroganov's bowdlerized reminiscences. The whole truth was
to be found in the suppressed dedication to *Marino Faliero* lying
*perdu* in Albemarle St. 'There let it lie', the merciful will murmur.
But the House of Murray which had done its fair share in the past
to queer the relationship between the two poets had another shot
in its locker in the shape of that same dedicatory letter reposing in
its archives, where John Murray Junior (John Murray III) unfortunately discovered it, and still more unfortunately omitted to
read it. This enterprising if thoughtless young man visited the
Continent in 1829, a visit which inspired the conception of the
famous Murray Handbooks; and among other objects of note on
his tour he went to see Goethe in Weimar. This was now incum-
bent on travellers with any pretensions to culture; for Goethe had
attained to a degree of celebrity which vied with the attractions
of the great public or national monuments. It was not unlike
entering a museum nowadays to be shown into his study, deco-
rated with copies of the Elgin Marbles and other specimens of
Greek art. Here Murray found 'the hale old man . . . attired in a
brown dressing-gown, beneath which shone the brilliant whiteness
of a clean shirt; a refinement not usual among German philosophers'[2] – and not always to be found on Goethe either, to judge
by Bancroft's experience.

---

[1] *Gespräche*, ii, p. 637. August 23/September 9, 1829. Communicated by V. Pavie in
French.

[2] Ibid., ii, p. 651. October 14, 1829.

Sixty years later Murray was under the impression that he had on this occasion presented Goethe with the manuscript of Byron's 'suppressed dedication of *Werner* to him';[1] ironically enough picking out the only one of the three (and that one almost certainly not by Byron) which had never been suppressed. Sixty years is a long time; and John Murray III had forgotten not only what had really occurred, but his own resultant state of mind, perhaps a Freudian forgetfulness. For he had rashly and irresponsibly promised Goethe the unpublished dedication to *Marino Faliero*, of whose existence Goethe was in utter ignorance, and of whose nature Murray was equally in the dark. His dismay can be imagined when, on returning to London, he belatedly read the document he was committed to present to its addressee. How would the patriarch of German letters receive a posthumous tribute marred by so much blithe irreverence? Having had the honour of a personal interview with Goethe, the young man must have been fully aware of the enormity of bringing it gratuitously to his notice; and he may have been strongly tempted to take a leaf out of his father's book and put the whole matter out of his mind. But that simple solution was impracticable because he had also lightheartedly promised to send Goethe Moore's forthcoming *Life of Lord Byron* which was to contain the dedicatory epistle with the omission of the passages directed against Wordsworth and Southey, because forsooth:

... the unmeasured severity poured out in it upon the two favourite objects of his wrath and ridicule compels me to deprive the reader of some of its most amusing passages.[2]

*Their* feelings were to be spared; but to omit all the passages guying Goethe would reduce the letter to mere rows of asterisks; and although Tom Moore was no niggard of those, there were limits beyond which even he could not go. Omit the letter altogether from the *Life*? But Moore would never consent to that, because it was such a priceless letter; and as Murray Junior had told Goethe that it was to figure in the biography, *he* would never rest content until he had seen it. There was nothing for it: the misbegotten manuscript must go to Goethe with a tactful covering letter:

In transmitting to you the dedication of Lord Byron's Tragedy of *Marino Faliero*, which I mentioned when you allowed me the honour of an interview in October last, I must beg to observe, that not having read it at that time, I was not aware of the nature of its contents. Could

---

[1] Cf. *Murray's Magazine*, November 1889. The mistake has been rectified in Beutler's edition of the *Gespräche*; but it was still in Biederman, op. cit., iv, p. 176.
[2] Moore, p. 459.

I, however, for a moment suppose, that it would in any way tend to give offence, I should be tempted to refrain from fulfilling the promise I then made, of sending it to you. But, although written in the playful style in which Lord Byron was so frequently in the habit of indulging, it is at the same time characterized by the same expressions of respect for you, Sir, and admiration of your works, which accompany the mention of your name in every part of Lord Byron's writings and I hope that it will be gratifying to you to possess such a literary curiosity.[1]

'Letter from Murray from London with a Byron manuscript',[2] Goethe noted laconically in his diary for January 30, 1830, and then sat down to wrestle with it. The handwriting probably gave him some trouble; but, especially in view of Murray's warning, it is unlikely that he called in anyone to help him decipher it; so that the painful process of enlightenment will have been slow:

For *MARINO FALIERO*.[3]

## DEDICATION TO BARON GOETHE, ETC., ETC., ETC.

Sir, – In the Appendix to an English work lately translated into German and published at Leipsic [Wagner's *Manfred*], a judgment of yours upon English poetry is quoted as follows: 'That in English poetry, great genius, universal power, a feeling of profundity, with sufficient tenderness and force, are to be found; but that *altogether these do not constitute poets*', etc., etc. I regret to see a great man falling into a great mistake. This opinion of yours only proves that the *Dictionary of Ten Thousand living English Authors* has not been translated into German. You will have read, in your friend Schlegel's version, the dialogue in *Macbeth* –

'There are *ten thousand*!

Macbeth: *Geese*, villain?
Answer:         *Authors*, sir.'

Now, of these 'ten thousand authors', there are actually nineteen hundred and eighty-seven poets, all alive at this moment, whatever their works may be, as their booksellers well know; and amongst these there are several who possess a far greater reputation than mine, although considerably less than yours. It is owing to this neglect on the part of your German translators that you are not aware of the works of [William Wordsworth, who has a baronet in London who draws him frontispieces and leads him about to dinners and to the play; and a Lord in the country, who gave him a place in the Excise – and a cover at his table. You do not know perhaps that this Gentleman is the greatest of all poets past – present and to come – besides which he has written an *Opus Magnum* in prose – during the late election for Westmoreland. His principal publication is entitled *Peter Bell* which he had withheld from the public for '*one and twenty years*' – to the irreparable

---

[1] Brandl, op. cit., pp. 31 f. Albermarle St, London, January 1830.
[2] *Tagebücher*, xii, p. 189.
[3] *Letters and Journals*, v, pp. 100 ff. Dated from Ravenna, October 14, 1820. The two passages in square brackets are those which Moore omitted from the *Life*.

loss of all those who died in the interim, and will have no opportunity
of reading it before the resurrection.] There is also another named
[Southey, who is more than a poet, being actually poet Laureate, – a
post which corresponds with what we call in Italy *Poeta Cessareo*, and
which you call in German – I know not what; but as you have a
'*Caesar*' – probably you have a name for it. In England there is no
*Caesar* – only the Poet.]

By this time Goethe must have been asking himself impatiently
why Byron should be wasting his time over two quite irrelevant
poets, whom he had no intention of reading, knowing quite
enough about Southey from *The Vision of Judgment*, and nothing
whatsoever about Wordsworth. As to the allusions to the Excise
and so on, he could make neither head nor tale of them, and
didn't want to:

I mention these poets by way of sample to enlighten you. They form
but two bricks of our Babel, (WINDSOR bricks, by the way,) but
may serve for a specimen of the building.

Goethe was quite ready to take this on trust, WINDSOR bricks
and all; but why should it be supposed to concern him?

It is, moreover, asserted that 'the predominant character of the
whole body of the present English poetry is a *disgust* and *contempt* for
life'. But I rather suspect that by one single work of *prose, you* yourself,
have excited a greater contempt for life than all the English volumes
of poesy that ever were written. Madame de Stael says, that 'Werther
has occasioned more suicides than the most beautiful woman'; and I
really believe that he has put more individuals out of this world than
Napoleon himself, except in the way of his profession.

A heavy frown was beginning to darken Goethe's broad
Olympian brow. To find Byron teasing him about the suicides
supposedly occasioned by *Werther*, and quoting that maddening
woman Germaine de Staël, was enough to put him out of all
patience. Was he never to hear the end of that unfortunate novel?
And what did Byron mean by raking it up in a dedicatory letter'
A 'playful style' was one thing, but sweeping assertions fringi‧
the libellous were quite another; and now listen to this:

Perhaps, Illustrious Sir, the acrimonious judgment passed by a
celebrated northern journal upon you in particular, and the Germans
in general, has rather indisposed you towards English poetry as well
as criticism. But you must not regard our critics, who are at bottom
good-natured fellows, considering their two professions – taking up the
law in court, and laying it down out of it. No one can more lament
their hasty and unfair judgment, in your particular, than I do; and
I so expressed myself to your Friend Schlegel, in 1816, at Coppet.

Goethe's friend Schlegel? Say rather his renegade disciple, dis-
loyal to the core, and probably in his heart as pleased as Punch
about that article in *The Edinburgh Review*. But to suppose for one
moment that Goethe could be influenced in his literary opinions
by any fatuous judgments of the journalists was to show how little
Byron really knew him, quite apart from the fact that the passages
quoted had been written earlier. No wonder young Murray had
feared that Goethe might take offence; he was more than half
inclined to do so; but meanwhile he read on:

In behalf of my 'ten thousand' living brethren, and of myself, I have
thus far taken notice of an opinion with regard to 'English poetry' in
general, and which merited notice, because it was YOURS.

There was something soothing about those capitals; and after
all Goethe *had* rather emphasized the gloomy side of English
literature in general, and of Byron in particular. His brow began
to clear:

My principal object in addressing you was to testify my sincere
respect and admiration of a man, who, for half a century, has led the
literature of a great nation, and will go down to posterity as the first
literary Character of his Age.

This was more promising, and Goethe smiled:

You have been fortunate, Sir, not only in the writings which have
illustrated your name, but in the name itself, as being sufficiently
musical for the articulation of posterity. In this you have the advantage
of some of your countrymen, whose names would perhaps be immortal
also – if any body could pronounce them.

The smile wavered and vanished. This was too much; another
sign of that lack of respect in Byron which his high rank unfortunately created:

It may, perhaps, be supposed, by this apparent tone of levity, that
I am wanting in intentional respect towards you; but this will be a
mistake: I am always flippant in prose. Considering you, as I really
and warmly do, in common with all your own, and with most other
nations, to be by far the first literary Character which has existed in
Europe since the death of Voltaire, I felt, and feel, desirous to inscribe
to you the following work, – *not* as being either a tragedy or a *poem*,
(for I cannot pronounce upon its pretensions to be either one or the
other, or both, or neither,) but as a mark of esteem and admiration
from a foreigner to the man who has been hailed in Germany 'THE
GREAT GOETHE'.

> I have the honour to be,
> With the truest respect,
> Your most obedient and
> Very humble servant,
> BYRON.

BYRON. . . . Not very humble, and not truly respectful; and yet animated by a feeling for Goethe which had prompted him to inscribe not only *Marino Faliero* but *Sardanapalus* and *Werner* as well to 'the first literary Character of his Age'. And now here was a postscript which would probably undo all the good the last paragraph had done:

I perceive that in Germany, as well as in Italy, there is a great struggle about what they call '*Classical*' and '*Romantic*', – terms which were not subjects of classification in England, at least when I left it four or five years ago. Some of the English Scribblers, it is true, abused Pope and Swift, but the reason was that they themselves did not know how to write either prose or verse; but nobody thought them worth making a sect of. Perhaps there may be something of the kind sprung up lately, but I have not heard much about it, and it would be such bad taste that I shall be very sorry to believe it.

Little did Byron know that the struggle between classical and romantic which he thought in such bad taste was to be symbolized by THE GREAT GOETHE in a *Classical-Romantical Phantasmagoria*, in which, as the idolized offspring of both, he was cast for the part of a falling star. Ten years ago since he wrote those scornful words over which Goethe was brooding now; ten years ago, and six since he had died; and the letter he himself had never sent had found its way in the end. The wheel had come full circle at last.

But it had not come to rest. Its immediate effect upon Goethe can only be imagined; for he did not confide in Eckermann nor anyone else. *This* dedication was not handed about and shown to his friends. It was received, read and digested in silence, whilst Goethe came to terms with the bitter fact that the brightest jewel in his crown of fame was flawed by mischief and mockery. And unhappily this was not knowledge which he could keep to himself. A year later, in January 1831, he received from John Murray Junior the promised copy of Byron's *Life*; and there was the letter in print; 'written', said Tom Moore airily, 'in the poet's most whimsical and mocking mood'.[1] This publicity was all the harder to bear because Goethe himself had taken such pains to instruct public opinion fully on the subject of Byron's admiration and esteem, both in the Memoir written for Medwin's *Conversations* and also in his unsolicited contribution to this very book, purveyed by Crabb Robinson:

The complete edition of Byron's works, including the *Life* by Moore, contains a statement of the connection between Goethe and Byron. At the time of my interviews with Goethe, the *Life* was actually under his

[1] Moore, p. 459.

biographer's hands. Goethe was by no means indifferent to the account which was to be given to the world of that connection, and was desirous of contributing all in his power to its completeness. For that purpose he put into my hands the lithographic dedication of *Sardanapalus* to himself and all the original papers which had passed between them. He permitted me to take them to the hotel with me, with liberty to do with them what I liked; in other words, I was to copy them. And I added to my copies such recollections as I was then able to supply of Goethe's remarks on Byron. These filled a very closely written folio letter. On my return to England I enquired of Mr Murray, to whom I sent the letter, whether he had received it. At first he said he had, and that it had come too late to be of use. Then he said that Moore had had it. But, seeing Moore at Sam Rogers', he assured me that he had never heard of it.[1]

Things were evidently going on in Albemarle St in much the same way as during Byron's lifetime. But Crabb Robinson's timely enquiry must have jogged someone's memory; for Byron's letter to Goethe from Leghorn appeared in the *Life*, taken from Robinson's copy. Moore also gave a translation of Goethe's contribution to Medwin's *Conversations* with the poem in the original German; so that one way and another the picture was fairly complete. From Goethe's point of view indeed it was too well documented; for, in addition to the dedication of *Marino Faliero*, Moore mischievously printed an English version of the review of *Manfred* with a galling introductory comment:

The grave confidence with which the venerable critic traces the fancies of his brother poet to real persons and events, making no difficulty even of a double murder at Florence to furnish grounds for his theory, affords an amusing instance of the disposition so prevalent throughout Europe, to picture Byron as a man of marvels and mysteries, as well in his life as his poetry. To these exaggerated, or wholly false notions of him, the numerous fictions palmed upon the world . . . have, no doubt, considerably contributed; and the consequence is, so utterly out of truth and nature are the representations of his life and character long current upon the Continent, that it may be questioned whether the real 'flesh and blood' hero of these pages . . . may not, to the exalted imaginations of most of his foreign admirers, appear but an ordinary, unromantic, and prosaic personage.[2]

The venerable critic, thus blandly convicted of palming sensational fiction about Byron on the world, was suffering a belated Nemesis, which Tom Moore had long intended should overtake him; but to Goethe it must have appeared a piece of audacity on

---

[1] Robertson, op. cit., p. 109; quoting Crabb Robinson's unpublished *Reminiscences* in the Dr Williams Library. Cf. also Sadler, ii, p. 434; and Biedermann, op. cit., v, p. 107.
[2] Moore, p. 448.

a par with his printing the dedication to *Marino Faliero* which Byron had suppressed, keeping all the jokes at Goethe's expense and omitting the far more telling ridicule poured over Wordsworth and Southey. What is more, not a word was said in the whole of the *Life* about the flattering dedication to *Sardanapalus*, a copy of which, as Goethe well knew, was in Moore's hands. It would have needed the temper of a saint to take all this in good part, and:

... the old gentleman is now eighty years old, and so it is hardly surprising that the clouds of incense sometimes go to his head, and that it is then incomprehensible to him how other people have the nerve to exist at all.[1]

Leaving Byron out of it (and he had after all withdrawn the dedication), Tom Moore had displayed considerably more nerve than that by publishing the 'literary curiosity', and should if possible be made to smart for it. Dignity forbade recriminations but demanded satisfaction; and Goethe procured this indirectly by writing cordially and composedly to John Murray Junior fourteen months after receiving his letter and enclosure and three months after the arrival of Moore's *Life of Lord Byron*:

It is now more than a year, my very dear Sir, since I received your kind letter with its agreeable enclosure; and now, although late in the day, let me assure you that the remarkable manuscript missive of the highly honoured Lord Byron was and has remained of the utmost value to me. For every utterance of such a man is important, particularly when he indulges in mischievous invective and lively polemical satire.[2]

The allusion to the Wordsworth-Southey passages was clear enough; Goethe proceeded to underline it:

The sheet you have sent me has now gained greater importance, since it has lately been printed, but with the omission of certain passages, which I, who possess the whole, am in a position to supply. From these passages I learn what his attitude was towards persons whose productions it was quite impossible for him to admire, even though a wide public finds them to its taste.

The implication is obvious: these two poets (whose works were unknown to Goethe) were clearly beneath contempt, since Byron despised them; and that being the case, it could do no harm to hint that should the occasion arise, Goethe would print the passages deriding them. It was more important at the moment, however, to focus attention on the letter from Leghorn, whose

[1] K. v. Holtei, *Vierzig Jahre*, 4th ed., Breslau, 1898: II, p. 205. Johanna Schopenauer to Karl von Holtei from Weimar, February 19, 1829.
[2] *Briefe*, xlvii, pp. 164 f. March 29, 1831. Original in German.

tone was certainly warranted to take the sting out of the mockeries publicized in Moore's *Life*:

I have attempted to prove my interest in that important work by sending through Mr Robinson a copy of that much prized letter with which Lord Byron rejoiced my heart from Leghorn, and it has accordingly now been printed.

As for Moore's insolent assumption that, because Goethe was a foreigner, he was unable to understand 'the social, practical-minded, and, with all his faults and eccentricities, *English* Lord Byron',[1] there was an obvious answer to that:

But I feel sad to think that Lord Byron, who showed himself so impatient with the fickle public, did not live to learn how well the Germans understood him and how highly we value him.

Yes indeed; and one of them could have written a far better appraisal than Moore's and had half a mind to try:

In our country all the transient tittle-tattle of the world counts for nothing, and the man and his talent alone remain resplendent in their glory. And in this connection I venture to assert that whoever, now or in the future, succeeds in forming an approximately true estimate of this extraordinary personality, recognising it in all its uniqueness, without praise or blame, will be able to congratulate himself on the enrichment of his life. I at least for my part find extreme pleasure in this endeavour.

Goethe, with that double murder at Florence on his conscience, should have been the last person to adopt a high and mighty tone about tittle-tattle. But it is difficult to withhold admiration on reading his rousing tribute to Byron which was at the same time by implication the annihilation of Tom Moore; and it is also difficult not to rejoice that the Irishman was there as a whipping-boy, deputizing on this occasion for the British aristocracy; and as Tom dearly loved a Lord he had no real cause to complain. Better Goethe's wrath with him than an eleventh-hour rejection of Byron after so many attempts had been withstood to wean him from his idol, efforts in which the idol himself had so perversely collaborated: by his hypochondria, by *Don Juan*, by his disastrous expedition to Greece, by his revolutionary leanings, and now by his irreverence, hardest of all to forgive. Medwin's *Conversations* had hinted at feet of clay; General Congreve and Crabb Robinson had muttered about wood and stone. But Goethe had been proof against all this and had been sustained by other factors: the inscription to *Sardanapalus*, the letter from Leghorn, Parry with his *Last Days of Lord Byron*, the English nobility in the guise of scape-

[1] Moore, p. 448.

goats, and now Thomas Moore, whose wicked sense of humour recoiled upon himself and resulted in Goethe's last defiant tribute to a genius resplendent and unique.

A few days later the old poet and the crazy angel were bending together over a red portfolio, looking through the papers concerning Byron which were then entrusted to Ottilie 'for further ordering'.[1] So the 'little collection' was to be published at last, but whether the 'literary curiosity' were to be included or not we cannot tell, since the contemplated edition never saw the light of day; but we may be sure that Ottilie would have lent 'her' note to swell the slender volume. Otherwise there was nothing in Byron's handwriting but the inscription to *Sardanapalus* and the letter from Leghorn; for that was all there had ever been.

[1] *Tagebücher*, xii, pp. 56 f. April 3, 1821.

# PART III

## SYNTHESIS

# CHAPTER VI

# Life and Literature

THE unpredictable nature of life is strikingly apparent in the drama of the human relationship played out *sub rosa* between Byron and Goethe; so much *sub rosa* indeed that posterity has remained unaware of it until the present day, and unaware, too, of the resultant effect upon twentieth-century life. Nothing could have been more dependent on the workings of mere chance than the beginning, middle and end of an action which, had it been engaged between ordinary mortals, would have left no trace behind. If young Theodore Lyman had not presented Goethe with a copy of *Manfred* . . . if someone called Rupprecht had not been moved to send Byron a pile of *Deutsche Gazettes* . . . if Wagner's uncle had not felt impelled to write a plaguy long dissertation, the tangled tale of the dedications would not be there to unravel; and there would be far less unravelling to do but for the frenzied imagination of Caroline Lamb, the malice of Ticknor, the haverings and waverings of Murray and Kinnaird, the unwitting interposition of George Bancroft, the tenacity of Professor Benecke and the rashness of John Murray III. The one constant factor throughout was Goethe's indestructible regard for Byron; the irresistible force came from Byron, in whose hands the initiative lay during his lifetime and after. For even when he was dead he kept in touch with Goethe: through Medwin, through Parry, through Kinnaird and Benecke, through Stroganov and through John Murray Junior: praising him and stinging him; goading and flattering; venerating and teasing, and finally telling him those home truths which he had suppressed when alive. Goethe's emotional reactions were no less varied; grief, vexation and enchantment struggled for mastery, till the mounting tide of enthusiasm swept all before it, including Byron's light-hearted mockeries.

For it was no longer even in Byron's power to alienate Goethe; and it seems safe to assume that he would no more have withstood the English poet in person than he had done in print. They would have been obliged to converse in Italian, since Byron could manage neither German nor French and Goethe was tongue-tied in English. Goethe's Italian was getting rather rusty; Byron spoke it fluently, indeed almost like a native. Who would have held the floor? There is no knowing and no telling. But if those two great personalities had ever found themselves together in the chaise which once carried Goethe and Stroganov, something even more remarkable than the transformation the Russian had witnessed would have taken place, for

Byron's power of attaching those about him to his person was such as no one I ever knew possessed. No human being could approach him without being sensible of this magical influence. There was something commanding, but not overawing in his manner. He was neither grave nor gay out of place, and he seemed always made for that company in which he happened to find himself.[1]

Leigh Hunt for one and Trelawny for another would have disagreed vociferously about the 'magical influence'; but Mary Shelley (as has been seen) would have subscribed to it; and it is particularly reassuring to hear from Byron's life-long friend that he would not have been 'gay out of place'. That one danger removed, one can only presume a greater state of enchantment in Goethe than before.

And Byron? Goethe could be quite as irresistible as the younger man when the spirit moved him. He completely conquered Cogswell and Stroganov and many others who were violently prejudiced against him, by his personal charm. He would have deployed it to the full for Byron; there would have been no stiffness and dignity to overcome. Meeting on equal terms, each would have made an indelible impression on the other; but it is more than likely that only Byron's effect upon Goethe would have borne fruit. That the older man would have been refreshed, rejuvenated and inspired by the encounter seems certain from all that has been said and shown; but the result for Byron is less easy to gauge; so elusive, so lonely was that enigmatic spirit, that perhaps only Shelley among his contemporaries ever came close enough to affect it. Certainly Leigh Hunt's sanctimonious observations, tinged with malignancy, do not carry much conviction:

I believe that if anybody could have done good to Lord Byron, it was Goethe and his correspondence. It was a pity he did not live to have more of it. Goethe might possibly have enabled him, as he wished he could, 'to know himself', and do justice to the yearnings after the good and beautiful inseparable from the nature of genius. But the danger was, that he would have been influenced as much by the rank and reputation of that great man, as by the reconciling nobleness of his philosophy; and personal intercourse with him would have spoilt all. Lord Byron's nature was mixed up with too many sophistications to receive a proper impression from any man; and he would have been jealous, if he once took it in his head that the other was thought to be his superior.[2]

---

[1] Broughton, op. cit., iii, p. 41. May 16, 1824.
[2] L. Hunt, *Lord Byron and some of his Contemporaries*, London, 1828, pp. 89 f.

What Leigh Hunt did not know (and the knowledge would have greatly disconcerted him) was the extent of the power Byron exercised over Goethe's mind, a strange remote control which was to affect both literature and history, and which completely precluded any such influence of Goethe over him. The 'reconciling nobleness' of Goethe's philosophy, on the contrary, was to be given a Byronic bias towards the end.

The power was real enough; but it was not generated by any profound knowledge of the literature created by Byron, nor by any true understanding of it, although a significant exception must be made for the complex of apocalyptic writings. The reviews of *Manfred* and *Don Juan* were mere temperamental reactions to Byron's personality as revealed in those two works; but the review of *Cain* is in a different category. This was not only because, when Goethe read it, he was passionately predisposed in Byron's favour on account of the dedication to *Sardanapalus*; it swayed his judgment for another reason, appealing together with *Heaven and Earth* and *The Vision of Judgment* to those rebellious depths within himself which answered to the call of the insurgent depths in Byron. This was crucial: what is sometimes labelled Satanism, for which Goethe was to find a different name, was responsible for the fact that the review of *Cain*, written in 1824, was the only full-length statement of any value about a work of Byron's which ever came from Goethe's pen, and as such it demands an extended quotation:

This poet, whose burning spiritual vision penetrates beyond all comprehension into the past and the present and, in their train, also into the future, has now conquered new worlds for his boundless talent; and no human being can foresee what he will achieve with them. His method on the other hand can already be defined with some exactitude.

He holds to the letter of the Biblical tradition. By making the first human pair barter their original purity and innocence for a guilt mysteriously induced, and by making the penalty thus incurred the inheritance of all their descendants, he lays an enormous burden on the shoulders of Cain as the representative of disaffected humanity, plunged into abject misery owing to no transgression of its own. The primeval son of man, bowed down beneath this load of sin, is tormented by the thought of death, of which he has yet no conception; and although he may wish the end of his present wretchedness, to exchange it for a state utterly unknown seems to him still more repugnant. From this it is already clear that the full burden of a dogmatic theology, expository, interposing, and perpetually in conflict with itself – a theology which still preoccupies us – has been laid on the shoulders of the first distressful son of man.

These calamities, to which humanity is no stranger, surge in his soul and cannot be allayed by the resigned meekness of his father and brother, nor by the loving and soothing ministrations of his sister-wife.

To aggravate them beyond endurance, Satan now appears, a power-fully seductive spirit, who first unsettles him morally and then leads him miraculously through all worlds, showing him the past as colossally great, the present as small and trivial, the future without consolation.

He returns to his own people, more distraught but not worse than he was before; and finding everything in the family going on in the same way, he feels the importunity of Abel in forcing him to take part in the sacrifice to be utterly intolerable. We say no more than that the scene in which Abel is killed is wonderfully prepared, and what follows is equally great and beyond praise. There lies Abel! This is death, of which we have heard so much, and the race of man knows just as much about it as before.

But we must not forget that through the whole piece there runs a kind of presentiment of the coming Saviour, and that in this as in all other points, the poet has succeeded in approximating to our inter-pretations and doctrines.

Of the scene with the parents, when Eve finally curses the silent Cain, a scene which our Western neighbour has so admirably singled out for praise, there is nothing more to be said; we can only approach the conclusion with awe and admiration.

A gifted lady of our acquaintance, akin to us in her great esteem for Byron, expressed the opinion that everything that can be said religiously or morally in the whole world is contained in the last three words of the piece.[1]

The gifted lady was almost certainly Ottilie, whose defence of the piety of *Cain* was noted by Chancellor Müller; and Goethe evidently agreed with her in seeing a profound significance in the concluding line:

> CAIN:   And *he* who lieth there was childless! I
>         Have dried the fountain of a gentle race,
>
> .     .     .     .
>
>         O Abel!
> ADAH:   Peace be with him!
> CAIN:                    But with *me*![2]

It is clear enough from this review that Goethe was heart and soul with Byron in his implicit protest against the mercilessness of the old dispensation; and his particular dislike of the English clergy (inflamed to fever-heat in his clash with the Bishop of Derry) lent still greater ardour to his championship of *Cain*:

'One sees', he said, 'how the inadequacy of the Church doctrines preyed on such a free spirit as Byron's, and how he sought to free himself by means of this work from a doctrine which had been forced upon him. The English clergy will probably not thank him for doing so; but I shall be surprised if he does not go on to treat kindred Biblical

[1] Cf. *Werke*, xli, 2, pp. 94 ff., for the complete text. 'Our Western neighbour' was the author of the French review. See above, pp. 95f.

[2] *Poetry*, v, p. 275.

subjects, such as the destruction of Sodom and Gomorrha, which he will surely not allow to escape him.'[1]

I said that I had been reading *Cain* during the last few days, and had particularly admired the third act and the motivation of the murder.

'Yes indeed,' said Goethe, 'the motivation is admirable and so unique in its beauty as not to be found a second time in the world.'

'*Cain*,' said I, 'was nevertheless prohibited in England at first; but everyone reads it now, and travelling young Englishmen generally have a complete Byron with them.'

'What folly it was,' said Goethe, 'for at bottom there is nothing in the whole of *Cain* that the English bishops do not teach themselves.'[2]

... Goethe preferred to all the other serious poems of Byron, the *Heaven and Earth*, though it seemed almost satire when he exclaimed: 'A bishop might have written it!' He added, Byron should have lived to execute his vocation. 'And that was?' I asked. 'To dramatise the Old Testament. What a subject under his hands would be the Tower of Babel!' ... It was the devilish parts of these Old Testament poems that he excessively praised. He called Adam a Philistine and Abel a country parson.[3]

– 'you must not take it evil, but Byron owes these fine views of the Old Testament to the ennui he suffered at school. – He must have been terribly annoyed at the absurdities and in his own mind he ruminated over them and turned them to account.'[4]

'It was the devilish parts'; allowing for Robinson's choice of epithet, this squares completely with Goethe's enthusiasm for *The Vision of Judgment*; and if he overestimated *Cain*, he did so in good company. Walter Scott declared that in this 'very grand and tremendous drama' Byron had matched Milton on his own ground; and Shelley hailed it as an apocalyptic vision not hitherto communicated to man. Goethe, equally awe-stricken, acclaimed the religious rebel in Byron whom he viewed with entirely different eyes from the political liberator; but they were two complementary elements of the one nature, witnessing to the basic principle of Byron's thought and the unity and integrity of his being. Yet *Cain* has not worn so well as the testimonies of Goethe, Shelley and Scott seemed to predict. The boldness of the onslaught on Church dogma has done its work. It is impossible today to recapture either the sense of outrage or of release which the dramatic mystery produced in its own times. Moreover (*pace* Sir Walter) Byron utterly failed to attain to the grand manner of Milton; and more to the point he fell noticeably short of his own highest level. This

[1] Eckermann, p. 87. February 24, 1824.
[2] Ibid., p. 251. June 20, 1827. Cf. Medwin, p. 150. 'I ... made the snake a snake, and took a Bishop for my interpreter.'
[3] Sadler, ii, p. 435  August 1829.
[4] *Gespräche*, ii, p. 609. August 17, 1829, Crabb Robinson.

is all the stranger because the whole power of his mind was behind the drama, but it was a mind which could not master the medium of dramatic blank verse. With the possible exception of *Manfred*, where he was sustained by the passionate lyricism of *The Dream* and *Darkness*, all his dramas exhibit the same fatal flaw, and give the impression of a right-handed man attempting to write with his left. Innately and intensely subjective, and yet imbued with the sense of universal, indeed cosmic, tragedy, he aimed at communicating this in his plays by dramatic objectivity; but he only achieved it partially and at the expense of all the poetry that was in him. The incomparable strength and energy, the soaring eloquence of his great works in rhymed metres are absent from his blank verse dramas. At his best he is rhetorical in this medium; at his second-best he is laboured; and at his worst he is pedestrian, as too often, and with dire effect, in *Cain*. As far as *Cain* was concerned, this was hardly noticed by his contemporaries, too much stunned, dazzled or scandalized by the content to be susceptible to the form. But, even if only by its subconscious effect, Byron's blank verse is surely responsible to a great extent for his still persisting failure to capture the stage. For neither are all his dramas negligible, nor are they all undramatic. When attentively read and analysed with the skill and care of Samuel Chew, or the imaginative sympathy of Wilson Knight, the Venetian dramas and *Sardanapalus* reveal surprising depths and intense dramatic power. Any producer worth his salt could prove that, if slightly shortened, they are perfectly fitted for the stage. But who could speak them? Who could infuse the breath of real poetic life into their lagging rhythms? *Sardanapalus*, most fascinating of themes, might inspire the actors; but even then the blank verse would be a formidable obstacle to interpretation.

This bar to understanding and enjoyment did not operate with Goethe; he was tone-deaf to the sound of Byron's dramas and judged them by their sense. Judging on those grounds, he saw Byron's main achievement to lie in the field of tragedy and ranked him with Shakespeare, at times only just below him, at other times at some considerable distance. After reading Medwin he told Müller that, though Byron was a giant beside Pope or Wieland, he was only a dwarf beside Shakespeare. Few will quarrel with that order of merit; but Goethe did not keep to it, declaring to Eckermann somewhat later that Byron was Shakespeare's equal in everything but 'pure individuality'. Byron was well aware of this, he added, and rarely referred to Shakespeare, although he knew whole passages off by heart; but he would have liked to deny him because Shakespeare's serenity stood in his way. This is a transparent allusion to the occasion recorded by Medwin when Byron, having spoken disparagingly of Shakespeare, quoted a whole speech in *Troilus and Cressida* as an example of fine poetry, adding disconcertingly:

But what has poetry to do with a play, or in a play?[1]

It was perhaps a half-confession that his own dramas were barren of poetry; but Goethe did not miss its presence, or at least not consciously; yet it only needed a book of engravings representing Shakespeare's characters for the power of the great Elizabethan to overwhelm him completely and almost obliterate Byron in the process:

It is awe-inspiring to glance through this book and realise again the infinite richness and greatness of Shakespeare. There is not a single aspect of the life of man which he has not represented and given expression to. And everything with such ease and mastery! Words fail one when it comes to Shakespeare; they are totally inadequate. I dabbled about with him in my *Wilhelm Meister*, but what did it signify? He is not a poet for the theatre, he never thought of the stage which was far too narrow for his mighty mind; indeed the whole visible world was too narrow for him. He is too bewilderingly great and rich. A creative poet should only read one of his plays a year unless he wishes to be annihilated. I did well to rid myself of him in my *Götz von Berlichingen* and my *Egmont*; and Byron was well advised not to be overawed by him, but to go his own way. How many excellent Germans have not been ruined by Shakespeare; by him and by Calderon.[2]

The notion that Shakespeare did not write for the stage was a fixed idea with Goethe at the time; and it was one of the characteristics which, in his view, Byron shared with Shakespeare:

... I had been enraptured, during a dialogue about the great Briton which had lasted longer than usual one afternoon in the garden, by the manner in which he had concentrated and mastered the whole being and essence of such a genius. We had come to Shakespeare from Lord Byron, the points of contact being so near and then again so far. I had remarked how extraordinary it was that Byron, who had been occupied for some time with theatrical management, had yet completely misunderstood its nature, as all his dramas clearly proved; and that even *Marino Faliero* and *The Two Foscari*, produced as he had written them, would fail altogether of their effect on the general public. – 'My dear child,' answered Goethe in that well-known way of his, 'I will tell you something: Shakespeare didn't understand the stage either, but that didn't matter, for he didn't need it.'[3]

---

[1] Cf. Eckermann, p. 149. February 24, 1825, and Medwin, pp. 105 ff. The quotation was taken from Act III, Scene iii.
[2] Eckermann, p. 167. December 25, 1825.
[3] *Gespräche*, ii, p. 542; 1826 or later. O. L. B. Wolff, improvisor and author.

It is clear from these allusions that Goethe gave Byron Shake-spearean rank as a dramatist. *Cain* had won for Byron a place by Goethe's side, and *Marino Faliero* a position near Shakespeare's. Some time back we left him telling Eckermann that, had he still been the director of the Weimar theatre, he would have made it his business to produce that drama:

> It is true that the piece is too long and would have to be shortened; but nothing in it should be cut out or eliminated. The content of every scene should be assimilated and then reproduced in a shorter form. In that way the piece would be pulled together without being injured by alterations, and it would gain throughout in powerful effect, without losing any of its essential beauty.[1]

The technique of 'boiling down' as against 'cutting out' had already been advocated by Goethe when speaking about *Hamlet* in *Wilhelm Meister*; it shows how far from sacrosanct the actual language of either dramatist was to their would-be producer. It was the characterization, the dramatic invention and the local colour (as he pointed out to General Congreve) which impressed him in *Marino Faliero*, the objective historical reality:

> Byron too, in spite of his strongly dominant personality, had on occasions the power to suppress himself completely, as can be seen in some of his plays and particularly in *Marino Faliero*. When reading this piece, one completely forgets that it was written by Byron, or indeed by an Englishman. We live in it wholly in Venice and wholly at the period when the action takes place. The *dramatis personae* speak entirely in accordance with their characters and circumstances, without having anything of the subjective feelings, thoughts and opinions of their author. That is the right way.[2]

It is indeed difficult to remember that Byron was the author of *Marino Faliero*, bereft as it is of his most shining qualities; but, although *The Two Foscari* is in like case, there is a strong subjective element in Jacopo Foscari's laments on the theme of unwilling exile and the cruelty of his native land. But this was not the reason why Goethe, although he admired it greatly, did not rank this play among his favourites:

> We then spoke of *The Two Foscari*, and I made the remark that Byron drew women excellently.
> 'His women,' said Goethe, 'are good. But then womanhood is the only vessel which has remained to us moderns into which to pour our ideals. There is nothing to be done with men. In Achilles and Odysseus, the bravest and the wisest, Homer has anticipated us all.'
> 'In addition,' I continued, '*The Two Foscari* has something dis-

---

[1] Eckermann, p. 145. February 24, 1825.
[2] Ibid., pp. 728 f. March 14, 1830.

quieting about it on account of the pervasiveness of the torture and the rack; and indeed it is difficult to understand how Byron could live at the heart of such a painful subject long enough to finish the play.'

'That kind of thing was absolutely Byron's element,' said Goethe; 'he was an eternal self-tormentor and such subjects were always his favourite themes, as you can see in all his works where there is hardly one serene subject to be found. But all the same, you will agree that the presentation of *The Two Foscari* is admirable too?'

'It is excellent,' I said, 'every word is strong, significant and going straight to the point. And in fact I have not yet found one weak line in Byron's works. He always seems to me to be coming up out of the waves of the sea fresh, and impregnated with elemental power.'

'You are quite right,' said Goethe, 'it is so.'[1]

Eckermann has sometimes been suspected of fathering his own opinions on Goethe; but in this case it almost looks as if the reverse process had taken place. At the very least, however, Goethe emphatically confirmed the statement that there was not one weak line in Byron's works; and this of the poet, uniquely notorious among great poets for his sins in that respect; and this, too, in connection with his dramas, so much disfigured by weak lines, to give them no harsher description.

In so far as Goethe's opinions about Byron's poetry were ever impersonal and dispassionate, his views about the two Venetian tragedies can be said to have been so. He sympathized too deeply with the trend of the Biblical dramas for completely objective criticism; and personal pride blurred his vision when he read *Werner*, causing him to refer to it publicly as one of Byron's most admirable works, and bracketing it together with *Sardanapalus* in private conversation. *Werner* is a turgidly romantic drama deriving from a German tale, a fact which would certainly not have recommended it to Goethe, had he been judging it dispassionately. *Sardanapalus* is in a different category altogether: psychologically absorbing and deeply moving, it represents Byron's high-water mark as a dramatist. As such Goethe acclaimed it on receiving his dedicatory copy, giving reasons for calling it his favourite among all Byron's dramas, which show that it had in some special way captured his imagination; and one would be willing to concede that this was a critical rather than a subjectively biased judgment, were it not that only a few months later he was to be heard paying an even greater tribute to *The Deformed Transformed*:

'I have', he said, 're-read his *Deformed Transformed*, and I must say that the greatness of his talent grows upon me more and more. His devil derives from my Mephistopheles, but it is no imitation. Every-

---

[1] Eckermann, pp. 255 f. July 5, 1827. John Nichol actually attributed this paragraph to Goethe. Luckily Arnold, who was very severe on Nichol for omitting Goethe's stricture on Byron's childishness, did not notice this blunder.

thing is absolutely original and new, everything is concise, excellent and brilliant. There is not one weak passage in the whole piece, not a spot as large as a pin's head devoid of invention and genius. Were it not that his hypochondria and negative attitude stand in his way, he would be as great as Shakespeare and the Ancients.' I expressed my surprise. 'Yes', said Goethe, 'you can take it from me. I have been studying him afresh, and I feel more and more obliged to concede this to him.'[1]

Eckermann, considerably taken aback, made all haste to read this masterpiece, and brought up the subject again a few weeks later:

'I am right, am I not?' said he. 'The first scenes are great, and not only that, but poetically great. The rest, where it falls apart and comes to the siege of Rome, I will not praise for its poetry, but its brilliance must be granted.'

'In the highest degree,' said I; 'but it is easy to be brilliant if one has no respect for anything.'

Goethe laughed. 'You are not altogether wrong,' he said; 'It must be allowed that the poet says more than one likes. He speaks the truth, but it makes us uncomfortable and one would prefer him to be silent. There are things in the world that it would be better the poet should conceal rather than reveal. But then that is Byron's nature, and one would destroy him if one wanted him to be different.'

'Yes,' I said, 'he is superlatively witty. For instance, what a striking passage this is:
"The Devil speaks truth much oftener than he's deemed,
     He hath an ignorant audience".'

'That is certainly quite as frank and free as anything my Mephipheles ever said.'[2]

Allowing, as at this point I think it must be allowed, that Goethe when discoursing about Byron's poetical works was not unlike a blind man talking about colours, one cannot help suspecting that it was partly because an insufferable young man called 'Schelle' had incited Byron to commit to the flames this 'Faustish kind of drama', that Goethe was now giving it pride of place; but mainly because the author had stated in the Advertisement that it was founded 'partly on the Faust of the great Goëthe'; on such extraneous circumstances do aesthetic judgments at times depend. Goethe's on Byron were more than usually at the mercy of chance; and indeed the breathless impression of watching a race accompanies the effort to follow his shifting preferences among the poems and dramas in the field.

In 1817 Manfred, the favourite, led off in fine style and kept the lead until 1820, when it was overtaken by Polidori's Vampyre, a

[1] Eckermann, pp. 181 f. November 8, 1826.
[2] Ibid., p. 183. November 29, 1826.

rank outsider pounding past, and leaving that dark horse *Don Juan* almost at the post. In 1823 *Sardanapalus* and *Werner* raced forward, outdistancing *Manfred* whose pace was slackening, and who seemed hardly in the running when *Cain* shot ahead, only to be overhauled almost immediately by *Heaven and Earth*. Meanwhile *English Bards and Scotch Reviewers*, although sadly handicapped, was giving proof of more stamina than *Don Juan*; but both fell behind when *The Vision of Judgment* thundered by them, flashed forward and led the field, with another outsider, Wolfe's *General Moore*, hot on its heels. It was anyone's race in 1826, although one would have put one's money on the drama, with *Sardanapalus*, *Cain* and *Heaven and Earth* all in a bunch together, *Marino Faliero* and *The Two Foscari* panting close behind them, and that ungainly colt *The Deformed Transformed* (anything but a thoroughbred) gaining on them all. But finally in 1829 *The Vision of Judgment* was racing neck and neck for the winning-post with *Heaven and Earth*; *The Deformed Transformed* and *Cain* were half a length behind, *Manfred* was faint but pursuing, *Don Juan* was making a final spurt, and *Sardanapalus* had dropped out.

'But where is Harold?' as Byron so frequently asked during the course of that famous poem. Could the Childe have been a non-starter, or was he among the also-rans? Incredible though it must seem, he was never even entered, for he was consistently ignored by Goethe from beginning to end. He may have read the first two cantos; he certainly read Scott's review of Canto III in *The Quarterly* for February 16, 1816; and, as a fortnight later he announced the arrival of 'the newest things by Byron',[1] he probably possessed a copy; but the only reference he ever made to it was on June 18, 1817, when sending a book to Ottilie to give to her mother. In a covering note he announced that there were 'still all kinds of Harold-children, Chillon-prisoners and Dreams in the background';[2] and that was all. The most essentially Byronic of all the works, endowed with a momentum which sent it sweeping tumultuously onward through canto after canto to its magnificent conclusion escaped Goethe's notice entirely as far as one can tell; and the same holds good for the vast majority of the poems. Goethe read *The Corsair* and *Lara* with enthusiasm, *The Age of Bronze* and *The Island* without recorded comment; he remarked that *The Prisoner of Chillon* was modelled on the Ugolino episode in Dante's *Inferno*; but he had nothing to say about *The Giaour*, *The Bride of Abydos*, *The Siege of Corinth*, *Parisina*, *Prometheus*, *Tasso*, *The Dream*, *Churchill's Grave*, *The Monody on the Death of Sheridan*, *Darkness*, *Beppo*, *The Curse of Minerva* and *Mazeppa*. The

---

[1] *Tagebücher*, vi, p. 62. June 2 and 3, 1817.
[2] *Briefe*, xxviii, p. 131.

only lyrical poem he mentioned by name was in reality by Wolfe, although he certainly read some of the 'domestic' pieces. Except as a dramatist and a satirist Byron provoked no response from Goethe; and one can only marvel at so deep an impression created by an author, one of whose greatest works was ignored and the other viewed with disfavour; whilst the silence observed about *Tasso* and *Prometheus* is particularly perplexing. Goethe possessed copies of both; for *Prometheus* was bound up with *Chillon*, and Edward Everett had presented him with *Tasso*, two themes which Goethe had treated himself.

This coincidence (for neither knew anything about the other at the time of writing) is all the more remarkable because both poets so clearly identified themselves with their heroes, in the case of *Prometheus* under the cloak of mythological symbolism. Goethe represented the defiant, dynamic, rebellious and above all creative genius which possessed him in a dramatically lyrical outburst:

> Hier sitz' ich, forme Menschen
> Nach meinem Bilde,
> Ein Geschlecht, das mir gleich sei,
> Zu leiden, zu weinen,
> Zu geniessen und zu freuen sich,
> Und dein nicht zu achten,
> Wie ich!
>
> .        .        .        .
>
> Here I sit and form men
> In mine own image,
> A race to be like me:
> To suffer, to weep,
> To laugh and rejoice,
> And not to regard thee,
> Like me!

Language apart, the defiance has a Byronic flavour; but the exhilarating triumph of the challenge is Goethean, as that epithet was used in his youth; and so is the contemptuous side-glance at the indifference of the lord of the universe to the sufferings of mankind:

> Ich dich ehren? Wofür?
> Hast du die Schmerzen gelindert
> Je des Beladenen?
> Hast du die Tränen gestillet
> Je des Geängsteten?
>
> .        .        .        .
>
> Honour thee I? And why?
> Hast thou once lightened
> The pains of the burdened?
> Hast thou once tempered
> The tears of the wretched?

It was this aspect of the martyred Titan, the compassion for oppressed humanity, the Aeschylean aspect, which appealed to Byron and which he coloured with his own sufferings and sorrows:

> Titan! to whose immortal eyes
> The sufferings of mortality,
> Seen in their sad reality,
> Were not as things the gods despise;
> What was thy pity's recompense?
> A silent suffering, and intense;
> The rock, the vulture, and the chain,
> All that the proud can feel of pain,
> The agony they do not show,
> The suffocating sense of woe,
> Which speaks but in its loneliness,
> And then is jealous lest the sky
> Should have a listener, nor will sigh
> Until its voice be echoless.[1]

Goethe's youthful and vociferous Titan dwindles in the presence of Byron's tragic saviour, who is the creation of a much maturer mind, although the English poet was only two years older than Goethe had been when composing his dramatic monologue. But a whole world of suffering separated them, and the same is true of the two *Tassos*, in spite of the fact that the maturity here is all on Goethe's side. Byron's version is, like Goethe's *Prometheus*, an impassioned soliloquy; Goethe's *Tasso* is a five-act play which ranks with his major classical works. Both poets were once more drawing on their personal experience. Goethe was dramatizing the ceaseless and wearing conflict between two irreconcilable sides of his nature, and also his sufferings as a poet in the court circles of Weimar, symbolized by the much more excruciating situation of Tasso at Ferrara. Byron, pierced to the heart by the sight of the dungeon of Sant' Anna where Tasso lived under restraint for many years, was overcome by the bitter sense of his own persecution and ostracism and the nightmare fear of madness. Goethe's drama is a finished work of art, absorbing, indeed fascinating, subtle and penetrating; and yet, almost in the manner of Henry James, imbued with a certain deliberate subservience to current social values. Byron's *Lament*, much less finely wrought, is under no such restraint, giving the painful impression of listening-in to the ravings of the real Tasso, and inducing the shameful desire to stop one's ears. Goethe offered a precarious solution which might temporarily shelve an insoluble problem, and combined it with the metaphysical consolation that poets can express their agony in art. Byron's anguished hero also believes that his works will endure; but this brings no relief to his distracted mind.

[1] *Poetry*, iv, pp. 48 f.

Both Byron and Goethe adopted the legend of Tasso's passion for Leonore d'Este, and gave it an overriding part in the situation. Byron's torrential monologue therefore challenges a comparison with the three increasingly moving, despairing and distraught soliloquies of Goethe's Tasso in the fourth act. Contrasted with this delicate poetical sublimation, Byron has all the crudeness of stark reality which can never bear comparison with art, and which Goethe in particular shrank from contemplating. But if *The Lament of Tasso* is almost unbearable and distressingly strident, the half-demented hero is a tragic figure; and so, although one of much greater stature, is Byron's Prometheus. This is possibly the reason why Goethe passed them by in silence; for in his heart he was inimical to the tragic view of life, the metaphysical content of Byron's poetry as a whole, which Goethe deprecated as hypochondria. He might therefore have liked Byron less had he known his poetry better; and the more one reflects, the less that knowledge appears. Very slightly acquainted with his lyrics, disregarding *Childe Harold*, dismissing *Don Juan* and ignoring nearly everything else: what then remained? There remained the dramas, which he overestimated in bulk and misjudged in detail; there remained *English Bards and Scotch Reviewers*; and there remained the apocalyptic writings, first and foremost *The Vision of Judgment*. Mere literary criticism is silenced here. One need not and indeed one cannot go to Goethe for valid estimates of Byron's individual works, nor yet for a survey of his work as a whole. But one can, and I think one must agree with Robertson's judgment that Goethe's unswerving faith in the heaven-scaling genius of Byron was eternally to his credit.[1] Where that unswerving belief was finally to lead may appear no matter for general rejoicing; but the faith has a beauty of its own.

\*     \*     \*

Byron's knowledge of Goethe's works belonged to the region of hearsay and translation (whether oral or written), a world of muffled rumours and poetical shapes looming through the mists of an unknown language which he felt no irresistible desire to learn. As a lyrical poet, Goethe meant even less to Byron than Byron to Goethe, so that one could almost say he hardly knew Goethe at all. Moreover nothing less than a complete list of Goethe's works (which take up fifty-five volumes of the Weimar edition), omitting only *Werther*, *Faust* and *Die Wahlverwandtschaften*, could adequately illustrate Byron's ignorance of the works of his greatest contemporary. And yet he was alive and alert to their

[1] Cf. Robertson, op. cit., p. 124.

epoch-making nature, and full of an ardent desire to know more about *Faust* and its author:

Are there not designs from *Faust?* Send me some, and a translation of it, – if such there is. Also of Goethe's life if such there be; if not – the original German.[1]

Murray acted promptly for once, dispatching almost by return of post *A Series of Twenty-six Outlines illustrative of Goethe's Tragedy of Faust. . . . And an Analysis of the Tragedy* by F. A. M. Retzsch, London, 1820. Evidently the whole Pisan circle studied them, and Shelley for one was delighted with them:

We have just got the etchings of *Faust*, the painter is worthy of Goëthe. The meeting of him and Margaret is wonderful. It makes all the pulses of my head beat. . . . We have seen here a translation of some scenes, and indeed the most remarkable ones, accompanying those astonishing etchings, which have been published in England from a German master. It is not bad – and faithful enough – but how weak! how incompetent to represent *Faust.* . . . What etchings those are! I am never tired with looking at them; and, I fear, it is the only sort of translation of which *Faust* is susceptible.[2]

This must have been bad news for Byron, who had evidently caught fire from Shelley in the matter of *Faust*, but probably did not share Shelley's raptures over the etchings, which in reproduction hardly justify such enthusiasm. What with Shelley and Retzsch, however, Byron was now much better acquainted with Goethe's masterpiece than he had been when writing *Manfred*. The result was *The Deformed Transformed* where the influence is clearly apparent, but never a sign of inspiration. 'Only insufficient knowledge is creative', Goethe once declared; and here is proof of his assertion. Lewis's oral translation of *Faust*, if not precisely the germ of *Manfred*, was one of the seeds scattered on to fertile soil; whereas Shelley's illuminating comments and wonderful verse-renderings fell upon stony ground. They heightened Byron's admiration for *Faust* and impelled him to conscious imitation, where earlier he had been unconsciously swept along by the Faustian current which was the law of his own inner being; for the kinship between himself and Goethe lay in the restlessly questioning and searching spirit manifest in Goethe's masterpiece and in Byron's work as a whole. In so far as Byron was able half-intuitively to grasp the workings of Goethe's mind in *Faust*, he accorded him the same kind of homage which Goethe had given to *Cain*, saying for instance of the conjuring up of Mephistopheles,

---

[1] *Letters and Journals*, v, p. 488. To Murray from Pisa, December 4, 1821.
[2] *The Letters of P. B. Shelley*, ed. cit., ii, pp. 931 and 954. To J. Gisborne from Pisa, January 1822 and April 10, 1822.

o

that it was 'one of the finest and most sublime specimens of human conception'.[1] Significantly enough, it was 'the devilish parts' which each singled out for the highest possible praise in the work of the other.

During their own lifetimes and posthumously too, the rough and ready justice meted out to poets by popular acclaim fixed upon Goethe as the creator of *Werther* and *Faust*, and upon Byron as the author of *Childe Harold* and *Don Juan*. Almost totally ignorant of Goethe's works as he was, Byron was nevertheless vividly aware of *Werther* and realized to the full that *Faust* was Goethe's supreme achievement. Whereas Goethe, so much better informed and so much better equipped, by-passed *Childe Harold* and recoiled before *Don Juan*.

[1] J. Kennedy, *Conversations on Religion with Lord Byron*, London, 1830, p. 154.

CHAPTER VII

# Hellenism and Philhellenism

IT is not from Goethe's *obiter dicta* about Byron, revealing though these are, that the true extent and depth of the creative inspiration proceeding from the younger man can be gauged. It is from an outburst of astonishing poetry and in the shaping of Goethe's latter-day vision of life. Both are impregnated with signs of the conflict, never quite resolved, between something elemental in the two poets: Goethe's affirmation of life here and now, and Byron's denial and rejection, the Will to Life and the Will to Death engaged in a hand-to-hand encounter. Here, too, the onslaught came from Byron; with Goethe it was a case of stubborn resistance in order to maintain a precarious balance which Byron's writings no less than his personality disturbed; and his political antagonism sprang from the deeply rooted desire to preserve the equilibrium of the world he knew which Byron aimed at destroying. Goethe opposed him unconditionally here until Parry's *Last Days of Lord Byron* revealed something of the glory of ancient Greece playing round the figure of the hero and emblazoning the scene of his exploits. The immediate result was the 'Parry' poem, a bubble on the surface of the waters, heralding yet another spring-tide of the mysterious and unfathomable sea which ceased from ebbing and flowing only with Goethe's death. It broke on the legendary shore of the *Helena*-act in *Faust II* and, retreating, left behind all that was both mortal and immortal in the poet who had sacrificed himself for Greece.

In the earliest statement of the Faust legend (the Faustbook of 1587) the union between Helen and Faust had been blessed, if that is the right word, with issue: a fantastic little being called Justus Faustus who could foretell the future and who vanished away with Helen when his father died. This semi-supernatural imp played no organic part in the whole, and Marlowe and his successors allowed him to drop out of their versions. But Goethe saw that, as the child of Helen and Faust, he had a symbolical significance; and he set out to portray him under the significant name of Euphorion as the personification of the spirit engendered by the fusion between the ancient and modern worlds, or more narrowly between classical and romantic poetry. Nothing could well sound less promising, more abstract and more frigidly alle-

197

gorical; and to judge by the outline of the Euphorion episode roughed out in 1816 it would have been merely a symbolical fairy-tale dramatically presented:

A son is born of this union, who, as soon as he comes into the world, dances and sings and fences in the air with his hands. Now it must be known that the castle is surrounded by a magic boundary within which alone these half-realities can exist. The growing boy gives his mother much pleasure, and everything is permitted him except to cross a certain stream. One feast-day he hears music beyond the stream and sees soldiers and country-folk dancing. He crosses the boundary, mingles with them and becomes embroiled with them. He wounds many, but is finally slain by a consecrated sword. The steward of the castle, who is a magician, rescues the corpse. The mother is in despair; she wrings her hands and in doing so strips off the ring and falls into Faust's arms; but all he can grasp is her empty robe. Mother and son have vanished.[1]

Poetized by Goethe, it would have passed muster; and the death of Euphorion was functionally useful since it removed Helen as well and sent Faust forward and onward to new experiences. Goethe's infanticide was therefore justified, and hardly to be deplored since he was not aiming at the emotions when he first pondered the conclusion to this episode visualized in a world of 'half-realities' unrelated to the heart. But the mood of playful make-believe which was uppermost in large portions of *Faust II* was not easy to maintain on the subject of Greece with which Euphorion was so closely connected; and it was shattered irretrievably by Byron's death in the country of Goethe's dreams, a real and tragic event in Goethe's own life, but which he finally came to see was treasure-trove for his masterpiece:

I could use no one but him as the representative of the most modern poetic era, for without question he must be regarded as the greatest talent of the century. And then Byron is not antique and not romantic, but he is like the present day itself. I had to have someone like that. Besides he suited me exactly because of his dissatisfied temperament and his warlike tendencies which caused him to perish at Missolonghi. ... I had conceived of the end quite differently before and had developed it along several lines, one of which was quite good, although I won't reveal it to you. But then time brought me this with Lord Byron and Missolonghi, and I gladly let all the rest go.[2]

The modern spirit, restless, dissatisfied and warlike, had been embodied in the fairy-tale child and had caused his untimely death, in which Greece, whether ancient or modern, played no part. When 'time brought this with Lord Byron and Missolonghi'

[1] *Werke*, xv, 2, p. 176.
[2] Eckermann, p. 256. July 5, 1827.

Goethe realized how wonderfully his personality and the manner and place of his death fitted his conception of Euphorion. They were indeed uncannily appropriate, and even more so probably than Goethe knew; for by a strange fatality he seems never to have read any of those works in which Byron's Philhellenism reveals itself clearly as an aspect of that passionate Hellenism Goethe had experienced so deeply and so long:

> And yet how lovely in thine age of woe,
> Land of lost Gods and godlike men, art thou!
> Thy vales of evergreen, thy hills of snow,
> Proclaim thee Nature's varied favourite now:
> Thy fanes, thy temples to thy surface bow,
> Commingling slowly with heroic earth,
> Broke by the share of every rustic plough. . . .
>
> . . . . . . . . . . . . . . . .
> Where'er we tread 'tis haunted, holy ground;
> No earth of thine is lost in vulgar mould,
> But one vast realm of Wonder spreads around,
> And all the Muse's tales seem truly told,
> Till the sense aches with gazing to behold
> The scenes our earliest dreams have dwelt upon. . . .[1]

The emotional content of the *Helena*-act is incurable grief for a vanished ideal of heroic beauty which cannot be caught and held except as a mirage in the modern world; and Goethe therefore could hardly have failed to respond to those lines, or to have echoed the plaint in *The Isles of Greece*:

> Eternal summer gilds them yet,
> But all, except their Sun, is set.[2]

He might even have seen something more than mere hypochondria in the lament in *The Giaour*:

> So fair, so calm, so softly sealed,
> The first, last look by Death revealed!
> Such is the aspect of this shore;
> 'Tis Greece, but living Greece no more![3]

As far as one can tell, the poems in which these evocations of Greece occur were among the number which Goethe never read; but a striking statement quoted by Parry shows how deeply rooted in Hellenism Byron's Philhellenism was:

The cause of Greece . . . naturally excites our sympathy. The very name of the country is associated in our minds with all that is exalted

---

[1] *Poetry*, ii, pp. 155 and 157. *Childe Harold II*.
[2] *Poetry*, vi, p. 169.
[3] Ibid., iii, p. 90.

in virtue, or delightful in art. From it we have derived our knowledge, and under the guiding hand of its wisdom, did modern Europe make its first tottering and feeble steps towards civilization. In every mind at all embued with knowledge, she is regarded with the affection of [sic] a parent. . . . There never was a cause which, in this outline view of the matter, had such strong and commanding claims on the sympathy of the people of all Europe. . . .[1]

This was language after Goethe's own heart; and Byron's self-immolation in the cause of Greece appeared to him now as an act dictated by a spirit compounded of all that was most representative of the ancient and modern worlds: classically heroic and tragically romantic. He might even have been deeply moved at this juncture by the famous stanza:

> The Mountains look on Marathon –
> And Marathon looks on the sea;
> And musing there one hour alone,
> I dreamed that Greece might still be free. . . .[2]

There is something poignant in the memory that these lines in *The Isles of Greece* followed so hard on the heels of the stanza in *Don Juan* in which Goethe loped past on Pegasus; for neither did Byron know that 'old Goethe' had any spiritual affinities with Greece, nor did Goethe know that Byron had paid him a compliment and cocked him a snook just before glorifying Hellas. Yet Goethe, Greece and Byron, in fortuitous proximity here, were to be magically merged together in the *Helena*-act, the third act of *Faust II*. This opened with the arrival of Helen before the palace of Menelaus in Sparta to learn her fate; but in reality it is the shade of Helen in radiant yet ethereal beauty against the legendary background of Greece in her golden age of glory. It continued with the entry of Faust as a medieval hero to rescue her from the peril of death, and Gothic splendour surrounds the mythical mating of this symbolical pair. But a note of anti-climax marks the appearance of their offspring Euphorion, who makes his entry in the manner prefigured in the fairy-tale sketch: hopping and skipping, singing and dancing and playing childish games with the enraptured chorus. His ecstatic but anxious parents, however, watch his ever-growing wildness with dismay; and gradually the onlooker realizes that there is some fearful compulsion behind the apparent fantasy; that there is danger in the situation, real danger, and that Goethe himself is sounding the note of alarm, of peril mounting steadily as Euphorion recklessly climbs upward and out of sight. Reality ('which must be kept strictly apart from the ideal')

---

[1] Parry, op. cit., p. 170.
[2] *Poetry*, vi, p. 169.

has broken in disruptingly even before the liberation of Greece
and Byron's will to death mingle together in wild, clamorous,
exultant verse, pealing out for danger, for doom and for death:

HELENA, FAUST und CHOR
Wolltest du den Gemsen gleichen?
Vor dem Falle muss uns grauen.

EUPHORION
Immer höher muss ich steigen.
Immer weiter muss ich schauen.
        Weiss ich nun, wo ich bin!
        Mitten der Insel drin,
        Mitten in Pelops Land
Erde – wie seeverwandt.

CHOR
Magst nicht in Berg und Wald
Friedlich verweilen?
Suchen wir alsobald
Reben in Zeilen,
Reben am Hügelrand;
Feigen und Apfelgold.
Ach in dem holden Land
Bleibe du hold!

EUPHORION
Träumt ihr den Friedenstag?
Träume, wer träumen mag.
Krieg! ist das Losungswort.
Sieg! und so klingt es fort.

CHOR
Wer im Frieden
Wünschet sich Krieg zurück,
Der ist geschieden
Vom Hoffnungsglück.

EUPHORION
Welche dies Land gebar
Aus Gefahr in Gefahr,
Frei, unbegrenzten Muts,
Verschwendrisch eignen Bluts;
Dem nicht zu dämpfenden
Heiligen Sinn,
Alle den Kämpfenden
Bring' es Gewinn!
.  .  .  .  .  .  .  .

CHOR

Heilige Poesie,
Himmelan steige sie,
Glänze, der schönste Stern,
Fern und so weiter fern,
Und sie erreicht uns doch
Immer, man hört sie noch,
Vernimmt sie gern.

EUPHORION

Nein, nicht ein Kind bin ich erschienen,
In Waffen kommt der Jüngling an;
Gesellt zu Starken, Freien, Kühnen,
Hat er im Geiste schon getan.
Nun fort!
Nun dort
Eröffnet sich zum Ruhm die Bahn.

HELENA und FAUST

Kaum ins Leben eingerufen,
Heitrem Tag gegeben kaum,
Sehnest du von Schwindelstufen
Dich zu schmerzenvollem Raum.
Sind denn wir
Gar nichts dir?
Ist der holde Bund ein Traum?

EUPHORION

Und hört ihr donnern auf dem Meere?
Dort widerdonnern Tal um Tal,
In Staub und Wellen Heer dem Heere,
In Drang um Drang zu Schmerz und Qual.
Und der Tod
Ist Gebot,
Das versteht sich nun einmal.

HELENA, FAUST und CHOR

Welch Entsetzen! welches Grauen!
Ist der Tod denn dir Gebot?

EUPHORION

Sollt' ich aus der Ferne schauen?
Nein! ich teile Sorg' und Not.

DIE VORIGEN

Übermut und Gefahr,
Tödliches Los!

EUPHORION

Doch! – und ein Flügelpaar
Faltet sich los!

Dorthin! Ich muss! ich muss!
Gönnt mir den Flug!
(*Er wirft sich in die Lüfte, die Gewande tragen ihn einen Augenblick,
sein Haupt strahlt, ein Lichtschweif zieht nach.*)

### CHOR
Ikarus! Ikarus!
Jammer genug!

(*Ein schöner Jüngling stürzt zu der Eltern Füssen, man glaubt in dem
Toten eine bekannte Gestalt zu erblicken: doch das Körperliche ver-
schwindet sogleich, die Aureole steigt wie ein Komet zum Himmel auf,
Kleid, Mantel und Lyra bleiben liegen*)

### HELENA und FAUST
Der Freude folgt sogleich
Grimmige Pein.

### EUPHORIONS STIMME AUS DER TIEFE
Lass mich im düstern Reich,
Mutter, mich nicht allein!
(*Pause*)

.   .   .   .

### HELENA, FAUST and CHORUS
Wouldst thou chamois-like aspire?
Fearful of thy fall are we.

### EUPHORION
I must clamber ever higher,
Ever farther must I see.
Where I am I now descry.
Right in the Isle am I,
And this is Pelops' land,
Kin both to sea and strand.

### CHORUS
Bide thou by grove and hill,
Peacefully, rather!
We from the vineyards will
Grapes for thee gather, –
Grapes by the ridges stand,
Figs and the apples' gold:
Ah, yet the lovely land
Loving behold!

### EUPHORION
Dream ye a peaceful day?
Dream on, and dream who may.
War! is the countersign;
Victory! Chime on chime.

CHORUS

He, who in days of peace
Wishes for war
Bids hope and gladness cease
For evermore.

EUPHORION

Those whom this land hath reared
And through fell dangers steered,
Freemen, and boundlessly brave,
Lavish of blood they gave,
May they with glorious
Unquenchable might,
Send us victorious,
Now, in the fight!

.  .  .  .  .  .  .  .

CHORUS

Mount, holy Poesy,
Skywards, and we shall see
Shining, the fairest star,
Farther and still more far!
Yet she shall reach us here
Still, for her voice we hear,
Welcome from far.

EUPHORION

No, 'tis no child whom thou beholdest, –
A youth in arms with martial brow!
In concert with the freest, boldest
And strongest, he hath pledged his vow.
I go!
For lo!
The path of glory opens now.

HELENA and FAUST

Out alas! from life he's turning,
Hardly warmed by day's glad beam,
And from giddy heights he's yearning
For the place of pain supreme!
Are then we
Naught to thee?
Is the lovely bond a dream?

EUPHORION

Hark to the thunder from the ocean!
From land the thunder-echoes call;
On land and sea, with fierce commotion
The armies shock, the heroes fall!
The command
Is sword in hand
To die: that's clear to one and all.

HELENA, FAUST and CHORUS
What affirightment! Who could bear it?
Is then death a law to thee?

EUPHORION
Shall I from the distance share it?
No! The fate be borne by me!

HELENA, FAUST and CHORUS
Recklessness danger brings,
Fatally bold!

EUPHORION
Yes! – and a pair of wings
See me unfold!
Thither! I must! – I must!
Grant me this flight!

(*He casts himself into the air; his garments bear him up for a moment, his head is illuminated and a streak of light follows.*)

CHORUS
Icarus! Icarus!
Heart-breaking sight!

(*A beautiful youth falls at the feet of his parents and a well-known figure seems recognisable in the dead body. But the corporeal part vanishes at once and the aureole rises like a comet towards heaven. The garment, mantle and lyre remain upon the ground.*)

HELENA and FAUST
Joy beyond reckoning
Brought bitterest woe.

EUPHORION'S VOICE FROM BELOW
Mother, I'm beckoning,
Leave me not here alone.

(*Pause*)

By concentrating his thoughts and emotions about Byron's life, character and fate into a few pages of headlong, semi-fantastic action and fear-stricken comment, Goethe achieved a poetical synthesis of Byron's meteoric career and of his own part as a by-stander: enthralled, apprehensive, helpless, shaken and agonized because he counted for nothing and was powerless to save when the tragic crisis came:

Are then we
Naught to thee?
Is the lovely bond a dream?

Tell him about me and mine, and the inexhaustible reverence, admiration and love which we feel for him. Speak out and tell him. . . .

But Byron had remained indifferent and unaware; the bond had been a dream.

It was whilst Goethe was sadly pondering over this that Kinnaird's letter arrived with its precious enclosure, something tangible and real, so real that the translucent shadow-world of the *Helena*-act grew dim, and the dirge sung by the chorus after Euphorion's last words took shape as a straightforward lament for Byron from which all trace of symbolism had disappeared:

Nicht allein! – wo du auch weilest,
Denn wir glauben dich zu kennen,
Ach! wenn du dem Tag enteilest,
Wird kein Herz von dir sich trennen.
Wüssten wir doch kaum zu klagen,
Neidend singen wir dein Los:
Dir in klar – und trüben Tagen
Lied und Mut war schön und gross.

Ach! zum Erdenglück geboren,
Hoher Ahnen, grosser Kraft,
Leider! früh dir selbst verloren,
Jugendblüte weggerafft.
Scharfer Blick, die Welt zu schauen,
Mitsinn jedem Herzensdrang,
Liebesglut der besten Frauen
Und ein eigenster Gesang.

Doch du ranntest unaufhaltsam
Frei ins willenlose Netz,
So entzweitest du gewaltsam
Dich mit Sitte und Gesetz;
Doch zuletzt das höchste Sinnen
Gab dem reinen Mut Gewicht,
Wolltest Herrliches gewinnen,
Aber es gelang dir nicht.

Wem gelingt es? – Trübe Frage,
Der das Schicksal sich vermummt,
Wenn am unglückseligsten Tage
Blutend alles Volk verstummt.
Doch erfrischet neue Lieder,
Steht nicht länger tief gebeugt:
Denn der Boden zeugt sie wieder,
Wie von je er sie gezeugt.

.     .     .     .     .

Not alone, where'er thou bidest;
Knowing thee for whom thou art,
And, though from the day thou hidest,
Still to thee will cling each heart.

Scarce we venture to lament thee,
Singing envious of thy fate;
For in storm and shine were lent thee
Song and courage, fair and great.

Born to taste of earth's full gladness,
Strength was thine and proud descent;
Early erring, lost in sadness,
Bloom of youth was from thee rent.
Sharpest eyes the world beholding,
Human hearts to thee were known,
Love of fairest women holding,
And a song thy very own.

Wildly rushing, uncontrolledly
In the net where will is law,
Thus thyself divorcing boldly
As from custom, so from law;
Till the noblest thought, sustaining,
Gave pure courage its full power,
And the prize was worth the gaining, –
'Twas not given thee in that hour.

Unto whom then? Question dreary;
And the fates will never say,
Whilst the people wounded, weary,
Silent mourn the tragic day.
Yet new songs shall still elate them,
Bow no longer and deplore,
For the earth will generate them,
As it has done heretofore.[1]

As a conclusion to the action which preceded it, this elegy lacks the visionary power which inspired Euphorion's end. In parts it might almost be a versification of certain conversations with Eckermann; but it affirms and acclaims the splendour of the antecedent episode in which the reckless heroism of the protagonist shed a sad and fearful beauty over the isles of Greece.

'The more I read Byron', said Eckermann, 'the more I admire his greatness; and you did quite right to erect that immortal monument of love to him in your *Helena*!'[2]

Eckermann found the right phrase when he called the Euphorion-scene in the *Helena*-act an immortal monument of love. In its more obvious aspect the dirge ranks with such tributes

[1] The English versions are based on Bayard-Taylor's translation of *Faust*. Cf. the Euphorion Books edition, London (1949), pp. 274–277.
[2] Eckermann, p. 256. July 5, 1827.

# 208    BYRON AND GOETHE

to brother-poets as Shelley's *Adonais*, Byron's *Monody on the Death of Sheridan* and Goethe's *Epilog zu Schillers Glocke*. But the scene as a whole also belongs to the love-poetry of the world: to the ballad-like laments of abandoned, desolate, bereaved or betrayed or rejected lovers with which the poetry of all peoples and ages abounds. The hidden power in such poems comes from the beloved personality whom the lover cannot sway. In this case as in so many others, it was inaccessible to prayers and supplications, being sunk beyond all human reach in the absolute indifference of death.

Another and an even deeper confession is contained in these scenes. When Euphorion died, Helen followed him to the shades and Faust's Greek dream-world vanished. Byron's death, but more than that his aspirations, had destroyed for ever Goethe's waning belief in the essential harmony and stability underlying the chaotic and stormy waste of waters which we call the world. His surety for that had always been the vision of ancient Greece; and his hopes had lain in its resurgence in modern times. But Byron had shown him what form that resurgence was most likely to take; he abandoned his hopes as delusory and his conception of classical Greece itself as based on an illusion. There was (as he had always really known) something dimly apprehended in the universe and in man warring against the realization of any such golden age, something incommensurable, terrible and mysterious, to which he now held the key.

# CHAPTER VIII

# Byronism and Daimonism

On the plane of poetry Goethe had glorified the Faustian nature of Byron's genius, but this was far from exhausting the vision which the total experience of the Byronic spirit had induced in him; this was developing and expanding along cosmological lines; for he felt that there was something greater in Byron than could be circumscribed by a single individual; and he therefore protested strongly when Soret expressed a priggish doubt that 'a positive gain for pure human culture' could be won from his works, however brilliant they might be:

'There I must contradict you', said Goethe; 'Byron's boldness, audacity and grandeur, are they not formative in themselves? We must beware of seeking for that quality only in what is decisively pure and moral. Everything great is formative, as soon as we are aware of it.'[1]

Goethe spoke feelingly, and well he might; for those particular qualities in Byron were proving themselves formative in Goethe and shaping a mythological system in which Byron would find a conspicuous place and a far more convincing label than hypochondriacal, negative, polemical, self-tormenting or licentious which had done duty in the past. Goethe had read the riddle of Byron; and the solution was contained in the epithet daimonic; history was entering upon the scene. He had carried the notion of daimonism about with him for a very long time, almost since his poetical beginnings, for he had always been aware of it and had recurred to it at intervals in his writings and conversations. But it was not until the *Helena*-act was completed that it began to impose itself in a mythological guise visible in the light (ominous, glorious, lurid) illuminating the fate of Euphorion and the hidden recesses of his own mind. The vision loomed nearer, and Goethe began to speak. Eckermann reports a long and fascinating conversation circling round the subject as having taken place on March 11, 1828. The date can be trusted, since he found the following entry in his diary for 1828 fourteen years later:

*Thursday, March 11.* Evening with Goethe. Interesting conversation, productivity, genius, Napoleon, Prussia.[2]

[1] Communicated by Eckermann, p. 306. December 16, 1828.
[2] Cf. Houben, op. cit., i, pp. 418 f., and ii, pp. 660 f.

These few but evocative words recalled a whole complex of strange and enigmatic sayings to Eckermann, and he began to delve in the deeper layers of his memory where they had lain dormant for so long. A month later he had, he believed, recovered them all and blended them, whether unconsciously or by design, with statements on the same subject made at other times to form (as was his habit) an aesthetic whole. With the unerring instinct of the somnambulist he found himself speaking Goethe's language and using Goethe's words, a gift which invariably came to his aid when he was writing from memory rather than from notes; for he had lived too many years hypnotized by the Master's conversation to falsify it now. But even had he misrepresented him (which I am far from suggesting), the effect upon posterity would have been exactly the same, since the conversations reported by Eckermann have been accepted by the world at large as genuine Goethean pronouncements; and indeed, particularly perhaps in the case under review, Eckermann was not the man who could have invented them.

On March 11, 1828, therefore, we must take it from him that he felt rather seedy and slack, a condition which had been dragging on for some time and which had finished by irritating Goethe because Eckermann refused to do anything about it:

'But we're all the same', he concluded; 'our periods of darkness and light constitute our fate. It would be well for us if the daimon had us daily on leading-strings and told us and urged us what to do. But our good angel deserts us and we are flabby and grope about in the dark.'[1]

How different was Napoleon (he continued), striding like a half-god from battle to battle and from one victory to the next. In all his acts he showed that productivity (or creativeness) which is the hall-mark of illumination, manifest predominantly in youth, the period of that divine state; and Goethe went on to instance his own most inspired years, during which he had written *Werther* and his love lyrics. Creativeness of this sort was imbued with a power that changes the face of the world, inciting to thoughts and deeds which continue to influence mankind long after the creator is dead. Mozart, Phidias, Raphael, Dürer and Holbein were still at work in men's minds, and so were the unknown architects of medieval cathedrals. Luther was a genius of this sort; the effect of his words and deeds continues today and will endure for countless ages yet to come. Frederick the Great and Peter the Great belonged to the same order of beings; but Napoleon, with his body of granite and his mighty mind, was clearly for Goethe the

---

[1] Cf. Eckermann, pp. 671–682, for the complete text of the conversation, which should be treated with some reserve for the reasons given above.

genius-hero and Shakespeare as clearly the genius-poet *par excellence*.

So far, indeed, the daimon and genius were almost synonymous terms; and in answer to Eckermann's eager questions, Goethe once more affirmed that youth was the period most propitious to genius; but he allowed the phenomenon of repeated rejuvenation to men whose entelechy was mighty enough to impel them to establish a claim to eternal youth; and he referred in this connection to his own Indian summer which had produced the *Westöstlicher Divan*. Eckermann, who ardently aspired to poetic fame, now begged to be told what means could be used to produce or intensify the creative mood; but Goethe's answer was not encouraging:

Every productivity of a higher nature, every significant revelation, every invention, every great thought that bears fruit and has results, – all this is in no man's power and is above all earthly might. Things of this sort must be looked upon as unhoped-for gifts from above, as pure children of God, which the recipient should take and honour with gratitude and joy. It is akin to the daimonic spirit, which all-powerfully does with a man what it wills, and to which he surrenders himself unconsciously, believing that he is acting on his own initiative. In cases like this a man is often to be regarded as the instrument of a higher world-order, as a vessel found worthy for the reception of a divine influence. I say this in consideration of the fact of how often one single thought has given to whole centuries another aspect, and how single individuals have by the power that proceeded from them given an imprint to their age recognisable to succeeding generations and continuing to be beneficently active.

In this passage the daimonic is so close to the divine that Eckermann should have despaired of obtaining a recipe for it. But he made another effort; and modestly declaring that a glass of wine had sometimes helped him to come to a decision, which was after all productivity of a sort, he enquired whether it might not also stimulate genius. Goethe gravely agreed that wine harboured creative powers; but he added warningly that circumstances alter cases and that one man's meat is another man's poison. Moreover there were other vitalizing forces: there was rest and sleep; there was the release of power in movement; water and the very air itself were productive of states of inspiration:

'Fresh air and open country are where we are really at home. It would almost seem as if the spirit of God were in direct contact with us there and as if a divine power inspired us. Lord Byron, who daily spent several hours out of doors, either riding along the sea-shore on horseback, or sailing, or rowing in a boat, and then bathing in the sea and thus exercising his bodily powers, was one of the most creative human beings who have ever lived.'

Goethe sat down opposite me, and we spoke of many other things. Then we came back to Lord Byron and the many misfortunes which had darkened his later life, until at last a noble ambition but an untoward fate had driven him to Greece and completed his undoing.

'Generally speaking', Goethe continued, 'you will find that in the middle of a man's life a turning-point will occur and that, just as in his youth everything favoured him and everything he did prospered, suddenly all this changes and one misfortune follows another.

'But do you know what I think about this? Such men must be destroyed! Every outstanding man has a certain mission which he has been sent to fulfil. When he has completed it, he is no longer necessary on earth in that particular form, and Providence makes use of him again for another purpose. But as everything here below happens in a natural way, the daimons trip him up again and again, until at last he is vanquished. That is what happened to Napoleon and many others. Mozart died in his thirty-sixth year, Raphael at almost exactly the same age, Byron only a little older. They had all fulfilled their mission completely, and it was therefore time that they went, so that there might be something left for others to do in this world which is calculated to last for a very long time.'

Although Goethe did not tell Eckermann what he conceived Byron's mission to be, we know from Crabb Robinson that it was to dramatize the Old Testament, and by so doing to unseal men's eyes to the mercilessness of the current Christian dogma based on the Bible, to destroy the fearful belief in eternal damnation. Byron's Biblical dramas and *The Vision of Judgment* had convinced Goethe that Byron, the religious rebel, was enacting the part of another Luther; and although he told Eckermann that he had completely fulfilled this mission, Crabb Robinson heard him lament: 'He should have lived to execute his vocation.'

In this conversation, in which Napoleon and Byron occupied central positions, Goethe began by naming each man's daimon as the source of his genius in the Greek manner, to which Hamann in the far-off days of the Storm and Stress had given wide publicity. When referring to the daimon's leading-strings, Goethe was indeed speaking in much the same sense as Shakespeare's Plutarchian soothsayer in *Antony and Cleopatra*:

> Thy demon, that thy spirit which keeps thee, is
> Noble, courageous, high, unmatchable. . . .

But Goethe's daimons had also another part to play, a destructive as well as a creatively inspiring part, annihilating men of destiny and genius when their mission was fulfilled; and for no better reason than that there should be something left for their successors to do. Apparently accepting this, Goethe was not really reconciled to it in Byron's case, and deplored it openly when speaking of the Duke of Weimar, whose dynamic personality secured him a conspicuous position among Goethe's daimonic heroes:

But is it not lamentable, that no distinction is made, and that even such a man must go so soon? Only a paltry century more, and how much he would have furthered the progress of his age, highly placed as he was! But do you know what? The world is not to be allowed to reach its goal as early as we think and hope. The retarding daimons are always there, interposing and opposing everywhere; so that, although on the whole there is progress, it goes very slowly. Just you go on living, and you will see that I am right.[1]

Karl August, who was eight years Goethe's junior, had died on June 15, 1828, aged seventy-one. They had been friends and associates for fifty-three years, and the loss was still sufficiently recent to darken Goethe's world, the little world of Weimar, the centre of his universe. The fantastic claim that 'a paltry century' should have been added to the allotted span of three score years and ten in the Grand Duke's case has a mythopoeic origin. Goethe was interpreting a personally shattering event as a daimonic interposition retarding the progress of the world for some inscrutable reason. Always deeply conscious of mystery in nature and life, he now associated it with the fateful action of daimonism, saying on one occasion that its native element was passionate love, and on another speaking of daimonic forces at work in the rage and despair which had led to the Wars of Liberation in 1813.[2] His own passion for Lili Schönemann had changed his whole fate by causing his removal to Weimar, he commented; but he was too old at sixty to share in that devastating hatred which had led to the Wars of Liberation. These statements show that Goethe's attitude towards daimonism was as ambivalent as he obviously felt that incalculable force to be. But so far the daimons he had instanced, whether inspiring, or retarding, or destroying, were presumed to be acting in concert with the world-order or world-planning as a whole; yet the conception was growing and subtly changing in the process.

In February 1831 when completing the last book of *Dichtung und Wahrheit*, which brought the story of his life up to the departure for Weimar in 1775, Goethe felt constrained to attempt a description of the phenomenon in its totality, not only as an inexplicable elemental force but also in its human manifestations. As early as 1813 he had noted in his diary: 'Conception of the daimonic and of *Egmont*', for he had partially represented one aspect of its fateful power in that drama; and as he had been

[1] Eckermann, p. 696. October 23, 1828.
[2] Ibid., pp. 723 and 731. March 5 and 14, 1830.

carrying *Egmont* in his mind on the eve of going to Weimar, it was an appropriate moment in his memoirs to introduce the subject. But almost insensibly as he began to reflect, the darker and more problematical side of daimonism imposed itself, the influence of Byron made itself felt; and the passage as a whole gives the impression of having crystallized round that core in Byron's being which had fascinated, perplexed, disturbed and half-repelled Goethe for so long: something irrational, powerful, dangerous, destructive and irresistible; something that, even as a very young man, he had been dimly aware of in the texture of life itself:

He thought to discover in nature animate and inanimate, with or without a soul, something that only manifested itself in contradictions, and could therefore not be confined to any conceptual category, far less defined in words. It was not divine, for it seemed irrational; not human for it appeared to be without a mind; not devilish, for it could be beneficent; not angelic, for it often betrayed malice. It resembled chance, being apparently causeless; yet it had some similarity with providence, for it hinted at connections. Everything that seemed to us limited was penetrable by this force, for it contracted time and extended space. It seemed that its dwelling-place was among impossibilities and that it rejected possibilities with scorn.

This being, which seemed to interpose itself between all other beings either to separate or unite them, I called daimonic after the example of the ancients and others who have thought like them. I tried to escape from this terrible being by taking refuge as was my practice in a symbol.[1]

This sibylline description reflects the perplexity of Goethe as a young man, brooding over the random, incalculable, perverse and inscrutable element in life. The symbol which he chose to incorporate this incomprehensible spirit was the figure of Egmont, whom he endowed with the gift of *attrativa* (as he labelled it) and whose character he impregnated with daimonism present also in the forces ranged against him. The retrospective interpretation of the drama now given by Goethe was conditioned by his deeper awareness of the mysterious power involved and appeals more directly to the imagination than the drama itself. For although ostensibly characterizing Egmont, Goethe was under the spell of another and more vital spirit, even more compelling, and more potent by far both for good and for ill. Turning away from Egmont, Goethe went forward into the present:

And therefore here too, for the sake of many a beloved reader, I will anticipate; and as I do not know how soon I shall be able to speak again, I will communicate something of which I only became convinced much later.

[1] Cf. *Werke*, xxix, pp. 173 ff., for the whole passage, *Dichtung und Wahrheit*, Book IV, Chapter 20.

Much later; and much water had run under many bridges since *Egmont* had been finished in 1787, bringing a great many strangely varied experiences to Goethe, which came crowding round him now:

Although the daimonic element can manifest itself in all material and immaterial things, and actually expresses itself in a most remarkable way in animals, nevertheless it is allied with mankind in a pre-eminently extraordinary manner, and represents a power which, if not actually opposed to the moral world-order, yet cuts across it, so that they can be regarded as the warp and the woof of life.

There are countless names for the phenomenon thus brought about; for all philosophies and all religions have tried to solve the riddle prosaically or poetically and have finally washed their hands of it, which they are still at perfect liberty to do.

But the daimonic element appears in its most terrifying aspect when it manifests predominantly in a human being. During the course of my life I have been able to observe several such men, sometimes closely, sometimes from afar. They are not always the most admirable persons, not necessarily the most intelligent nor the most gifted, and rarely are they remarkable for their goodness of heart; but an extraordinary force goes out from them, and they have an incredible power over all creatures, yes, even over the elements; and who can say how far such an effect may not extend? All the moral forces banded together are powerless against them; in vain do the more enlightened among mankind strive to render them suspect either as deceivers or as deceived; they attract the masses, and they can only be vanquished by the universe itself with which they are in conflict. It is from observations of this nature that the strange and terrifying saying probably arose: *Nemo contra deum nisi deus ipse.*

It is almost as if a premonition of things to come were guiding Goethe's hand as he traced this composite portrait, in which the features of Napoleon, Byron and Karl August were finally obliterated by the challenging countenance of Cagliostro, the man of marvels and mysteries whose eyes were reported to dart flames of ice. The demi-god of Paris at his zenith, he had perished miserably in the dungeons of San Leo in 1795, and Goethe had rejoiced over his downfall; for he believed him to be an arch-deceiver, and as such he had represented him in his comedy *Der Gross-Kophta.* Yet he had never been in any doubt as to the daimonic power wielded by the magus, which (he firmly believed) had helped to precipitate the outbreak of the French Revolution. The sinister element in daimonism was incarnate for him in the person of Cagliostro; his description evokes for the present-day reader the much more evil personality of Adolf Hitler, against whom all the moral forces banded together were of no avail until his hour had struck. But the majesty and magic in Goethe's phrasing are in telling contrast with the dwarfish spiritual monstrosity who was once the dictator of Germany.

The majesty and the magic are evocative of Napoleon and Byron; and indeed the passage as a whole, floodlighting the phenomenon of daimonism and its representatives, was dictated by Goethe's intense emotional preoccupation with the most dazzling of them all. They were in conflict with the universe, he said; this formula fitted Goethe's conception of Byron perfectly; it could obviously also apply to Napoleon and Cagliostro; but it could hardly be stretched to include Karl August. Such personalities, said Goethe, if not actually opposed to the moral world-order, yet cut across it, and could be regarded as the warp to the woof of life. Here again his deepest feelings about Byron found lapidary expression. Even more revealing is the fact that Goethe, though fearing it and blenching before it, paid awe-stricken homage to the terrifying, amoral, violently active and potentially annihilating force streaming out from the elect. It formed no part of his own nature, he assured Eckermann, adding, however, that he was subject to it (exposed to it, subjugated by it); and a truer description of his inner life and of his relationship to Byron could hardly be found.

It seems clear that in 1831 Goethe no longer thought of daimonism and genius as interchangeable terms; and in his subsequent conversations with Eckermann on the subject, the men of purely artistic or poetical genius are no longer in evidence, and the men of destiny (the coming Carlylean heroes) possess the field. Not that Goethe denied daimonism in poetry where, as he told Eckermann, it is always present, particularly in the almost unconscious kind which transcends reason. He also acknowledged its irresistible and inexplicable power in music; but, when it came to personalities, the men of destiny came forward alone; and the only poet who shared their company was Byron, who belonged there by right. For if destiny rather than genius is to be the touchstone, then Byron's precedence over Shakespeare is assured; since, however anomalous the position may be, it yet remains true that the greatest creative genius England has ever brought forth and one of the supreme creative poets of the world has had no discernible effect upon the course of history and the destinies of mankind. Whereas Goethe rightly sensed in Byron a power that might alter the trend of future events. Moreover it was his personality which had illuminated the scene where Napoleon, Frederick the Great, Peter the Great and the Duke of Weimar now occupied the centre of the stage; so that, having paid due tribute to these conquerors, rulers and kings, Goethe added thoughtfully:

In Byron too the daimonic element must have been present in a high degree, and that is why he possessed the power of attraction to such an extent that no one, least of all women, could resist him.[1]

Perhaps one might add 'least of all Goethe' in order to give its due weight to this penultimate tribute to Byron's personality. The last was still to come in the letter to John Murray Junior a few weeks later, when he fired a final salute across the water to the poet 'resplendent in his glory'; and the 'approximately true estimate' he was endeavouring to form of a character which he proclaimed to be unique was undoubtedly conditioned by the conception of daimonism which Byron and Byron's fate had helped him to disengage. And here we come to the parting of the ways between England and the Continent. It seems certain now that Goethe saw deeper and further than the English in penetrating through Byronism to daimonism. There is a world of difference between these two epithets. The first, even when pronounced tolerantly and benevolently, sounds as if one were sitting in judgment on insincerity and pose. The other resists ironical overtones, suggests danger and has an ominous yet alluring aura. Both concepts arouse attention and have gained adherents; but how different their history has been! Byronism in England, at one time all the rage, consisted largely of imitations of Byron's superficial affectations and foibles in literature and in life; it produced nothing of importance and gradually wore away, leaving behind it an impression that Byron himself was only a negligible poseur. Whereas the real Byron, the reckless, titanic and dynamic personality revealed in his writings and in his deeds (the daimonic Byron as Goethe would put it), has left an imprint on Continental history which has not yet passed away.

His passionate call to the Greeks to remember the past and throw off the foreign yoke in the second canto of *Childe Harold* and in the beginning of *The Giaour* had already, says Sir Harold Nicolson:

... by 1820 done more than all the intricate energies of the Greek intellectuals such as Korais, or the intrigues of the Phanariots such as Ypsilanti, to awaken European opinion to the existence of a Greek question, and to prepare men's minds for the upheaval which was so shortly to come. The trumpet call which Byron sounded, irresponsibly perhaps, and with no real conception of the consequences, echoed through England and through France, through Germany and Russia; it was taken up at Jena, at Göttingen, and at Zürich; it became the literary stimulus of the Philhellenic movement in Europe.[2]

But this outstanding fact was far from exhausting Byron's in-

[1] Eckermann, p. 472. March 8, 1831.
[2] Nicolson, op. cit., p. 49.

fluence on the Europe of his day. As Lord Russell truly says, he was the poet of the movement which asserted the right of rebellion in the name of nationalism, and of the splendour of war in defence of liberty, a movement of which Fichte, Carlyle and Nietzsche were the philosophers.[1] And even this was not all. His practical championship of the Carbonari was an inspiration to Mazzini, and his death at Missolonghi intensified the desire felt by the generation of French romantic poets to play an active part in the field of politics. Chateaubriand, Lamartine, Victor Hugo, even for a moment Alfred de Vigny, forsook the ivory tower of art to follow the footsteps of Byron into 'the *poetry* of politics' under the ghostly banner of Napoleon. His direct effect on the history of Poland was even more remarkable. His anti-Russian and pro-Polish sympathies expressed with vigour in *Don Juan* and in *The Age of Bronze* set the tone in Western European letters; but it was his personality, his poems and his fate which fired the inflammable mind of Adam Mickiewicz and produced *Konrad Wallenrod* (1828). That stormy and passionate epic, closely modelled on *The Corsair* and breathing the same spirit, acted as a call to arms to the Polish nation in the Insurrection of 1830–31. Yet Mickiewicz himself, great among Polish poets and among epic poets of all times, who longed to take a personal part in the conflict in which his very soul was engaged, hesitated and procrastinated, as Byron had done before him; but, unlike Byron, he hesitated until the end; although his creation of a Polish Legion in the 'forties shows that he was still vainly dreaming of repeating in his own country what Byron had done and suffered for Greece.

Liberation and revolt; 'rage, resistance and redress'; this was Byron's message to the enslaved peoples of the world, made all the more irresistible because he was not content with mere words. It will obviously always depend on the personal attitude of the observer of events as to whether his influence on this plane is to be acclaimed or deplored; to Goethe it appeared a disaster; since Byron was advocating and partly achieving the antithesis of everything he held dear. His stubborn adherence

> To this my plain, sworn, downright detestation
> Of every despotism in every nation,[2]

was gall and wormwood to Goethe, being the flat denial of the views he had upheld ever since 1789, when the French Revolution had threatened to annihilate all that he prized as irreplaceable in the civilization of the world. Apostles of freedom, he savagely declared, had always been abhorrent to him; and he tried to make

---

[1] Lord Russell, *A History of Western Philosophy*, London, 1946, p. 624.
[2] *Poetry*, vi, p. 381.

them equally abhorrent to others in his anti-revolutionary writings (1790–94) which represent the nadir of his genius, vainly struggling to stem the fearful flood-tide by deriding, or belittling, or impugning the manifestations of a spirit so incommensurable with his own. Recognizing its presence in Byron, he recoiled in dismay before something so darkly daimonic; but the spell cast over him was such that he learnt to accept and almost to acclaim, the liberation of Greece, and to exalt and magnify the champion. This effect of the impact of Byron's mind on Goethe's is a striking example of the power over his contemporaries and over succeeding generations wielded by the younger man. It has earned him a whole chapter in Lord Russell's *History of Western Philosophy*, in which work Goethe is barely mentioned. This reversal of the generally accepted verdict of their relative importance as thinkers is due to the latter-day emergence of Byron as one of those whose thoughts have perceptibly altered the course of events; or, to quote Goethe, 'have given an imprint to their age recognizable to succeeding generations'. Some may account for this by Byron's 'shallow, pitiable habit of being always intelligible';[1] others may echo the admirable phrase coined by Ernest Hartley Coleridge and say that it is because his reflections are coeval with reflection;[2] Lord Russell believes that he moved men's minds as other aristocratic rebels have done 'whose philosophy requires some greater change than their own personal success';[3] but perhaps Byron's own reason is the real one:

> I won't describe, – that is if I can help
>     Description; and I won't reflect, – that is
> If I can stave off thought, which – as a whelp
>     Clings to the teat – sticks to me through the abyss
> Of this odd labyrinth; or as the kelp
>     Holds to the rock; or as a lover's kiss
> Drains its first draught of lips: – but, as I said,
> I *won't* philosophise, and *will* be read.[4]

He has had his wish, to an extent which has made him one of the inescapable figures in European literature no less than in European history. He can be discerned under the mask of the *héros fatal* of French romanticism; he pervades the cosmic melancholy of Lenau and Heine; and he inspired the passionate liberal outbursts of the latter. He is to be found in the poems of Pushkin

[1] Charles Kingsley, quoted by Chew, *Byron in England*, p. 272.
[2] *Poetry*, ii, p. xiii.
[3] Russell, op. cit., p. 775. The chapter on Byron is placed between those on Hegel and Schopenhauer.
[4] *Poetry*, vi, p. 408.

and Lermontov, and he can be seen animating the heroes of Mickiewicz's epics and stimulating the patriotic fervour of the Italian romantic movement. Some may welcome his pervasive presence; others may regret it or scoff at it; but nowhere except in Germany under the guise of daimonism as interpreted by Goethe has it spelt disaster.

Goethe meant much more by this mythological symbol than could be contained in any one person; and Germany herself forgot about Byron when she was caught in the toils of daimonism; nevertheless it was Byron who opened up new vistas to Goethe down which he caught glimpses of the mysterious entity he had discovered or rediscovered in the cosmic scene: terribly potent, darkly alluring. Neither of them can be blamed for the dire effect this conception was to have in the future; retrospectively they appear as unconscious agents of the incalculable power of ideas which have outstripped their creators, whether for good or for ill especially visionary and mythological ideas. Byron, himself incapable of experiencing this kind of revelation, pierced the veil for Goethe who penetrated beyond it, seeking and finding traces of daimonism in the universe, in nature, in life and in the world at large. Most vividly of all he saw it incarnate in certain men, and pre-eminently among them in Byron: ceaselessly creative, irresistibly attractive, but in conflict with universal order and moral law. Byron, 'the most remarkable personality that could possibly be born', had convinced Goethe that he and his kind transcended humanity and that mortal men were powerless against them, a mythological conception already prevalent about Napoleon; for in the eyes of Europe he and Byron were members of the same fateful race. Goethe called them daimonic; and by the use of that one single word he gave 'to whole centuries another aspect' as he would have put it himself. For it fell on German ears and penetrated deeply into German minds, minds always avid for the absolute and intoxicated by ideas; and Goethe himself was half-intoxicated by Byron when he uttered the ominous rallying-cry.

'There was more of the devil in me than in Goethe', said Byron. Substitute daimon for devil, and the statement still holds good; for, although Goethe denied it to Eckermann, it was part of his nature too, breaking through as Faustianism and recognizing its counterpart in *Manfred*, *Cain* and *The Vision of Judgment*. He was therefore vulnerable both from within and from without when he found himself exposed in his old age to the assault of Byron's overpowering personality. It was a shattering and at the same time a revitalizing experience, arousing emotions both rapturous and searing, and inducing such anger with the English for their persecution of Byron as to inject into his innately tolerant and conciliatory organism the virus of Anglophobia. What shadow that may have cast on events to come is a matter for conjecture. It is one of the imponderables and escapes assessment. But the part Goethe's conception of daimonism was to play in the future as one of the great impersonal forces driving towards disaster is easier to discern. He had not only pronounced one of those words charged with a creatively destructive force, he had also seemed to sanction, by his haunting description, the dark and dangerous element he had suppressed in himself and had finally surrendered to in Byron. It no longer even needed the latter's name to wreak havoc in the world.

Nietzsche, who was strongly sympathetic towards Byron, called Eckermann's *Conversations with Goethe* the best German book ever written; he also quoted from the discussion about daimonism of March 11, 1828, in *The Birth of Tragedy*. The hero of that extraordinary rhapsody is the Dionysos of Euripides' *Bacchae*; but what Nietzsche baptized and worshipped as the Dionysiac element in life and art, a wild, ecstatic, frenzied, glorious yet terrible force, differs from Goethe's conception of daimonism only by something more orgiastic, less mysterious and of lesser cosmic resonance. But it had an even headier effect; for what Goethe had represented as an awe-inspiring element in life, Nietzsche boldly proclaimed as the highest ideal for mankind; and he then embodied the ideal in *Thus Spake Zarathustra*, announcing the advent of the superman in inspired prophetic language which cut straight across the moral world-order and won a signal victory for daimonism. It was by no means an isolated victory; but it was so decisive as to sweep everything before it, including the precarious sanity of daimon-driven dictators and their devil's disciples. Lord Russell sums up the situation incisively and lucidly in these words:

The romantic revolt passes from Byron, Schopenhauer and Nietzsche to Mussolini and Hitler. . . . The aristocratic philosophy of rebellion, growing, developing and changing as it approached maturity, has inspired a long series of revolutionary movements, from the Carbonari after the fall of Napoleon to Hitler's *coup* in 1933. . . . And in this way nationalism, Satanism, and hero-worship, the legacy of Byron, became part of the complex soul of Germany.[1]

Goethe's name should be added to this list; since it was daimonism rather than Satanism, daimonism with all the weight of Goethe's prestige behind it, which, joined to other and darker forces, incited Germany to megalomania and madness. Goethe would have recoiled in horror from the barbarous degeneracy of

[1] Russell, op. cit., pp. 746, 775 and 779.

daimon-worship in Nazi-ridden Germany; and Byron's horror
would probably have been greater still; for it needs no effort of
the imagination to hear the words with which the poet who wished
to 'teach, if possible, the stones/To rise against Earth's tyrants'
would have anathematized the Chancellor of Germany:

> 'Let there be Light! said God, and there was Light!'
> 'Let there be Blood!' says man, and there's a sea!
> The fiat of this spoiled child of the Night
> (For Day ne'er saw his merits) could decree
> More evil in an hour, than thirty bright
> Summers could renovate. . . .[1]

Both Goethe and Byron, whatever their personal velleities,
were men of exceptionally humane and enlightened dispositions;
and (egoists by the divine right of genius though both of them
were) each in his totally dissimilar way was far from indifferent to
the welfare of humanity. Goethe took endless time and trouble as
a servant of the state and of the people of Weimar; Byron lavished
his genius, his fortune and the last months of his life on a cause
which he believed would further human happiness. Yet from the
contact of these two minds a third energy came forth, focusing and
concentrating the dark rays of daimonism, an indescribably baneful force, sanctioning spiritual evil in high places, sinister and
grotesque.

That such a result should have been produced by Goethe's
spiritual surrender to Byron is a sobering reminder of the incalculable power latent in persons, emotions and ideas. One
would like to deny it in the present instance; but if in truth Byron's
legacy to Europe was Hitlerism, then it must also be allowed that
a vital contribution was made to it from Goethe's estate, and that
the conjunction of the two poets was ill-starred.

\*

\*        \*

Goethe once told Eckermann that there had been something un-
mistakably daimonic about his friendship with Schiller. They
might have met earlier or later; but that they actually came
together at the very moment when Goethe had his Italian
journey behind him and Schiller was beginning to tire of his
philosophical speculations was significant and had been productive of the greatest results for both of them. This is emphatically not the moment to embark on that pregnant, perennially
fascinating and certainly not neglected theme, the friendship
between the Dioscuri of Weimar. It made history in German

[1] *Poetry*, vi, p. 316.

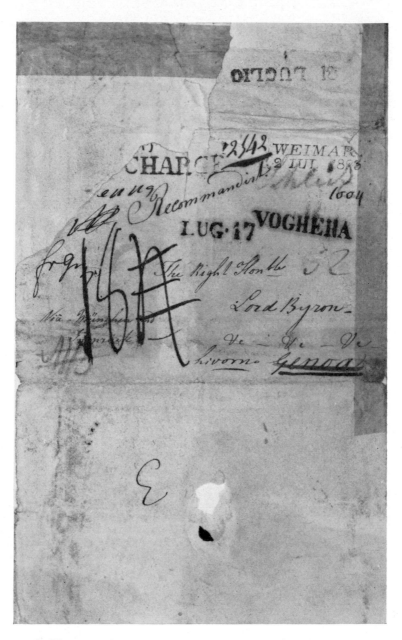

6. Photograph of envelope containing Goethe's poem to
Byron, by kind permission of Sir John Murray.

literature; but has it made history elsewhere? Unhappily for humanity it has not, or an era of widespread humanism, idealism, happiness and peace would have blossomed for mankind. Whereas Goethe's association with Byron has had such world-wide and disastrous after-effects, that one is predisposed to believe in the daimonic nature of their encounter.

As was the case with Goethe and Schiller, the meeting of their minds took place at the most favourable of all possible moments; when Goethe was mourning the loss of Marianne and Christiane, and Byron's home had been laid desolate by the separation from his wife. Yet if daimonic forces presided over the relationship as a whole, they often betrayed that malice of which Goethe speaks: thrusting *Glenarvon* into his hands simultaneously with *Manfred*, tripping him up over *The Vampyre* and forcing the suppressed dedication to *Marino Faliero* on his unwilling notice. The retarding daimons were also much to the fore, delaying vital publications and hindering by every means in their power the delivery of the *Sardanapalus* inscription; interposing in fact, as Goethe would say, to separate the two poets. But perhaps it was to unite them irrevocably. At the very moment when it could best accomplish this by dispelling the hostile apathy engendered by *Don Juan* which had paralysed Goethe's heart, the dedication made its belated appearance and transformed the situation. If ever an inanimate object were possessed of magical powers, it was the sheet of paper in Byron's handwriting, which reappeared again at a crucial moment to act as an inspiring factor in Goethe's memorial to the writer which will outlast 'the brass of both his epitaph and tomb'. Blind chance may have been at work in both cases; add them together and it begins to look like fate.

Yet what is one to think of the eleventh-hour arrival of Goethe's poem on board the *Hercules*? It is tempting to imagine a daimonic *deus ex machina* ensuring its delivery by means of contrary winds, and marking with an invisible '*Urgent!*' the envelope smothered with forwarding addresses and cancellation-stamps. But what might have been a real turning-point in their joint history mis-fired; for there was to be no close human contact between them, and attempts to establish it were thwarted at every turn. After Byron's death the final issue seemed to hang in the balance; for what with the expedition to Greece and the tone of Medwin's *Conversations* Goethe's feelings for Byron were threatened with an eclipse. But it was only so that they might burst forth more con-sumingly than ever when Parry's book and a mystery-volume containing *Sardanapalus* marked with Byron's 'own hand' rose upon his horizon. And could it be that Goethe's death was delayed, until he had passed on to posterity the vision of daimonism which

Byron's personality had engendered? When circumstances behave in this way: urging and thwarting, hindering and helping and seemingly in control, unseen agents are apt to be suspected; and no better name could be found for those which kept on interposing between Byron and Goethe than the name the German poet has made famous. Scepticism in the face of such an hypothesis is nonetheless justifiable and should perhaps be given the last word. This cannot unfortunately alter the subsequent historical facts.

Yet looking back for the last time over the ground traversed, reason rebels at the notion that something on the face of it so purely personal as Goethe's passion for Byron should have had such dire and disproportionate results. But then rebellious reason must perforce submit to Goethe:

Do you know what I think about this? . . . The world is not to be allowed to reach its goal as early as we think and hope. The retarding daimons are always there, interposing and opposing everywhere. Just you go on living, and you will see that I am right.

# INDEX

225